GEORG SIMMEL

Revised Edition

DAVID FRISBY

London and New York

First published 1984 by Ellis Horwood Limited
and Tavistock Publications Limited

This revised edition first published 2002
by Routledge
11 New Fetter Lane, London EC4P 4EE

Simultaneously published in the USA and Canada
by Routledge
29 West 35th Street, New York, NY 10001

Routledge is an imprint of the Taylor & Francis Group

© 1984, 2002 David Frisby

Printed and bound in Great Britain by
TJ International Ltd, Padstow, Cornwall

British Library Cataloguing in Publication Data
A catalogue record for this book is available from the British Library

Library of Congress Cataloging in Publication Data
A catalog record for this book has been requested

ISBN 0–415–28534–8 (Hbk)
ISBN 0–415–28535–6 (Pbk)

GEORG SIMMEL

Until recently little of Simmel's work was available in translation and certain key texts were unknown outside Germany. Here David Frisby provides not only an introduction to the major sociological writings of this important figure, but also an argument for a reconsideration of his work. The author outlines the cultural and historical context in which Simmel worked; reviews Simmel's most important writings; and examines his legacy to sociology by illuminating his links with Weber's theories and his influential relationship with Marxism.

Simmel, a central figure in the development of modern sociology, and a contemporary of Weber and Durkheim, was one of the first to identify sociology as a separate discipline. His ideas influenced Weber, the Chicago School, and many later sociologists. His introduction of a number of basic concepts to sociology, such as exchange, interaction and differentiation, attest to his intellectual stature and the far-reaching significance of his work.

David Frisby is Professor of Sociology at the University of Glasgow.

KEY SOCIOLOGISTS

Edited by PETER HAMILTON

Now reissued, this classic series provides students with concise and readable introductions to the work, life and influence of the great sociological thinkers. With individual volumes covering individual thinkers, from Emile Durkheim to Pierre Bourdieu, each author takes a distinct line, assessing the impact of these major figures on the discipline as well as the contemporary relevance of their work. These pocket-sized introductions will be ideal for both undergraduates and pre-university students alike, as well as for anyone with an interest in the thinkers who have shaped our time.

Series titles include:

EMILE DURKHEIM
Ken Thompson

THE FRANKFURT SCHOOL AND ITS CRITICS
Tom Bottomore

GEORG SIMMEL
David Frisby

MARX AND MARXISM
Peter Worsley

MAX WEBER
Frank Parkin

MICHEL FOUCAULT
Barry Smart

PIERRE BOURDIEU
Richard Jenkins

SIGMUND FREUD
Robert Bocock

Table of Contents

Editor's Foreword

Georg Simmel's sociology has always been tantalizingly elusive for the English-speaking reader. Although some of his best work was translated fairly soon after its first publication, a considerable amount had never been made available in translation until very recently. Simmel's work, fragmentary in its apparent structure because of the vagaries of translation, seemed also to suffer from the sheer variety of themes with which he dealt. Clearly a thinker capable of the most penetrating of insights – into, for example, the significance of common mealtimes, or the importance of eye-to-eye contact in interaction – the very richness of this apparently ephemeral material has for long sustained the impression that Simmel was little more than an idiosyncratic sociologist of form, whose work failed to grasp historical processes or mundane empirical reality. Despite the fact that contemporaries recognized Simmel's importance as the first academic sociologist in Germany, and that his theories of *sociation* were unquestionably influential in the development of symbolic interactionism in America, his reputation today does not generally rank him alongside his contemporaries Durkheim and Weber. However, the fruits of recent scholarship, and a veritable renaissance of Simmelian studies (of which this book represents one facet) have begun to salvage Simmel's work from the relative obscurity into which it had fallen.

David Frisby has been one of those most responsible for a return to Simmel, the unfairly neglected founding father of sociology. His contemporaries, Max Weber and Emile Durkheim, now appear as dominant figures in the rise of modern sociology, yet it is inappropriate to recognize their role without giving Simmel his due. Because his work was taken over quite rapidly in American sociology, especially by the 'Chicago School' sociologists, his influence in the emergence of such central concepts as *role*, *interaction*, *conflict*, *domination* and *subordination* has tended to be glossed over by virtue of its incorporation in the more systematic or empirically grounded theories of his successors. To take one quite well known example, Simmel's recognition (in his essay *The Metropolis and Mental Life* of 1903) that the city is 'not a spatial entity with sociological consequences, but a sociological entity that is formed spatially' can be seen to prefigure much of the later Chicago 'ecological' theory of urban society of Park, Burgess and Thomas. Moreover, Simmel's methodological starting point in constructing sociological theory, the assumption that society is a web of patterned interactions, is not seriously questioned by any contemporary paradigm of sociological theory.

It is commonplace to define Simmel's sociology as 'essayistic', over-concerned with the ephemeral and mundane and insufficiently systematic. The fact that Simmel wrote on many other subjects (especially philosophy, psychology and art) as well as sociology is frequently counted against him to further depress his importance, especially *viz-à-vis* the 'Holy Trinity' of Marx, Weber and Durkheim. However, as David Frisby shows in this book, these images of Simmel's sociological theories are misleading. Dr Frisby is a leading international scholar of Simmel's work, and his deep knowledge of the Simmelian *oeuvre* is brought into play to reveal a Simmel who is both more systematic and consistent than had hitherto been supposed. As a result of his work we can now see clearly how Simmel demarcated sociology as a distinctive intellectual discipline with a specific subject matter, and how this initial methodological procedure sets the scene for the rest of his work. The fact that Simmel's conception of sociology was highly rationalist, and tended to avoid any attempt at empirical generalization, was perhaps responsible for the impression that it provided little more than ingenious suggestions for further research. Durkheim's assessment of Simmel's *The Philosophy of Money* as a work 'replete with illegitimate speculation', a 'treatise on social philosophy' which contains 'a number of ingenious ideas, pungent views, curious or even at times surprising comparisons', seems to have been typical of one strand of critical response to Simmelian sociology in general. Perhaps more realistic was Weber's argument that virtually every one of Simmel's works 'abounds in important theoretical ideas and the most subtle observations'. David Frisby's treatment of Simmel starts from a similar point to Weber's assessment, and covers the whole range of Simmel's sociological work. It is able as a result to present a much more rounded picture of Simmel's claim to a central role in the development of modern sociological thinking than was hitherto possible. Frisby shows, for example, how *The Philosophy of Money* contributed to Weber's formulation of his 'Protestant Ethic' thesis, and how *Problems of the Philosophy of History* and other writings by Simmel provide a concept of the intentionality of social action which is close to Weber's notion of rational action. The impact of Simmel's ideas upon Georg Lukács, Ernst Bloch and Walter Benjamin also indicates that his influence extended into the realm of Marxist thought to an impressive extent.

But it is perhaps Simmel's status as the first sociologist of 'modernity' which is most interestingly developed by David Frisby. That this concern with the social effects of modern, cosmopolitan, and predominantly urban life should have been such a rich source of Simmel's theories and concepts is not surprising, given that much of his career was spent in Berlin at a time when that city was at the forefront of modernist culture. Its relationship to the way in which Simmel developed many of his most influential insights into modern life reminds us of the extent to which sociology is a reflection of (and upon) its socio-cultural locations. Simmel's intellectual heirs are many and varied, perhaps a consequence of the fact that no Simmelian school of sociology developed before or after his death, but also due to the fact that his most interesting ideas are capable of bridging gaps in historical time and social space. As David Frisby argues in this book, the time has come to re-examine Simmel's place in sociology and to allot more attention to the thinker who first developed so many concepts we now take for granted.

Peter Hamilton

Acknowledgements

I wish to thank the staff of the following libraries who provided material for this volume: Glasgow University Library, the British Library, the Universitätsbibliothek Konstanz and the Staatsbibliothek Preussischer Kulturbesitz (W. Berlin).

Completion of this study was facilitated by the generous renewal of my Alexander von Humboldt Fellowship at Konstanz University. In this connection, I wish to thank Horst Baier for his hospitality and assistance. Thanks are due to H. Jürgen Dahme and Klaus C. Köhnke.

Finally, I wish to thank Pru Larsen for typing the manuscript.

For the new edition, I wish to thank Gain Poggi for his invitation to give a paper to his seminar at the European University Institute, Fiesole, which helped me to outline some of the ideas presented in the Preface. And thanks are due to Maureen McQuillan for typing the new text.

Preface

INTRODUCTION

An introduction to the sociologist and social theorist, Georg Simmel (1858–1918), whose works range over twenty volumes and over three hundred essays and other pieces – and now in twenty-four volumes for his collected works in German [1] must necessarily be selective. This is all the more true of a theorist whose interests and impact encompassed philosophy, sociology, social psychology, aesthetics, cultural analysis, literature and art. The original text of this introduction sought to indicate some of the breadth of Simmel's influence in social theory and beyond. More specifically, with reference to sociology and social theory, a case was made for Simmel as indeed a contemporary of Emile Durkheim (1858–1917), insofar as he too was concerned with establishing sociology as an independent discipline in the early 1890s over a decade before Max Weber. The breadth of Simmel's early concerns has now been explored in detail in Klaus C. Köhnke's outstanding work on the young Simmel down to the mid 1890s. [2] The focus upon three of Simmel's major works – *On Social Differentiation* (1890) [3], *The Philosophy of Money* (1900) [4] and *Sociology* (1908) [5] – suggested, in the first case, that some central themes in his sociology were already outlined in 1890 along with an early foundation of sociology; in the second, that in his most systematic work in social theory (despite its title) he was able to explore, in a manner hardly excelled since, the interaction of a neglected aspect of the economy – the mediations of the money form – in such a way as to extend it to the whole of society and to modern culture (with its contradiction between subjective and objective culture) and thereby to outline a significant theory of modernity; and in the third case, that, despite the apparent heterogeneity of his explorations of diverse forms of social interaction or sociation, a case can be made for discerning a coherent sociological programme focusing upon the general properties of social interaction.

The examination of Simmel's foundation of sociology in chapter three took up the somewhat problematical relationship to social psychology. Here, we will focus upon Simmel's conception of society. Aside from the extensive treatment of a sociology of money, the discussion of Simmel's *Sociology* (1908) briefly explored his contributions to a sociology of sociability and of space. Here, other instances of his exploration of the forms of sociation and culture will be outlined to give a fuller idea of the breadth of Simmel's concerns. In the discussion of the money economy and in the brief outline of aspects of Simmel's essay on the metropolis, his contribution to a theory of modernity and modern culture were intimated but not developed. The intention here will be to expand upon these and other explorations of modernity. Finally, we will briefly examine the relevance of Simmel's contributions to a theory of modernity for more recent theories of postmodernity.

SOCIOLOGY

In essays published in 1890, 1894/1895 and 1908 (the latter three titled 'The Problem of Sociology') and elsewhere, Simmel sought to ground *sociology* as an independent social science discipline. [6] The basic principles of this foundation for sociology are ostensibly simple but also far-reaching. They can be summarised as follows. In the world everything interacts with everything else. This proposition is true of the social world too. Siegfried Kracauer argued that this was encapsulated in a core principle of the fundamental interrelatedness (*Wesenszusammengehörigkeit*) of the most diverse phenomena. A focus upon interaction is therefore a concern with relations between phenomena, with the reciprocal effect (*Wechselwirkung*) of phenomena with one another. Sociology must investigate the diversity of interactions and, from 1890, Simmel defines sociology as the study of the 'form of social interaction'. The diverse forms of social interaction signify our participation in the process of being members of society. Thus by 1894 (in the essay 'The Problem of Sociology' and in its 1895 expanded English version [7]), Simmel amplifies the study of forms of social interaction by introducing a further conceptualisation. This results in defining sociology as the study of the 'forms of sociation (*Vergesellschaftung*)', that is, the processes by which we engage in and are members of society. Sociology is concerned with the 'forms' rather than the 'contents' of social interaction and sociation because other social science disciplines already deal with these contents. For the purposes of analysis these forms are abstracted from their contents. Sociology is concerned with 'the investigation of the forces, forms and development of sociation, of the co operation, association and co-existence of individuals'. [8] It does not take as its starting point a pre existing society as totality. Rather it investigates how what we term society comes into being, and how it is possible. Sociology, in Simmel's sense, is 'the only science which really seeks to know only society *sensu strictissimo*', and that is really 'the study of that which in society *is* society'. [9] This discipline is grounded not so much in terms of its subject matter but in terms of its distinctive method, which relies upon abstracting the forms of sociation for sociological investigation. If sociation and social interactions occur anywhere in the social world, then the issue arises as to whether any of them should be privileged for sociological analysis. The universal existence of interactions leads Simmel to maintain that sociology should examine *any* form of sociation since none is too insignificant (whether it be interaction at mealtimes, the rendezvous, flirtation, etc.). All forms of sociation may be studied *historically* and *comparatively* in order to discover their *general features and properties* (a study which might focus upon the same form with different contents, as in the comparison of *conflict* in the economic and political spheres).

SOCIETY

Simmel's foundation for his sociology clearly has important implications for the way in which we study *society*. [10] As well as Simmel's exploration of the transcendental, quasi-Kantian question 'How is society possible?' (1908) [11] and his delineation there of the three apriories of role, individuality and structure (see pp. 120–3), it is possible to discover at least four conceptions of society in his work.

The first is that of society as *totality*, which Simmel rejects as the immediate object of sociology, insofar as it is viewed as 'an absolute entity' (explicitly arguing against Herbert Spencer, but also Durkheim). Rather, since society 'is only the synthesis or the general term for the totality of ... specific interactions', it must remain a 'gradual' concept until we have explored the myriad interactions that constitute it. Hence we can only answer the question 'what is society?' once we have investigated 'all those modes and forces of association which unite its elements'. [12]

This implies, therefore, that for Simmel society is a constellation of *forms of sociation*, including emergent as well as permanent forms. Thus, Simmel declares that 'I see society everywhere, where a number of human beings enter into interaction and form a temporary or permanent unity'. [13] The minimal 'number' that is crucial for Simmel is three. The properties of sociation can be explored with the interaction of three or more persons (though one of his students, Martin Buber, explored the significance of two – I and you). [14] The entry of the third person as Other and I and You as 'We' – is one of the crucial differences between the dyadic and triadic relationships. The variety of the forms of interaction explored by Simmel and their constituent features will be indicated more fully below. But it is worth pointing to two ideal or pure forms of interaction explored by Simmel: sociability as a pure form of sociation that must be devoid of serious content, and exchange as 'a sociological phenomenon *sui-generis*', and its reified form in money exchange.

A less fully developed but highly significant conception of society is to be found in the essays 'The Sociology of the Senses' (1907) [15], 'The Problem of Sociology' (1908) [16] and 'How is Society Possible?'. [17] There society is conceived as being *grounded in the experience and knowledge of its participants*. With respect to *experience*, it should be emphasized here that on many occasions Simmel highlights the importance of everyday experience. It is true that major formations and systems (classes, the state, religion, etc) appear to constitute that which we call society. But sociology should also be concerned with the less structured crystallizations of interactions that 'remain in a fluid state but are no less agents of the connection of individuals to societal existence'. [18] Indeed, if we confined our attention only to society's major formations, then 'it would be totally impossible to piece together the real life of society *as we encounter it in our experience*'. [19] Here and elsewhere Simmel points towards a *phenomenology* of the social world. With regard to *knowledge* of society, we have Simmel's reference in the essay 'How is society possible?' to 'the *epistemology* of society'. It is not merely the case that we ascribe meanings to the social world and its formations but also that society presupposes '*consciousness* of sociating or being sociated'. Such reflections could form part of the foundation for a sociology of knowledge. In fact, the discipline as it developed in Germany was associated with Simmel's contemporary Max Scheler, his student Karl Mannheim and later developed by Alfred Schutz in a phenomenological direction (whose work examined some specifically Simmelian themes such as the stranger). [20]

Society can also be conceived as an aesthetic *formation*. Indeed, the aesthetic dimensions of society and social interactions (already contained in the focus upon 'forms' of sociation) are one of the distinctive features of Simmel's sociology, so much so that one of his students suggested that for Simmel, society itself is 'a work of art'. [21] This concern with aesthetic dimensions of social life is signaled in his important essay 'Sociological Aesthetics' (1896) [22], which not merely explores aspects of the symmetry and asymmetry of social relations but also, as its title suggests, indicates a new avenue for sociological investigation. A sociological aesthetics 'will extended aesthetic categories to forms of society as a whole' (which would include society as aesthetic totality), as well as to each form 'in which "society" comes into being' (society as sociation). At the same time, however, the *totality* of which Simmel speaks here has its origin in the *fragmentary*. This is made explicit in the assertion that

> For us the essence of aesthetic observation and interpretation lies in the fact that the typical is to be found in what is unique, the lawlike in what is fortuitous, the essence and significance of things in the superficial and transitory ... To the adequately trained eye, the total beauty, the total meaning of the world as a whole radiates from every single point. [23]

Since society as totality is a gradual concept, this gives a further justification for focus upon the individual forms of sociation, however insignificant they might appear. This aesthetic intention is revealed in Simmel's major systematic work *The Philosophy of Money* which contains not merely over forty instances of aesthetic reflections but, more significantly, is held together as a textual totality by its primary aim: 'The unity of these investigations [lies] ... in the possibility ... of finding in each of life's details the totality of its meaning'. [24] Substantively, too, there are affinities between the aesthetic mode of perception and the sphere of money circulation and exchange. For Simmel, interpreting Kant, 'aesthetic judgement ... connects with the mere image of things, with their appearance and form, regardless of whether they are supported by an apprehendable reality or not'. [25] Money exchange relations are the abstract 'embodiment of a pure function' – a representation of values, 'the reification of the pure relationship between things, standing between the individual objects ... in a realm organized according to its own norms'. [26] Is there not a parallel here between the world of circulation and exchange of commodities and the world of aesthetic representation of the image, appearance and form of things? We will return to this argument later.

FORMS OF SOCIATION AND BEYOND

If we return for the moment to Simmel's definition of sociology as the study of forms of social interaction or sociation, it may be useful to give some indication of the diversity of the areas of sociology, social theory and cultural analysis to which he contributed. Yet any attempt to order such contributions must be aware that not only did Simmel never intend a taxonomy of forms of sociation (and still less a formal one, unlike some of his successors), but virtually all of the forms which he did explore could be located in a variety of *other* contexts. To give but one example, the study of *fashion* appears in the context of *The Philosophy of Money* as an instance of a form which the consecutive differentiation of commodities assumes. Yet the location of fashion in the modern metropolis might highlight its significance as a mode of individual differentiation, given the importance of external indicators of class, status, gender and culture in the fleeting interactions of the city. In other essays on fashion, it is explored more fully in relation to the dialectic of wishing to be like others whilst simultaneously differentiating ourselves from others and, establishing social boundaries. In these fuller treatments of fashion (1895, 1905) [27], its relationship to our experience of the presentness of modernity, to 'the specific "impatient" tempo of modern life' is made clear:

> The fact that fashion takes an unprecedented upper hand in contemporary culture – is merely the coalescing of a contemporary psychological trait. Our internal rhythm requires increasingly shorter pauses in the change in impressions; or, expressed differently, the accent of attraction is transferred to an increasing extent from its substantive centre to its starting and finishing points. [28]

Simmel's treatment of this accelerating ever-new and ever-transitory presentness that we experience in the pursuit of the fashionable has been summarised as follows:

> Fashion is the 'concentration of social consciousness upon the point' in which 'the seeds of its own death also lie'. Without an objective reason, a 'new entity' is 'suddenly' there, only to be instantly destroyed once more. Fashion is 'an aesthetic form of the drive to destruction, a totally 'present' 'break with the past'. In it, the 'fleeting and changeable element of life' stands in place of the 'major, permanent, unquestioned convictions' that 'increasingly lose their force' in modernity. [29]

The symbolic significance of fashion was not lost upon those who subsequently explored modernity such as Walter Benjamin, but this does still not exhaust the relevance of Simmel's analysis of fashion. It could, for instance, be located as an exploration of time consciousness.

Indeed, one of Simmel's early intentions was to examine the *basic categories of experience*. Although this was never fully realised, there are explorations of time in relation to modern society (on the tempo of life in *The Philosophy of Money*) and an important essay on the problem of historical time (which Husserl read closely). [30] The first substantial attempt at a sociology of *space* is provided by Simmel (see 4.4.3.2 below). Alongside critiques of historical necessity in his Problems in the *Philosophy of History* (1905), an important aspect of *causality* is explored as the teleology of means and ends in the money economy (*Philosophy of Money*, ch.3). The significance of number is analyzed in relation to its impact upon forms of social interaction. It could also be argued that *mass* is explored with reference to the extension and enlargement of social groups and its impact upon social interaction. [31] The phenomenological structure of experience itself is explored in such essays as that on the adventure (which also has relevance to the experience of presentness in modernity).

As well as studies of pure forms of sociation, such as exchange and sociability mentioned earlier, there are a whole range of analyses of *social processes* of interaction in Simmel's *Sociology* and elsewhere. These range from the processes of differentiation of individuals and social groups, the power relations of domination and subordination, group cohesion and development, the role of conflict and boundary maintenance and social distance, including the role of secrecy. Many of these processes have been subjected to empirical examination. [32] In addition, Simmel worked extensively on religion and belief systems as well as a neglected essay on the sociology of the family. [34]

How forms of sociation structure our *everyday experience* is studied by Simmel from several perspectives. Some social parameters of face to face interaction are explored in his sociology of the senses [35] and on the aesthetic significance of the face [36], his sociology of the mealtime [37], his brief excursus on face to face versus written communication [38] and, more broadly in his essays on sociability [39] and flirtation. [40]

Simmel's contemporaries praised his explorations of the *'inner life'* of individuals brought about by a variety of contexts of social interaction. Many of these studies, of varying length, also make Simmel one of the first to develop a sociology of the emotions. [41] Such studies take as their theme, for example, pessimism, shame, love, gratitude [42] and, with reference to the money economy in particular, the blasé attitude, greed and avarice. In some cases, attributes generate personality types such as the blasé person, the cynic, etc. The complexities of social typification are explored more fully with reference to the stranger [43] and the poor. [44] Probably his most famous essay on the metropolis examines its effect upon our 'mental life'. [45]

Less well known are Simmel's writings on *social issues*, often published anonymously or under a pseudonym and often in socialist journals and newspapers in the early 1890s. They include articles in support of free trades unions [46], socialized medicine [47], on prostitution [48], on the German women's movements [49] and on the structure of university education. [50] Simmel's political stance – which would later include initial support for the German position in the First World War [51] – raises a broader issue which will be addressed later, namely, whether there is an emancipatory intention in Simmels's sociology.

Many of these socio-political essays were published in the early 1890s prior to his important essay 'Sociological Aesthetics' (1896). [52] Although an aesthetic interest can be discerned already in the previous decade, this essay certainly draws our attention to *aesthetic dimensions* of life. These include the general aesthetics of spaces such as the landscape [53], the ruin [54], the bridge and the door [55] and the picture frame. [56] Specific places and their aesthetic attraction are covered in essays on the Alps [57], Florence [58], Rome [59] and Venice. [60] The works of artists and writers addressed by Simmel include Dante [61], Michelangelo [62], Rembrandt [63], Stefan George [64] and Rodin. [65] The distinction between the fine and applied arts is present in essays on art for art's sake [66], adornment [67], style [68] and the handle. [69] The display of art and other works is addressed in essays on art exhibitions [70], and the Berlin trade exhibition of 1896. [71] The aesthetics of modern life is also to be found in Simmel's *Philosophy of Money*, in his essays on culture and especially his treatment of the dialectics of subjective and objective culture. [72]

We can draw upon many of these contributions, and especially his *Philosophy of Money* and essays that relate to modern metropolitan existence, to outline a theory of modernity in Simmel's work. The *money economy* is therefore a crucial site for Simmel within which he explores exchange relations and their reification in money relations, consumption, the division of labour and production. If his *Philosophy of Money* concludes with a chapter on 'The style of life' – suggesting an aesthetic of modern life – it is presented within the context of an equally central theme in his delineation of modernity, namely the widening gap between subjective and objective culture, the creation of a culture of things *as* human culture.

CULTURAL FORMS

In this context, we should not forget that Simmel not merely makes a major contribution to sociology but that he is also a social theorist who at the turn of the century makes an influential contribution to a philosophy and sociology of *culture*. [73] Aside from the notion of a philosophical culture there are several relevant conceptualisations of culture with which Simmel works. The first is the crystallization or condensation (*Verdichtung*) of interactions into cultural forms – both transitory (as culture *in statu nascendi*) and enduring. This process of crystallization is associated with the process of giving form to particular contents. The second is the creation or cultivating (*Kultivierung*) of culture as process. Here the process is associated with the transcendence of subjectivity and the creation of objective forms. The third is the dialectic of subjective and objective culture. Objective culture stands over against and appears independent of human existence whilst, at the same time, these cultural forms are incorporated into subjective culture. The interaction between form and content, between subjective and objective culture is rarely perfect or harmonious. Rather, the latter's disjunction leads Simmel to refer at various points in his theory of culture to the *conflict*, *crisis* and *tragedy* of culture. In his later writings, the conflict between subjective and objective culture is transposed or, better, dissolved into an open metaphysical struggle between life and form. More sociologically relevant are, of course, Simmel's explorations of money in modern culture and urban culture at the two sites of modernity: the mature money economy and the modern metropolis.

Simmel insists that this objective culture is also a thoroughly *gendered* culture, and in his essay on female culture (1902) [74] argues that 'with the exception of a very few areas, our objective culture is thoroughly male', so much so that there is a 'human'–'man' identification exemplified in the fact that 'many languages even use the same word for both concepts'. [75] In this male-dominated objective culture, 'the naïve conflation of male values with values as such ... is based on historical power relations'. [76] This patriarchal system 'is grounded in a multifaceted interweaving of historical and psychological motives'. [77] Yet rather than fully explore these origins, Simmel asks whether it is possible to develop a female culture that is independent of this male dominated objective culture (whilst recognizing that women can adapt to this objective culture often through accepting differentiated tasks). Simmel finds the possibility of a distinctive female culture in the home – 'the immense cultural achievement of women'. [78] As many critics have pointed out, the exploration of male and female culture is grounded in an unsatisfactory ontological differentiation in terms of the differentiated male (by virtue of participation in the division of labour in objective culture) and the organic unity of the female. As such, the female role in modernity is problematical. [79]

In a later essay on culture. Simmel radicalizes the relationship between objective and subjective culture to the point at which objective culture becomes independent of subjective culture. By extending Marx's theory of commodity fetishism (in which commodities appear to circulate in an autonomous sphere) to cultural production, Simmel maintains that objective culture exists in an 'autonomous realm' following 'an immanent developmental logic'. [80] Because this disjunction between objective and subjective culture plays such a significant role in Simmel's delineations of modernity both in his analysis of money (especially in the last chapter of his *Philosophy of Money*) and the modern metropolis (see the opening paragraph to his 'Metropolis and Mental Life' essay), it is worth asking what some of the implications are of conceiving of objective culture as an autonomous sphere.

If this objective culture is reified, closed off from human subjects and developing according to its own 'internal' logic, then how is its investigation possible? Only at a distance? Only aesthetically? Is it merely there, without a meaning that connects with ourselves? This might give further justification for Simmel's study of social forms of interaction or sociation *in statu nascendi*, at the point of their emergence or crystallization (*Verdichtung*) when they are not fully objectified or reified. If *we* reify this autonomy of the objective cultural sphere, then any critique of this culture can be confined to a critique of culture (*Kulturkritik*) rather than a critique of the social formations that produced this autonomy (*Gesellschaftskritik*). This is an implication drawn out by Theodor Adorno in his essay 'Cultural Criticism and Society'. [81] If a feature of modernity (suggested in different ways by both Marx and Nietzsche) is a broken relationship with origin, then ostensibly we cannot search for the origin of this autonomous sphere within itself. Of course, the semblance of autonomy need not be identical with actual independence. The relationship between objective and subjective culture and the putative autonomy of the former is not merely an abstract issue for Simmel. It arises quite explicitly in his analysis of the modern money economy in which money is 'the reification of the pure relationship between things as expressed in their economic motion' and 'stands between the individual objects ... *in a realm organized according to its own norms'*. [82] It should be apparent, therefore, that such issues surrounding an autonomous culture not merely have social implications but are relevant to recent debates on the nature of modernity and postmodernity.

MODERNITY IN CONTEXT

In order to examine what is distinctive in Simmel's contribution to the study of modernity, it is useful to place it in the context of other broadly contemporary theories of modernity. First, however, it is necessary to make a number of distinctions. [83] All the social sciences have at various times developed theories of *modernisation* that seek to explain how what we term 'modern' society came into existence. Often these explanations focus upon long term developmental tendencies such as the process of rationalisation or the development of capitalism. Such theories can be framed *chronologically* and include stages of development or they can approach modernisation and modernity as a *process*. It may be useful to distinguish between such theories and explorations of *modernity* understood as modes of experiencing that which is new in modern society. In turn, we can distinguish this focus, analytically at least, from one upon *modernisms*, that is, the aesthetic representations of the experience of modernity. In practice, explorations of modernity have applied the concept of modernity both to the socio-cultural processes through which societies become modern as well as aesthetic representations of modern experience. Those theories of modernity that have signaled aesthetic dimensions have often come closer to examining modes of experiencing modernity than those that have focused upon long term processes of modernisation. In turn, there is a contradiction between theories of modernisation that focus, say upon rationalisation as a driving force in modernity, establishing a new social formation ordered by a rationality whose ends may be irrational and striving to create a *totality* and, in contrast, those theories or approaches that focus upon the disintegration of modes of ordering life forms and human experience that may, of necessity, have to commence with the *fragmentary*.

In this context, Simmel's contribution to the study of modernity is not distinguished by a developed theory of modernisation such as is found in the work of say, Marx and Weber. The long term tendencies towards increasing social differentiation and the development of a mature money economy do not compare with the historical analysis of Marx and Weber. Simmel's focus upon the mature *money economy* as the site of the extensification of the effects of modernity and upon the modern *metropolis* as the site of modernity's intensification certainly indicates a shift away from production or the modern industrial enterprise. At the same time, insofar as a significant dimension of experience of modernity on the *surface* of everyday life lies in the sphere of circulation, exchange and consumption, Simmel's focus upon these sites focuses upon spheres that are often indifferent to class, gender and ethnicity (most obvious in the sphere of circulation where *what* is circulated is without reference to persons – and their circumstances – engaged in the circulation and exchange process). One of Simmel's aims is to reveal the processes of social differentiation that may remain hidden beneath the surface of dedifferentiation.

Like some of his contemporaries, Simmel's approach to modern society drew attention to both the emergence of the mass and a crisis in individuality that was associated with increasing abstraction. Tönnies, in his *Gemeinschaft und Gesellschaft*, conceived of modern society as dominated by abstract contractual relations based upon an arbitrary will. Durkheim's concern with the pathologies of modern society drew attention to the weakened moral and social solidarity in society that insufficiently integrated or regulated the individual, and resulted in what he termed 'excessive individualism.' Weber's exploration of modernity focuses upon the historical development of modern western rationalism and its most significant product, modern western rational capitalism dominated by the formal rationality of means and the maximisation of efficiency, whose systems of purposive rational action permeated the life world of individuals and threatened other systems of meaning. The new spirit of calculability emphasized by Weber had already been examined by Sombart whose account of modernity around 1900 emphasized the significance of uncertainty, unrest and perpetual change, the emergence of mass phenomena (including mass consumption) and the development of a distinctive modern urban culture ('asphalt culture'). Though occasionally drawing upon Simmel's work on money, Sombart came to develop a dubious anti-modernity stance. [84]

In their critical and influential explorations of modernity, a later generation of theorists such as Kracauer (who had studied with Simmel) and Benjamin (who took up Simmel's work on money, fashion, etc.) responded to Simmel's attempts to capture modes of experiencing modernity rather than those of his contemporary sociologists. If we add to this Simmel's impact upon leading artists and writers then it confirms that his social theory and philosophy contributed to avant-garde movements in the twentieth century. Indeed, Manfredo Tafuri, maintains that 'Simmel's considerations on the great metropolis contained *in nuce* the problems that were to be at the centre of concern of the historical avant-garde movements'. [85]

INVESTIGATING MODERNITY

One of the approaches to Simmel's exploration of modernity, which we will examine below, is through his essay 'The Metropolis and Mental Life' (1903), an essay which outlines several strands of his argument from his investigation of the mature money economy (in *The Philosophy of Money*, 1900), the other site of modernity. An ostensibly less promising approach is his only 'definition' of modernity, whose essence is

> psychologism, the experiencing and interpretation of the world in terms of the reactions of our inner life and indeed as an inner world, the dissolution of fixed contents in the fluid element of the soul, from which all that is substantive is filtered and whose forms are merely forms of motion. [86]

Modernity is here conceived as being experienced as an inner world that is in flux and whose substantive contents are themselves dissolved in motion. It suggests the kind of transformation of experience that Benjamin later maintained was constitutive for modernity, namely from concrete, historical experience (*Erfahrung*) to inner, lived experience (*Erlebnis*). There is also implicit here the notion that the process of dissolution of experience results in fragmentation.

But there is, too, affinity between this 'definition' of modernity with its emphasis upon 'inner life', 'fluidity' and 'motion' and Simmel's exploration of metropolitan experience with its 'swift and uninterrupted change' in stimuli, 'the rapid crowding of changing images, the sharp discontinuity in the grasp of a single glance, and the unexpectedness of onrushing impressions', 'the threatening currents and discrepancies' – all of which result in 'the intensification of nervous stimulation'. [87] What is added here to the focus upon inner life is not merely the physical confrontations and shocks of metropolitan modernity but also their recurring immediacy and presentness in everyday interactions. Such a conception of modernity, which has some affinities with Bandelaire's notion of modernity as the discontinuous experience of time as transitory, space as fleeting and causality replaced by the fortuitous, poses specific methodological problems. [88]

Simmel's theoretical and substantive contributions to our understanding of modernity presuppose an object of study that is dynamic and in permanent flux, fragmentary, problematical, often internal and located in the everyday world. His conception of modernity is not that of a decisive unilinear process but rather one of interaction between contradictory dimensions, whose contradictions, in turn, are not resolved. In this sense, the experience of modernity being analysed is not merely one that is in flux, but also one in which the analysts themselves are also in motion. They too are in transit, transitional (Lukács in another context described Simmel as a 'transitional phenomenon').

We should also remember how often the titles of Simmel's explorations reflect the *problematical* status of the phenomena under investigation. Neither Durkheim, Weber or Tönnies wrote articles titled 'The Problem of Sociology', 'The Problem of Historical Time', 'Towards a Theory of ...', 'Some Reflections on ...' or 'How is society possible?' Durkheim was confident of knowing the answers, whilst Weber could at times regard his conceptual apparatus as basic (the *Grundbegriffe* that open his *Economy and Society*). So many of Simmel's essays retain that provisional, hesitant status that led his student Ernst Bloch to describe Simmel as 'the philosopher of perhaps'. The hypothetical nature of reality (also signalled in Vaihinger's *Philosophy of As If*) is reinforced by the frequency of 'What if' reflections in his writings. [89]

The *fragmentary* experience of modernity manifests itself in several ways, including the forms of his approach to reality. That which is of significance is often located in an aside, an intermediate reflection, an excursus (as in 'The Stranger' or other instances in his *Sociology*). Viewed substantially, the experience of modernity as fragmentary (e.g. the moments of immediate presentness) raises the question of the fragment's relation to the totality. First, can the fragments be (re) assembled into a totality? In his analysis of society, we have seen that, for Simmel, 'society is only the synthesis or the general term for the totality of specific interactions' [90] and that there does not exist a pre existing societal totality (except in the sense that we may presuppose it counterfactually). Second, Simmel argued that the analysis of the fragmentary, of the small insignificance units or 'threads' of sociation may give us greater insight into the nature of society than the analysis of its major institutions. Third, a aesthetic interpretation allows the totality to be distilled from the fragmentary, such that 'the *typical* is to be found in what is *unique*, the *law-like* in what is *fortuitous*, the essence and significance of things in the *superficial* and *transitory*'. [91]

Similarly, the analysis of experience of modernity as a *world in flux*, in motion, is also approached in a variety of ways. Addressing the issue of capturing metropolitan modernity, Baudelaire had praised the 'painter of modern life' for his rapid sketches of the latest new changes. The equivalent mode for Simmel lay in the essay form, of which he was a recognised master. In this context, his student Lukács declared that 'the essay can calmly and proudly set its fragmentariness against the petty completeness of scientific exactitude or impressionistic freshness'. [92] The dynamic, open-endedness of the world in flux is manifested too in the unresolved nature of the antinomies and contradiction which animate all Simmel's essays, perhaps leaving to the reader the task of intervening and resolving them. This dynamic is also captured by

Simmel in his short pieces entitled 'Snapshots *sub specie aeternitalis*', snapshots viewed from the perspective of eternity. [93] More basically, we can suggest that the use of relational concepts (such as *Wechselwirkung*, literally reciprocal or changing effect, but translated as social interaction) enables him to capture social forms in motion, including those that are fleeting. Finally, Simmel seeks to distill the forms of life, forms of interaction as a way of capturing general properties of interaction through separation from their varied contents.

The focus upon the *everyday world*, upon more than what Marx termed 'the daily traffic of bourgeois life', is a distinctive feature of Simmel's analysis. He was 'the first to accomplish the return of philosophy to concrete subjects, a shift that remained canonical for everyone dissatisfied with the chattering of epistemology or intellectual history'. [94] Viewed sociologically, this focus upon social relations in the everyday world as an object of study resulted, Mannheim argued, from 'an aptitude for describing the simplest everyday experiences with the same precision as is characteristic of a contemporary impressionistic painting' and an ability 'to analyse the significance of minor social forces that were previously unobserved'. [95] However, this everyday world is not already organised as a sociological problem since

> the world of things in no way confronts the mind, as it might appear, as a sum total of problems whose solution it has to gradually master. Rather, we must first extract them as problems from out of the indifference, the absence of inner connection and the uniform nature with which things first of all present themselves to us. [96]

This everyday world of things is, in turn, one in which phenomena are interrelated. In his study of money, for example, Kracauer argued that Simmel's intention was 'to reveal the interwoven nature of the assembled parts of the diversity of the world' without privileging or prioritizing any part (in contrast to social theories that take a foundation, such as the economy, for their analysis of society).

In these respects at least, Simmel's sociological and philosophical orientation was one that enabled him to access some of the features of modernity that his contemporaries either did not consider significant or were only able to deal with in a more abstract manner. To give some indication of his analysis of one of the site of modernity, we will focus upon the modern metropolis since a later chapter examines in some detail the money economy.

METROPOLITAN MODERNITY

Massimo Cacciari has made the bold claim that 'the problem of the Metropolis, as a problem of the relation between modern existence and its forms, is the point from which all of Georg Simmel's philosophy develops'. [97] Conceived in such general terms this may be plausible. But the more modest thesis will be examined here, namely, that in order to comprehend the extent of Simmel's explorations of metropolitan modernity we have to recognise that his famous essay on the metropolis should be viewed as an intersection of other texts on urban experience, as well as itself being a text containing silences and absences. [98]

The modern metropolis is the site of intensification or concentration of modernity (with the mature money economy as the site of its extensification, whilst *also* having its focal point in the modern metropolis). Rather than the mode of production or the industrial capitalist enterprise, the economic focus is upon the sphere of circulation, exchange and consumption in both sites of modernity. With regard to the metropolis, emphasis is placed upon the circulation of individuals, groups and commodities and their forms of interaction and modes of representation. The image of the metropolis is that of a complex web of criss-crossing interactions and a site of myriad intersections of social circles or networks and their social boundaries.

To conceive of the modern metropolis as dominated by circulation implies a focus upon forms of movement or motion. In turn, this means a movement away from the continuity and immediacy of experience to discontinuity, mediation and abstraction. These latter features are also highlighted by Simmel in his analysis of modern money economy and direct our attention not merely to the movement of commodities and our images of them, but also our increasingly indirect relation to things in the money economy (as the extension of the teleological chain in money transactions). In turn, for individuals metropolitans experience is also associated with movement, with new experiences of social spaces and the plurality and speed of contact with others. The changes in experience and perception in the modern metropolis stem, in part, from the fact that the observer/spectator is also in motion, as are the images of things, streetscapes and exhibitions. With respect to the latter, it should not be forgotten that the context for Simmel's essay on the metropolis was its origin as a lecture, one of a series on the metropolis, given in February 1903 prior to the opening of the first German Municipal Exhibition in Dresden, devoted to displaying features of the modern German city. [99]

Simmel was asked to lecture upon the mental or intellectual life of the city (though what was expected of him was emphasis upon its cultural, intellectual and artistic offerings), and this is one of his major concerns in the essay. However, when read in isolation it does not do justice to the extent of his other relevant investigations of the modern city and nor does it necessarily lead us to view its deficiencies. Since some of the essay's more obvious aspects have already been alluded to and are covered briefly later (in chapter 4), our intention here will be to highlight other aspects of metropolitan life that are either briefly mentioned in the 1903 essay or are absent but developed elsewhere.

The *spatiality* of social interactions that is made explicit in references to the role of social distance in the modern metropolis is examined more fully in Simmel's essays on space. Whilst the general features of his sociology of space are discussed below (see 4.4.3.2), it is worth emphasizing here that the somewhat formal aspects of space have relevance for the fleeting, variable and opposing dimensions of spatial relations in the metropolis: distance and proximity; separation and connection; boundary and openness; fixity and mobility; abstract and concrete space; unity and separation; and inside and outside. Social boundaries that are so significant in urban stratification exist alongside time/space distantiation, abstract spaces of circulation and exchange and the transpatial 'community' of the money economy.

The modes of *interacting with others* in the modern metropolis that are associated with the creation of social distance are amplified in other essays as the senses (and the crucial role of vision) sociability and the stranger. Sociability, as a play form of sociation based upon the form rather than content of interaction, already presupposes distance but not so dramatically as in the exploration of our confrontation of the stranger as Other. Our more abstract relationship to the stranger as Other, the sense of fortuitousness in our relations with the stranger, our relation to strangers in the city not as individuals but rather as strangers of a particular type, and Simmel's references to 'inner enemies' and the proximity/distance dialectic in the stranger's position creating 'dangerous possibilities', all indicate that this is a crucial discussion of Otherness implying that we are socialized as strangers in the metropolis.

How we *represent and reveal ourselves* to others and, in turn, how we are able to *read* others in the metropolis reveals a concern not merely with our 'mental life' but with our body life in the metropolis and its presentation. Crucial to that presentation of self is the face and our reading of and response to the Other. And as a face in the crowd, and in public transport systems it is the eye that expresses most rapidly our interactional intentions. The eye 'bores into things, it retreats back, it encompasses a space, it wanders around, it grasps the desired object as if behind it and draws it to itself'. [100] Within the city's on rushing impressions, the rapid gaze and increase in nervous stimulation, this eye, as Mattenklott has argued might be

> that of the hunter: highly mobile and yet motionless; alert but not disturbed; encompassing everything, but itself never grasped. It is the ideal eye of the city dweller and the sociologist. ... In order that the physiognomical gaze ... should not be continually caught up in individual contents, it must immunize itself against sympathy or aversion: a cold eye. [101]

Less menacingly, perhaps, our representation of self and recognition of others owes much to our external presentation, to *fashion*, whose focal point is the metropolis. As one of the 'fillings in of time and consciousness' – as Simmel terms leisure – that are offered in the modern metropolis, fashion has a close relationship to modernity with its increasing 'turnover-time', its reflection of the '"impatient" tempo of life', its transitory nature that 'gives us such a strong sense of presentness' and the dialectic through which it 'emerges as if it wishes to live for eternity' but in which, at its very moment of emergence the seeds of its own death are located. It appeals especially to those preoccupied with social mobility, social strata abundant in the metropolis. The aesthetic veil of newness clothes both ourselves and the commodities that we desire. [102]

There are few *figures* in the metropolitan cityscape highlighted in Simmel's 1903 essay. Alongside the blasé person, the cynic, the fashion addict and dandy, the eccentric individual are also present. Elsewhere in his writings, the stranger, the poor, the adventurer and the prostitute all have explicit or implicit connections – not always made by Simmel – with metropolitan modernity. And since the metropolis is the focal point of the money economy, its figures are also present – not merely the blase person but also the less well drawn figure of the calculating individual.

Yet there are a number of dimensions of modern metropolitan life that Simmel does not explore in his 1903 essay, some of which are explored elsewhere. The economic focus upon the money economy draws attention to the sphere of circulation, exchange and consumption rather than that of *production*. Like Benjamin's image of Berlin around 1900, there is little indication that Berlin was a major site of industrial and manufacturing production, including some of its most advanced sectors such as Siemens and AEG. Similarly, there are dimensions of social *stratification* and *power* relations that hardly feature in the metropolis essay. Although Simmel writes elsewhere on female culture (and argues that objective culture is totally male dominated), there is no reference to female metropolitan culture. [103] Elsewhere, Simmel analyses systems of domination and the maintenance of social boundaries. Insofar as the essay owes something at least to his experience of Berlin, Simmel was certainly aware of state bureaucracies in the capital city of the German Empire. As Robert Park's lecture notes for 1899 reveal, this administrative organisation's ambiguous relationship to modernity was not unknown to Simmel. Bureaucracies form a part of the expanding objective culture, one endowed with their own (illusory) independence:

> Bureaucracy ... is a formal structure that is indispensable, but nonetheless a formal one. Bureaucratic organisation must be schematic. This necessary schematism, however, often comes into conflict with the requirements of real social life that cannot be forced into it. The machinery of bureaucracy stands perplexed confronted by very complex and individually distinctive cases. In addition, the slow pace at which it works is often a stumbling block. Yet if such

an organ forgets its merely subservient role and regards itself as
the purpose of its own existence, then a contradiction must emerge,
the impossibility of the coexistence of the two forms of life alongside
on another. In the abyss between the self-forgetting bureaucracy and
the requirements of practical life there lies many partly humorous,
partly tragic frictions'. [104]

Already anticipating aspects of Weber's later analysis, Simmel implies that the
illusory autonomy of this expanding mode of organisation constitutes a
significant dimension of objective culture in the modern metropolis.

If bureaucracies are one of the modes in which the state represents itself to
us, then world *exhibitions* can be modes of representing not merely commodities
but also metropolitan centres. The city as spectacle figures in explorations of art
exhibitions and the Berlin Trade Exhibition of 1896. [105] The art exhibition,
with its juxtaposition of contradictory representations, produces an 'overloading'
of impressions that is not dissimilar from the effect of the streetscape from which
the visitor has seemingly escaped. The trade exhibition of 1896 – which
symbolised Berlin's elevation to a world city (*Weltstadt*) – displayed an even
more heterogeneous array of commodities whose only unifying element was
'amusement'. Such exhibitions were a form of sociation into 'the culture of
things', sociation into a form of consumption of dead commodities.
Consumption is viewed here as compensation for the monotony of work, a mode
of consumption dependent upon visual stimuli and new modes of representing
commodities. At the same time, such exhibitions encouraged the consumption of
representations of the modern metropolis in which 'a single city has broadened
into the totality of cultural production' and through which the exhibition
has become 'a *momentary* centre of world civilization'. The momentary and
transitory is reflected in 'the temporary purposes' of exhibition architecture,
thereby being recognizing as transient structures of modernity. Here it is worth
noting that this is one of the few places in which Simmel addresses aspects of the
aesthetics of the *modern* metropolis which, elsewhere he maintained could never
constitute a landscape. [106]

Somewhat like his contemporary Durkheim, (though nothing like
Durkheim's detailed analysis) Simmel makes reference to some of the
pathologies of metropolitan modernity, many of which he sees originating in the
money economy. But alongside neurasthenia, hyperaesthesia, anesthesia and
perhaps the blase attitude (a pathology rendered *normal*) the specifically modern
urban pathology is agoraphobia (briefly discussed in *The Philosophy of Money*),
itself subject to major debate in the late nineteenth century. And insofar as
modernity generates a focus upon an eternal *present* this implies a forgetting of
the past and the possibility of amnesia. [107]

With the exception of the blasé attitude, however, these are not the
tensions that animate the 1903 metropolis essay. The preceding brief analysis

has sought to show how the intersection of texts (and thematics) can provide a fuller account of Simmel's contributions to the delineation of metropolitan modernity that explore *interalia*, interactions with others (distanced, fortuitous, calculating, functional, sociable) mediated by our senses and spatial relations; knowledge of others through typification and representations (face work, body, fashion, adornment); pathologies; and our relationship to metropolitan objective culture (in monetary transaction, representations of commodities, systems of domination and bureaucratic administration and a gendered objective culture).

Simmel's metropolis essay concludes with the possibility for individual freedom and emancipation in the metropolis. A less often asked question is the extent to which his sociology is emancipatory. At issue is not Simmel's overt political stance (such as his early association with socialist aims) nor his muted political references on class structure and systems of domination. In contrast to Marx's emancipatory intent that aimed at the transformation of his object of study or to Durkheim's reformist response to social problems, the emancipatory potential of his sociology is much more muted. A case can be made for suggesting that it lies in the use that we can make of his analysis of the general properties of forms of social interaction, including those that we encounter in systems of domination and conflict and in our everyday interactions. Our recognition of these properties of interaction and how they function may liberate us from their oppressive effects and enable us to 'play' more freely in a society whose forms and rules of interaction we are consciously aware of. Simmel's unresolved tension and contradictions that provide a dynamism to his essays also encourages *our* participation in conceiving of possible resolutions to their guiding antinomies.

ANTICIPATING POSTMODERNITY

The continuing relevance of aspects of Simmel's explorations of modernity have led some to claim him as a postmodern theorist. [108] His critical response to modernity does not, however, make him a postmodern theorist. However, there are aspects of his analysis of modernity that are relevant for theories of modernity. If we take Lyotard's delineation of the postmodern condition as one that designates 'the state of our culture following the transformation which, since the end of the nineteenth century, have altered the game rules for science, literature and the arts', [109] then Simmel remains in some respects a contemporary theorist. The abandonment of grand narratives and the substitution with a plurality of language games is partly heralded with the Neo Kantian plurality of value spheres and Wittgenstein's mature philosophy. Simmel did theorize the fragmentation of both individuals and discourses, and a breakdown in unified contact with the past which now, he argued, 'comes down to us only in fragments' as a past that 'can come to life and be interpreted only through the experiences of the immediate present'. However, our experience of the immediate present is one of discontinuity, flux and fragmentation.

There are, however, three areas amongst others in which features of Simmel's delineation and explorations of modernity are relevant for theories of postmodernity. They are the contrality of focus upon the spheres of circulation, exchange and consumption; the growing autonomy of the cultural sphere; and a re-emphasis upon the aesthetic domain.

The shift from a focus upon production (implied in those theories of postmodernity that imply a post-production and post-industrial society) to one upon circulation, exchange and consumption may be viewed as a mode of theorizing the economy that took place over a century ago with the so-called Marginalist Revolution in economics, a shift towards a 'subjective' theory of value and the consumer as source of value-creation. Simmel's analysis of the money economy does take up some assumptions of marginalist theory, though in a critical manner, as in the central role of exchange as a sociological phenomenon. His treatment of the extension of commodification to leisure and human experience itself finds echoes in some postmodern discourse. The shift from production is certainly signaled in the metropolis and the money economy as the sites of modernity. The experiential analysis of the money economy and the phenomenal forms of the spheres of circulation, exchange and consumption implies, too, that Simmel, unlike Marx, remains longer with 'the daily traffic of bourgeois life', with 'the movement which proceeds on the surface of the bourgeois world'. [110]

Unlike Marx, Simmel does not go in search of the 'laws of motion' of the capitalist mode of production that will explain why the phenomenal forms of capitalist society (in the spheres of circulation and exchange) appear to us in the manner in which they do so. However, Simmel's analysis does view money as obliterating distinctions between use values, as the form in which value exists as a seemingly autonomous exchange value, and does recognize that the sphere of circulation appears to us an autonomous sphere, one that seems to be guided by its own laws. Such a self referential system comprising self-referential signifiers points towards a concern with the representational forms of commodities whether it be the ever-new face of the commodity creating the external and unstable illusion of modernity in fashion or fashion's co-production of the aesthetic veil or aesthetic attraction of things. This symbolic significance of money and commodities can be seen as anticipating some of Bandrillard's contemporary concerns. [111]

The apparent autonomy of the sphere of circulation, exchange and consumption has affinity with the autonomy of the sphere of objective culture, as Simmel indicated in his 1911 essay on culture when he asserted that

> The 'fetishistic character' which Marx attributed to economic objects
> in the epoch of commodity production is only a particularly modified

> instance of this general fate of the contents of our culture. These
> contents are subject to the paradox ... that they are indeed created by
> human subjects and are meant for human subjects, but follow an
> imminent developmental logic ... and thereby become alienated from
> both their origin and their purpose. [112]

The contents of this objective culture acquire an 'ominous independence'
somewhat akin to the commodity form in the sphere of circulation for Marx. But
for Simmel cultural forms stand in opposition to life forms and generate an
artistic and intellectual opposition to the reification of cultural forms that
manifests itself, for instance, in 'the modern feeling against closed systems', in
artistic movements such as Expressionism that seek to represent inner life and
experience and in the dissolution of formal religious life into religiosity.

For Simmel, the contradictions within modernity can be transcended in the
work of art, which is one reason for the attention he gives to the *aesthetic sphere*,
both within everyday life as well as the great art work – indeed more than any of
his sociological contemporaries. As we have seen, his sociology reveals as
aesthetic dimension in social interaction, one that we do not immediately
perceive in our everyday life, composed as it is of diverse and intersecting
interactional frames. Simmel is thus able to reveal aesthetic constellations and
configurations that both exist in but are often hidden in 'the flat surface of
everyday life'.

In his reading of Kant's philosophy, the aesthetic realm 'connects with the
mere image of things, with their appearance and form, regardless of whether they
are supported by an apprehendable reality'. Such a reading reveals an affinity
with the sphere of circulation and exchange (the circulation of images of things)
of commodities, and anticipates a concern in much postmodern theory. But to
remain with Simmel's intentions, aesthetic dimensions of the everyday world are
revealed, for instance, in his explorations of the fragmentary as a key to the
whole, the significance of distance, symmetry and asymmetry, the processes of
form-giving, the contrasts between the applied work of art (for us) and the work
of art (for itself), the picture frame and the process of framing, the modern
preponderance of style as disguise, as 'a veil that imposes a barrier and a
distance', in the stylization of forms of life (the last chapter of his study of money
is titled 'The style of life'), in the generation of a plurality of styles in which
'each style has it own syntax', as well as the dialectics of fashion. Much
postmodern theory may have other aesthetic concerns but some, at least, are
already anticipated in Simmel's work.

As the present introductory study indicates, Simmel had a significant
impact upon a whole range of sociological, philosophical and artistic fields:
through Small and Park upon the Chicago School, in philosophy through
students such as Husserl and Buber, in critical theory and sociology

through students such as Lukács, Bloch, Kracauer and Mannheim, in art history through Wilhelm Worringer and Max Raphael, in architecture through Erich Mendelsohn, Martin Wagner, and in literature Hugo von Hoffmansthal and Robert Musil. Though not a student of Simmel's, Walter Benjamin's prehistory of modernity and some of his other work contains more than traces of his work. [113]

Almost a century after Simmel's work was completed, there may be some justification for taking seriously Albion Small's reflection in 1924 that 'prophecy would be rash, but it is quite possible that Post-Simmelism will prove to be a pillar in the ultimate sociology. [114] Yet no doubt Simmel would have wished to point out that in modernity there can be no 'ultimate' sociology.

NOTES AND REFERENCES

[1]   Over half of the *Gesamtausgabe* (hereafter cited as GA with appropriate volume number) has been published under the general editorship of Otthein Rammstedt by Suhrkamp Verlag, Frankfurt.

[2]   See Klaus C. Kohnke, *Der junge Simmel – in Theoriebeziehungen und sozialen Bewegungen*, Frankfurt, Suhrkamp (1996).

[3]   *Uber sociale Differenzierung* (editor H.J. Dahme), GA 2 (1989), pp. 109–296.

[4]   *Philosophie des Geldes* (editors D.P. Frisby and K.C. Kohnke), GA 6 (1989); in English as *The Philosophy of Money*, (edited by D. Frisby), London, Routledge (2002).

[5]   *Soziologie* (editor O. Rammstedt) GA 11 (1992). Much of this volume is available in English in K.H. Wolff (editor), *The Sociology of Georg Simmel*, Glencoe, Free Press (1950).

[6]   See chapter 3 below.

[7]   See 'The Problem of Sociology', *Annals of the American Academy of Political and Social Science*, Vol. 6, 1895, pp. 412–23; reprinted in D. Frisby (editor), *Georg Simmel. Critical Assessments*, London, Routledge (1994), Vol. 1, pp. 28–35.

[8]   *Georg Simmel. Critical Assessments*, op. cit., p. 34.

[9]   See p. 54 below.

[10]   See D.P. Frisby, *Simmel and Since. Essays on Georg Simmel's Social Theory*, London, Routledge (1992), ch. 1.

[11]   G. Simmel, 'How is Society Possible?', in K.H. Wolff (editor), *Georg Simmel 1858–1918*, Columbus Ohio, Ohio State University Press (1958), pp. 337–56.

[12]   See *Simmel and Since*, ch. 1, p. 11.

[13]   *Ibid.*, p. 12.

[14]   Martin Buber, *I and Thou*, (trans. by R.G. Smith), Edinburgh, T. & T. Clark (1937).

[15] G. Simmel, 'Sociology of the Senses' in D. Frisby and M. Featherstone (editors), *Simmel on Culture. Selected Writings*, London, Sage (1997), pp. 109–120.

[16] G. Simmel, 'The Problem of Sociology' in K.H. Wolff (editor), *Georg Simmel 1858–1918*, op. cit., pp. 310–336.

[17] *Ibid.*, pp. 337–56.

[18] G. Simmel, 'Sociology of the Senses', p. 109. New translation.

[19] *Ibid.*, p. 110.

[20] On Scheler and Mannheim see my *The Alienated Mind. The Sociology of Knowledge in Germany 1918–1933*, (second edition), London, Routledge (1992). See Alfred Schutz, *Collected Papers*, 3 Volumes, The Hague, Martinus Nijhoff (1964, 1966, 1967).

[21] Arthur Salz, cited in *Simmel and Since*, p. 16.

[22] G. Simmel, 'Sociological Aesthetics' in *The Conflict in Modern Culture and Other Essays*, (editor P. Etzkorn), New York, Teachers College Press (1968), pp. 68–80.

[23] *Ibid.*, p. 69. Translation amended.

[24] G. Simmel, *The Philosophy of Money*, p. 55.

[25] G. Simmel, *Kant*, Leipzig, Duncker & Humblot (1904), p. 166.

[26] G. Simmel, *The Philosophy of Money*, p. 176.

[27] For the fullest treatment see G. Simmel, 'The Philosophy of Fashion' in D. Frisby and M. Featherstone, *Simmel on Culture*, pp. 187–211.

[28] Cited in *Simmel and Since*, p. 126.

[29] H. Brunkhorst, 'So etwas angenehm frisch Gekopftes. Mode und Soziologie' in S. Bovenschen (editor), *Die Listen der Mode*, Frankfurt, Suhrkamp (1986), p. 408. Cited in English in *Simmel and Since*, p. 75.

[30] G. Simmel, *Das Problem der historischen Zeit*, Berlin, Reuther & Reichard (1916).

[31] See 'Quantitative Aspects of the Group' in K.H. Wolff, *The Sociology of Georg Simmel*, pp. 87–99.

[32] For some examples see D. Frisby, *Georg Simmel. Critical Assessments*, Section 7.

[33] These are now collected in H.J. Helle (editor), Georg Simmel, *Essays on Religion*, New Haven, Yale University Press (1997).

[34] G. Simmel, 'On the Sociology of the Family', *Theory, Culture & Society*, Volume 15, nos. 3–4, 1998, pp. 283–93.

[35] *Simmel on Culture*, pp. 109–120.

[36] G. Simmel, 'The Aesthetic Significance of the Face' in K.H. Wolff (editor), *Georg Simmel 1858–1918*, Columbus, Ohio, Ohio State University Press (1958), pp. 276–81.

[37] G. Simmel, 'Sociology of the Meal' in *Simmel on Culture*, pp. 130–35.

[38] G. Simmel, 'Written Communication', in *The Sociology of Georg Simmel*, pp. 352–5.

[39] *Ibid.*, pp. 40–57.

[40] G. Simmel 'Flirtation', in *Georg Simmel: On Women, Sexuality and Love*, (editor, G. Oakes), New Haven, Yale University Press (1984), pp. 133–52.

[41] See *Simmel and Since*, chapter 2; also J. Gerhards, 'Georg Simmel's Contribution to a Theory of Emotions', *Social Science Information*, 25, 1986, pp. 901–24.

[42] See, for example, 'On Love' in *Georg Simmel: On Women, Sexuality and Love*, pp. 153–92; 'Faithfulness and Gratitude' in *The Sociology of Georg Simmel*, pp. 379–95.

[43] G. Simmel, 'The Stranger' in *The Sociology of Georg Simmel*, pp. 402–8.

[44] G. Simmel, 'The Poor' in L. Coser, 'The Sociology of Poverty', *Social Problems*, 13, 1970, pp. 140–48.

[45] G. Simmel, 'The Metropolis and Mental Life', in *The Sociology of Georg Simmel*, pp. 409–24; also in *Simmel on Culture*, pp. 174–85. There is another translation in G. Simmel, *On individuality and Social Forms*, (editor D.N. Levine), Chicago, Chicago University Press (1971), pp. 324–39.

[46] G. Simmel, 'Ein Wort über soziale Freiheit', *Sozialpolitisches Zentralblatt*, 1, 1892, pp. 333–35.

[47] G. Casparis and A.G. Higgins, 'Georg Simmel on Social Medicine' in *Georg Simmel. Critical Assessments*, Volume 3, pp. 168–73.

[48] Anon., 'Einiges über die Prostitution in Gegenwart und Zukunft', *Die neue Zeit*, 10, 1, 1892, pp. 517–25.

[49] G. Simmel, 'Der Frauenkongress und die Sozialdemokratie', *Die Zukunft*, 17, 1896, pp. 80–4.

[50] Anon.,'Zur Privatdozenten Frage', *Die Zeit*, 7, 1896. Now in D. Frisby (editor), *Georg Simmel in Wien. Texte und Kontexte aus dem Wien der Jahrhundertwende*, Vienna, WUV Universitätsverlag (2001), pp. 54–60.

[51] See D. Frisby, *Sociological Impressionism. A Reassessment of Georg Simmel's Social Theory*, (second edition), London, Routledge (1991), chapter 5; also P. Watier, 'The Wartime Writings of Georg Simmel', *Theory, Culture & Society*, 8, 3, 1991, pp. 219–33.

[52] G. Simmel, Sociological Aesthetics' in *The Conflict in Modern Culture and Other Essays*, pp. 68–80.

[53] G. Simmel, 'Philosophie der Landschaft', GA 12, 1 (editors R. Kramme and A. Rammstedt) (2001), pp. 471–82.

[54] G. Simmel, 'The Ruin' in *Georg Simmel 1858–1918*, pp. 259–66.

[55] G. Simmel, 'Bridge and Door' in *Simmel on Culture*, pp. 170–4.

[56] G. Simmel, 'The Picture Frame: An Aesthetic Study', *Theory, Culture & Society*, 11, 1, 1994, pp. 11–18.

[57] G. Simmel, 'Zur Aesthetik der Alpen', in GA 12, 1(2001), pp. 162–9.

[58] G. Simmel, 'Florenz', in GA 8, 2 (editors A. Cavalli and V. Krech) (1993), pp. 69–73.

[59] G. Simmel, 'Rom', in GA 5 (editors H.-J. Dahme and D.P. Frisby)(1992), pp. 301–10.

[60] G. Simmel, 'Venedig' in GA 8, 2 (1993), pp. 258–62.

[61] G. Simmel, 'Dantes Psychologie', in GA 1 (editor K.C. Kohnke) (1999), pp. 91–178.

[62] G. Simmel, 'Michelangelo als Dichter', in GA 2 (editor H.-J. Dahme) (1989), pp. 37–48.

[63] G. Simmel, *Rembrandt*, Leipzig, Kurt Wolff, 1916.

[64] G. Simmel, 'Stephan George. Eine kunstphilosophische Betrachtung', in GA 2 (1989), pp. 287–300.

[65] G. Simmel, 'Rodin', in *Philosophische Kultur*, Leipzig, Klinkhardt (1911), pp. 185–206.

[66] G. Simmel, 'L'art pour l'art', in GA 13, 2 (editor K. Latzel) (2000), pp. 9–15.

[67] G. Simmel, 'Adornment' in *The Sociology of Georg Simmel*, pp. 338–44.

[68] G. Simmel, 'The Problem of Style', *Theory, Culture & Society*, 8, 3, 1991, pp. 63–71.

[69] G. Simmel, 'The Handle' in *Georg Simmel 1858–1918*, pp. 267–75.

[70] G. Simmel, 'Über Kunstausstellungen', *Unsere Zeit*, 26.2.1890, pp. 474–80.

[71] G. Simmel, 'The Berlin Trade Exhibition', in *Simmel on Culture*, pp. 255–58.

[72] The major essays on culture are now in *Simmel on Culture*, pp. 33–107.

[73] See my introduction to *Simmel on Culture*, pp. 1–31; also B. Nedelmann, 'Individualization, Exaggeration and Paralysation: Simmel's Three Problems of Culture', *Theory, Culture & Society*, 8, 3, 1991, pp. 169–94.

[74] G. Simmel, 'Female Culture', in *Georg Simmel: on Women, Sexuality and Love*, pp. 65–101. For the context, see Oakes's introduction to this volume.

[75] *Ibid.*, p. 67.

[76] *Ibid.*

[77] *Ibid.*, p. 69.

[78] *Ibid.*, p. 92.

[79] For a critique of Simmel's position see R. Felski, *The Gender of Modernity*, Cambridge, Harvard University Press (1995), chapter 2.

[80] *Simmel on Culture*, p. 70.

[81] T.W. Adorno, 'Cultural Criticism and Society', *Prisms*, London, Spearman (1967), pp. 17–34.

[82] G. Simmel, *The Philosophy of Money* (second edition edited by D. Frisby), London, Routledge (1990), p. 176. My emphasis.

[83] See my *Fragments of Modernity*, Cambridge, Polity; Cambridge, Mass., MIT Press 1986, chapter 1.

[84] On Sombart see F. Lenger, *Werner Sombart 1863–1941*, Munich, Beck (1994); also, J. Herf, *Reactionary Modernism*, Cambridge, Cambridge University Press (1986), chapter 6.

[85] M. Tafuri, *Architecture and Utopia*, Cambridge, Mass., MIT Press (1968), p. 88.

[86] The context is Simmel's essay on Rodin. For a discussion see my *Fragments of Modernity*, chapter 2; on the metropolis in detail see my *Cityscapes of Modernity. Critical Explorations*, Cambridge, Polity (2001), chapter 3.

[87] *Simmel on Culture*, p. 175.

[88] For a brief discussion of Baudelaire in this context see *Fragments of Modernity*, chapter 1.

[89] Hans Vaihinger, *Die Philosophie des Als Ob*, Leipzig, Meiner (1911).

[90] See *Simmel and Since*, chapter 1.

[91] 'Sociological Aesthetics' in *The Conflict in Modern Culture and Other Essays*, p. 69.

[92] G. Lukács, 'The Essay as Form', cited in my *Sociological Impressionism*, p. 71.

[93] On the significance of these pieces see O. Rammstedt 'On Simmel's Aesthetics: Argumentation in the journal "Jugend", 1897–1906', *Theory, Culture & Society*, 8, 3, 1991, pp. 125–44.

[94] T.W. Adorno, 'The Handle, the Pot, and Early Experience', *Notes to Literature*, volume 2, New York, Columbia University Press (1991), p. 213.

[95] Cited in *Sociological Impressionism*, p. 95.

[96] G. Simmel, 'Üeber Massenverbrechen', in GA 1 (1999), p. 388.

[97] M. Cacciari, *Architecture and Nihilism*, New Haven, Yale University Press (1993), p. 3.

[98] For a fuller treatment see *Cityscapes of Modernity*, chapter 3.

[99] For details see *Cityscapes of Modernity*, pp. 130–43.

[100] Cited in *Cityscapes of Modernity*, p. 136.

[101] *Ibid.*, p. 140.

[102] On fashion see B. Nedelmann, 'Georg Simmel as an Analyst of Autonomous Dynamics: The Merry-Go-Round of Fashion' in M. Kearn, B. Phillips and R.S. Cohen (editors), *Georg Simmel and Contemporary Sociology*, Dordrecht, Kluwer (1990), pp. 225–42.

[103] See R. Felski, *The Gender of Modernity*, chapter 2. More generally, see T.R. Kandal, *The Woman Question in Classical Sociological Theory*, Miami, Florida International University Press (1988), chapter 4.

[104] *Soziologische Vorlesungen von Georg Simmel. Gehalten an der Universität Berlin im Wintersemester 1899*, University of Chicago, Society for Social Research, Series I, Number 1 (1931), p. 19. On Park's relationship to Simmel see the excellent study by R. Lindner, *The reportage of urban culture. Robert park and the Chicago School*, Cambridge, Cambridge University Press (1996).

[105] On the 1896 exhibition see *Cityscapes of Modernity*, pp. 100–114.

[106] G. Simmel, 'Philosophie der Landschaft', GA 12, 1, p. 471.

[107] On forgetting in the metropolis see C.M. Boyer, *City of Collective Memory*, Cambridge, Mass., MIT Press (1996); on agoraphobia see 'Psychopathologies of Urban Space' in A. Vidler, *Warped Space*, Cambridge, MIT Press (2000), pp. 25–50; on gendered pathologies see E. da Costa Meyer, 'La Donna e Mobile', in L. Durning and R. Wrigley (editors), *Gender and Architecture*, Chichester, Wiley (2000), pp. 155–70.

[108] See D. Weinstein and M.A. Weinstein, *Postmodern(ised) Simmel*, London, Routledge (1993)

[109] J.-F. Lyotard, *The postmodern Condition*, Minneapolis, University of Minnesota Press (1984), p. xxiii.

[110] For a brief summary of Marx in this context see my *Fragments of Modernity*, chapter 1. More fully see D. Sayer, *Capitalism and Modernity*, London Routledge (1991).

[111] A close reading of Simmel's *Philosophy of Money* might indicate how his treatment of money anticipates some of Baudrillard's analysis of the commodity.

[112] *Simmel on Culture*, p. 70.

[113] See F. Jameson 'The Theoretical Hesitation: Benjamin's Sociological Predecessor', *Critical Inquiry*, 25, 2, 1999, pp. 267–88. For an overview of Simmel's impact upon avant-garde groupings see R.M. Leck, *Simmel and Avante-Garde Sociology. The Birth of Modernity 1880–1920*, New York, Humanity Books (2000).

[114] A.W. Small, 'Individuum und Gesellschaft', *American Journal of Sociology*, 30, 1924, p. 353.

1

Introduction

Today, over a century after Georg Simmel commenced publishing works on psychology, philosophy and, later, sociology, it is difficult to imagine how significant Simmel was in the development of sociology. Contrary to our conception of the development of the social sciences in Germany, sociology as an independent discipline emerged relatively late compared with its neighbouring disciplines. For a variety of reasons, some of them political, sociology was not taught in German universities until the end of the nineteenth century. And quite probably the first to do so was Georg Simmel. This appears to be the verdict of his contemporaries. At the Paris Exhibition of 1900 – to which sociologists also presumably went to exhibit their wares – a report was prepared by the American sociologist Lester Ward and others on the state of sociology in the United States, Russia and Europe. After commenting on the absence of any chairs of sociology in Germany – a situation which continued until 1918 – Paul Barth reported with regard to sociological instruction that is was

> the representatives of the older sciences allied to sociology, or the ones out of which it has sprung . . . who admit the study of social theories in their courses. Nor do these all do so; but a certain number do something of the kind . . . In

this connection mention ought to be made of the work of Simmel, of the university of Berlin, who has been giving a course in sociology nearly every semester for the last six years. [1]

Still earlier, in a report by Thon in the newly founded *American Journal of Sociology* on 'The Present Status of Sociology in Germany', Simmel is again singled out for special mention. Aside from Ernst Grosse in Freiburg and Barth in Leipzig – neither of whom taught courses exclusively on sociology as an independent distinctive discipline – Thon emphasized the work of Simmel who

has an audience that is increasing in numbers each semester. For several years he has read in the summer semester on social psychology, and in the winter semester a special course on sociology. Everyone who knows his *Einleitung in die Moralwissenschaften* will guess that in his lectures on ethics he introduces and suggests many sociological ideas and points of view. Besides this he conducts a seminar for sociological practice. Here reports are made on sociological books and independent dissertations are read. Simmel himself usually conducts the discussions. This is for the moment very agreeable to the listeners, but it is pedagogically by no means advantageous. [2]

A few years later in 1899, Simmel himself declared to Bouglé that his 'sociology is a very specialised discipline, for whom there is no representative in Germany apart from myself'. [3] But it was not merely in the teaching of sociology in Germany that Simmel was already well-known by the mid-1890s.

Aside from his own publications in Germany, Simmel's articles were quickly translated abroad. Between 1896 and 1910 no fewer than nine of Simmel's sociological essays, largely due to the initiative of Albion Small, appeared in the newly established *American Journal of Sociology*. In the mid-1890s Simmel was also a member of the 'Institute Internationale de Sociologie', recently founded by René Worms. The very first issue of *L'Année Sociologique* in 1896 – edited by Emile Durkheim – contained as its second article an essay by Simmel. Durkheim often criticized Simmel's conception of sociology but respected his work nonetheless. Simmel corresponded with another member of the Durkheimian School, Celestin Bouglé, who not merely reported on Simmel's work to a French audience as early as 1894 but took up some aspects of Simmel's conception of sociology in his own works.

Simmel's institutional position within German sociology is reflected much later in his being one of three original executive members of the German Sociological Association at its inception early in 1909. At the first congress which commenced on 19 October 1910 the first preliminary talk was given by Simmel – questionably apposite in the light of sociological congresses – on 'The Sociology of Sociability'. Already in 1908 Simmel had given the opening address to the Viennese Sociological Society on 'The Nature and Task of Sociology'. [4] But this institutional acclaim took place when Simmel's interest in sociology was already on the wane. As Tönnies reported, 'in the autumn of 1913 . . . Professor Simmel left the executive committee [of the German Sociological Association, D.F.] because of other directions in his studies'. [5] Simmel did return to sociology briefly whilst in Strasbourg during the First World War. This is indicated by the course in sociology he taught there and the publication of his slender volume on *Basic Questions of Sociology* (1917). But it is open to question whether, had he lived beyond the war (he died in 1918), he would have continued to develop this interest in sociology. His last wartime writings do indeed suggest that 'other directions' preoccupied him.

But although there is little doubt that Simmel may be counted amongst the principal figures in the foundation of sociology as an independent discipline, there remains even today a tendency to see Simmel as a somewhat marginal figure within the sociological establishment. Caplow has pointed out [6] that 'for a founding father, Simmel seems curiously remote from organized sociology' and seems to remain a neglected figure. This impression, it is argued, 'may stem from a discrepancy between Simmel's style of thought and the prevailing sociological idiom' which has come to be dominated by detailed and refined empirical research and specialized modes of conceptualization that 'can only be used by professionals'. In contrast, Caplow maintains, Simmel 'seems to have envisaged sociological progress to be an increase of understanding by the sheer process of ratiocination and not to have attached any importance to the accumulation of descriptive facts'. Indeed, Simmel goes so far as to state in his *Sociology* that although the work is replete with actual empirical and historical examples that illustrate his propositions, he could just as well have used fictitious ones. In this respect, Simmel is the first sociologist to apply the philosophy of 'As-If' to the sociological domain. [7]

In Simmel's sociological work we therefore confront the paradox of the social theorist who, especially in the 1890s, sought to establish sociology as an independent discipline whilst at the same time rejecting the aims of many contemporary sociologists 'who want to describe the human sector of the universe as accurately as possible, uncovering hidden regularities for science's sake, or to enlarge man's control over the environment'. [8] Compared with the work of Durkheim or Weber, Simmel's sociological writings do not display an explicit concern with the role of sociology in society.

It is all the more remarkable then that after his death attempts were made to order his sociological writings under the rubric of 'systematic' sociology, despite his persistent and explicit aversion to all forms of system. In the philosophical realm, with which Simmel more closely identified himself, it was said of him that he is 'not so much a philosopher as a philosophizer'. Similarly, in sociology Simmel sought not merely to avoid reifying society but also to express an aversion for the preoccupation with the role of the professional sociologist. Even within a single short piece of work Simmel was not merely the master of the essay form but also of the shifting perspective of the philosopher, the sociologist, the psychologist and the aesthete. This is another reason why 'to the modern experimenter, Simmel is an exasperating godfather'. Perhaps in part because of the then unbounded and disputed terrain, Simmel refused to confine himself to participation within a strictly 'sociological' discourse. Even those of his contemporaries who admired his work were often bewildered by the variety of perspectives that it contained. As one of those admirers – Max Adler – pointed out, a full understanding of Simmel's work was impaired not merely by

> problems of style but also the largely merely fragmentary assessment of his work for which he himself was in large part to blame. Because he wrote upon the philosophy of history at one time, at another upon money and then again upon Schopenhauer and Nietzsche as well as upon Rembrandt without an apparently recognisable system, it might appear as if his frame of mind exhibited the same erratic jumps of thought as the immediacy of the diversity of objects with which he concerned himself. [9]

We might also add here that there is sometimes an apparent diversity of theme and perspective even within the same work.

Yet there is a positive side to this seemingly bewildering array of themes and perspectives. As 'a guest, a wanderer', Simmel possesses 'the capacity for association, the gift of seeing the connectedness and meaningful unification of arbitrary phenomena. Simmel is an eternal wanderer between things; an unlimited capacity for combination allows him to step out in any direction from any single point'. [10] The reader of Simmel's sociological and philosophical essays must be struck by his ability to draw connections between the most diverse phenomena such that the patterns of social relationships in society always appear as an intricate web in his work. The danger, however, is that the reader becomes lost in this eternal wandering from one aspect of social life to another.

Such a danger is amplified by the changing meaning that Simmel often gives to his central concepts. In turn, the essayistic form of much of Simmel's writing reveals a further feature of his thought. Simmel's essays are almost never accompanied by footnotes and other references to the sources of his examples. This is just as true of his major sociological works as it is of his essays. As one of his contemporaries pointed out, Simmel's works

> are distinguished even in their external form from the scientific working community. They are free creations of a free mind that never require reference to the results of predecessors or verification by co-researchers ... One cannot extract from the works themselves when they appeared, which impulses might have had their effect upon them, where they might have engaged in the course of scientific development and which standpoints and theories they might be opposing. They are, as it were, autonomous, timeless forms that ... preserve the 'pathos of distance' in all directions in a proud and exclusive reserve. [11]

In this respect too Simmel's works are very different from those of his contemporaries such as Durkheim and Weber. The essay form takes up the anti-systematic impulse of intellectual creativity that proves annoying to orthodox members of the scientific community. It is more suited to a different conception of sociology which Nisbet has somewhat loosely described as 'sociology as an art form'. [12]

Even though Simmel outlined and defended his conception of sociology as an independent discipline, there is seldom any sense of his being engaged in the major academic controversies of his time. One would be hard pressed to elicit Simmel's position in the methodological dispute in political economy (the *Methodenstreit*) or in the debate on the role of values in social science (the *Werturteilsstreit*). Unlike Weber, Simmel never engaged in such controversies and they do not explicitly shape his formulation of the nature and tasks of sociology. Where Simmel does take up academic issues and debates they relate to other spheres as free trades unions, foreign students, women and untenured lecturers in Prussian universities.

But if all this is true, what is it about Simmel as a sociologist that excited his contemporaries? Simmel was certainly one of the first sociologists in Germany to establish sociology as a circumscribed, independent discipline. As with succeeding generations of sociologists, his contemporaries applauded him for the wealth of insights into social life that his sociological and philosophical works provided. These include not merely the study of the preconditions for social relations (space, mass) but also of the fundamental features of social organization (domination and subordination, conflict). In some of his works, especially in *The Philosophy of Money*, there is also a more general social theory of modernity and a sociology of modern life (especially metropolitan life). There are also in his works an astonishing array of sensitive analyses of the seemingly most insignificant aspects of everyday life (mealtimes, writing a letter) as well as of some apparently marginal but illuminating social types (the stranger, the adventurer). And from his very earliest works onwards, Simmel proved to be a master of the analysis of psychological states (pessimism, the blasé attitude, etc.).

Yet it was not merely the wide range of themes that impressed his contemporaries. Time and time again they praised the mode of presentation of these themes. It was said of *The Philosophy of Money*, for instance, that 'in its form and content, Simmel's book must be characterised as masterly, one might say written as a virtuoso. The psychological analysis of semi- or completely unconscious processes . . . is as brilliantly carried out as it is presented'. [13] That virtuoso quality, that aesthetic attractiveness of the mode of presentation which Simmel's work shares with the best works of writers such as Theodor Adorno or Walter Benjamin – themselves both masters of the essay form – has its pitfalls for those who seek to present and summarize Simmel's sociological work. As another contemporary pointed out,

> Just as the best of a work of art is lost when one attempts to reproduce its content in a language other than that of the artist, so too the content of many of Simmel's cultural-philosophical works appears to be so bound up with the inimitable personal art of their creator that it disappears in its translation into the impersonal form of a scientific report. [14]

If the present introduction to Simmel's work acknowledges this limitation, then it should also indicate that there is no substitute for reading the original texts wherever possible. If it succeeds in its task then it should stimulate a reading or re-reading of them.

Aside from the attempt that is made to indicate some of the central features of Simmel's life and social theory, a task that can only be performed in summary form, the intention in what follows is also to highlight some of the lesser-known features of Simmel's work that are not readily available to the English reader. In particular, emphasis is placed on Simmel's early development in order to show – as was intimated at the outset – how far Simmel's sociological project was an original one that predates many subsequent developments in sociological theory and research.

NOTES AND REFERENCES

[1] See 'Sociology at the Paris Exposition of 1900', *Annals of the American Academy of Political and Social Sciences*, Vol. 19, 1902, pp. 170–175, esp. p. 173.

[2] O. Thon, 'The Present Status of Sociology in Germany', *American Journal of Sociology*, Vol. 2, 1896/7, pp. 567–800, esp. pp. 799–800. Thon was a student of Simmel.

[3] Letter to C. Bouglé of 13.12.1899. See W. Gephart, 'Verlorene und gefundene Briefe Georg Simmels' in H. J. Dahme and O. Rammstedt (editors), *Georg Simmel und die Moderne*, Frankfurt, Suhrkamp (1984).

[4] See 'Sociologische Gesellschaften', *Monatsschrift für Soziologie*, Vol. 1, 1909, p. 59.

[5] F. Tönnies, 'Die Deutsche Gesellschaft für Soziologie', in his *Soziologische Studien und Kritiken*, 2nd Collection, Jena, Gustav Fischer (1926), P. 151.

[6] T. Caplow, *Two Against One*, Englewood Cliffs, N.J., Prentice-Hall (1968), pp. 12ff.

[7] See I. Nissen, 'Vergesellschaftung als Einstellung', *Annalen der Philosophie und philosophische Kritik*, Vol. 5, 1925/26, pp. 77–108. Nissen was the first to systematically draw the connection between Simmel's work and Vaihinger's *Philosophy of As-If*.

[8] T. Caplow, *Two Against One*, pp. 13–14.

[9] M. Adler, *Georg Simmels Bedeutung für die Geistesgeschichte*, Vienna/Leipzig, Anzengruber-Verlag (1919), p. 6.

[10] S. Kracauer, *Georg Simmel*, ms., p. 37.

[11] M. Frischeisen-Köhler, 'Georg Simmel', *Kantstudien*, Vol. 24, 1920, pp. 6–7.

[12] R. Nisbet, *Sociology as an Art Form*, London, Heinemann (1976).

[13] A. Vierkandt, 'Einige neuere Werke zur Kultur- und Gesellschaftslehre', *Zeitschrift für Sozialwissenschaft*, Vol. 4, 1901, pp. 640–1.

[14] M. Frischeisen-Köhler, 'George Simmel', p. 6.

2

Life and Context

2.1 THE DEVELOPMENT OF SIMMEL'S WORK AND CAREER

Hans Simmel relates that

> . . . on March 1st 1858 my father Georg Simmel was born in the house that formed the north-west side of the intersection of the Leipzigerstrasse and Friedrichstrasse. Then still to the west of the old city centre, these two streets were later to become the most characteristic and important commercial streets; one could not, as it were, be 'even more' of a local of Berlin than when one was born on the corner of the Leipziger- and Friedrichstrasse. [1]

If the location of Simmel's birthplace was later to epitomize metropolitan Berlin at the turn of the century, then it also symbolized the life of someone who 'lived in the intersection of many conflicting currents, intensely affected by a multiplicity of intellectual and moral tendencies. He was a modern urban man, . . . an alien in his native land. Like the stranger he described in one of his most brilliant essays, he was near and far at the same time, a "potential wanderer"'. [2] He was also to become the most articulate sociologist of 'metropolitan culture'. Indeed, starting out from the image of a

metropolitan crossroads one can create the central motifs and sometimes the conceptual apparatus of Simmel's sociology. From its vantage points, it is not difficult to view society as consisting of ceaseless
interactions and to analyse this web of interactions in terms of social
networks. It is impossible not to be impressed by the differentiation
of individuals engaged in interaction and the extent to which individuals are fragments of a wider social whole that is only partly
visible in the intersection of diverse social milieux and groups.

But, in order to understand these images of the mature Simmel
as 'the adventurer' into hitherto unresearched intellectual and social
spheres who looks at them from a distance as a 'stranger', we need to
examine the diverse development of his intellectual and social life.
For this 'stranger in the academy' (Coser) displayed no unilinear
development that culminated in his recognition as a major sociologist. Indeed, amongst his contemporaries, Simmel was recognized not
merely as a sociologist but also – and often just as much – as a
philosopher, psychologist, aesthetician and essayist. In contrast,
amongst those with institutional power in the universities, Simmel's
achievements were often not recognized at all. Only in 1914, at the
age of 56, did he secure a chair in philosophy (and not sociology) at
the then somewhat marginal University of Strasbourg.

It was, however, in Berlin that Simmel spent the greatest part
of his academic life and it was its metropolitan culture which often
provided the inspiration for his work. As Simmel himself retrospectively remarked, 'Perhaps I could have achieved something that was
also valuable in another city; but this specific achievement, that I
have in fact brought to fruition in these decades, is undoubtedly
bound up with the Berlin milieu.' [3] In terms of intellectual output,
Simmel's achievements were certainly impressive. By the year of his
death in 1918 he had published 25 books of varying lengths – including a volume on ethics, *Einleitung in die Moralwissenschaft* (893 pages),
a volume on money, *Philosophie des Geldes* (554 pages) and a volume
on sociology, *Soziologie* (782 pages) – and around 300 articles,
reviews and other pieces. But if we turn to the main outlines of
Simmel's life and career we find that this prodigious intellectual
production stands in contrast to the progress of his career. This is
evident even in Simmel's early development. In stark contrast to his
own wide-ranging interests, Simmel 'always insisted that no one in
his parents' house had a notion of genuine intellectual culture'.
Instead, his own cultural and intellectual interests were stimulated
either by his own studies at Berlin University, through other personal contacts such as Sabine Lepsius (a member of the Stefan

George circle), or the friend of the Simmel family, Julius Friedländer, a successful music publisher who helped the young Simmel through his studies after his father's death (Simmel dedicated his doctoral dissertation to him). Simmel commenced his studies at Berlin University in 1876 first with history under Theodor Mommsen and then moving on to psychology under Moritz Lazarus (under whom Wilhelm Dilthey and Wilhelm Wundt also studied). After studying ethnology under Adolf Bastian, Simmel's interests turned 'without knowing how' to philosophy (under Eduard Zeller and Friedrich Harms). Not surprisingly Simmel's earliest work was in the fields of psychology and philosophy. His study of the origins of music entitled 'Psychological and Ethnographic Studies on Music' was rejected as his dissertation in 1880. In connection with this study, the last section on yodelling (!) is based on what must be one of the earliest questionnaires, which Simmel published in the journal of the Swiss Alpine Club in 1879. His examiners, however, were not impressed either with Simmel's initiatives or with 'the numerous misspellings and stylistic errors' and one of them – Helmholtz – concluded that with regard to this study 'we would be doing him a great service if we do not encourage him further in this direction'. [4] Nonetheless, in 1881 Simmel did obtain his doctorate on the basis of an essay entitled 'Description and Assessment of Kant's Various Views on the Nature of Matter' for which he had received a prize in the previous year. After submitting a further study on Kant and giving the obligatory public lecture Simmel was granted his Habilitation in January 1885 which enabled him to teach as a *Privatdozent* in Berlin University – a position he held until 1901.

This early phase of Simmel's work up to and even after the publication of his first major work *On Social Differentiation* (1890) was until recently unresearched. But it is likely that many of Simmel's key concepts were already being developed in this period, despite the very different context in which they appeared. At first sight, the interests and influences upon the young Simmel seem untypical of our image of him:

> The *young Simmel* starts out from pragmatism, social Darwinism, Spencerian evolutionism and the principle of differentiation. Fechner's atomism and Spencer's 'definite differentiation' lead him . . . to the problem of the individual. Through his teachers Lazarus and Steinthal . . . however, Simmel already early on became acquainted with the 'objective spirit'. The fact that, in this first phase,

Simmel exercised little influence and that he himself turned away from it has hardly been investigated at all. [5]

Some of these early interests are worthy of closer examination here.

In the winter semesters of 1886/87 and 1888/89 Simmel was holding seminars on 'The Philosophical Consequences of Darwinism'. It is always quite likely that discusion of Darwin (and, in another context, Fechner) was also contained in seminars and lectures held four times between 1887 and 1891 on 'Recent Philosophical Theories, especially in their Relationship to the Natural Sciences'. As late as 1895, Simmel published an essay 'On the Relation between the Doctrine of Selection and Epistemology'. In a more muted form, Darwin's theory of species preservation becomes an issue in Simmel's sociology within the context of the self-preservation of social groups – first developed in his *On Social Differentiation* (1890). [6]

Although Simmel never lectured exclusively on Herbert Spencer, there is little doubt that both his evolutionism and the principle of differentiation played a central role in the early formulation of the basic tenets of Simmel's theory of society. Spencer's *First Principles* (1862), which appeared in German in 1875, contains not merely his law of evolution with its emphasis upon the transition from homogeneity to heterogeneity, the persistence of force, a theory of continuous motion, the doctrine of relativity – all of which appear under a different guise in Simmel's early social theory – but also the principle of social differentiation and its relationship to social integration. Recent research also suggests that Simmel's early formulations of his theory of society owe much to Fechner's logical atomism, though this may be less true of Simmel's early psychology. [7]

In this context, it is necessary to point to the almost total neglect of Simmel's early psychology in contrast to his later writings in this area (most obviously on dyadic and triadic relationships). Simmel himself later 'characterised Steinthal and Lazarus, the founders of *Völkerpsychologie*, as his two most important teachers in his student days'. [8] Simmel's earliest essays 'Psychological and Ethnological Studies on Music' (1882) and 'Dante's Psychology' (1884), together with a number of book reviews, appeared in the psychology journal edited by Steinthal and Lazarus. Between 1882 and 1909 Simmel published a dozen or so articles concerned in various ways with psychology. A strong psychological component is also to be found in *On Social Differentiation* (1890), *Problems of the Philosophy of History* (1892), *Introduction to Moral Science* (1892–93),

The Philosophy of Money (1900) as well as in several essays that make up his *Sociology* (1908). Furthermore, between 1889 and 1909 – roughly the same period as Simmel's greatest interest in sociology – Simmel taught 13 courses concerned in varying degrees with psychology (including, intriguingly, on four occasions a course entitled 'Social Psychology, with special reference to Socialism'). [9]

These same early years of Simmel's academic career are also characterized by an, at first, parallel interest in sociology and an attempt to ground sociology as an independent discipline. In 1887 Simmel was already lecturing on 'Ethics with Special Reference to Sociological Problems', though the first course simply entitled 'Sociology' was not given until 1894 for which 152 students were enrolled. Thereafter, Simmel taught a course on sociology every year until 1908 (the year of the publication of his *Sociology*) and subsequently only in 1909/10, 1911/12 and 1917/18 (in 1917 his *Basic Questions of Sociology* appeared).

What this suggests and what his publications also seem to confirm is that the period of Simmel's greatest interest in sociology is from the late 1880s to 1908. It has also been argued, with some justification, that the fundamental features of Simmel's sociology were outlined in the decade 1890 to 1900, that is, between the publication of *On Social Differentiation: Sociological and Psychological Investigations* (1890) and *The Philosophy of Money* (1900). To this important argument we must return later. [10] But even if this is the case, we should guard against the view that sociology was Simmel's sole concern in these years. Though an often parallel interest in psychology has also been emphasized, this too does not exhaust the breadth of Simmel's interests. Simmel continued to lecture fairly consistently upon Kantian philosophy from 1885 until the first decade of the twentieth century. A further interest, confirmed by frequent publications, is the philosophy and psychology of pessimism derived from Schopenhauer and, in the 1890s, an increasing interest in the philosophy of Nietzsche and its consequences. The two were later to be combined in a volume on *Schopenhauer and Nietzsche* (1907). Indeed, there are many more occasions upon which one can find Simmel identifying himself as a philosopher rather than as a sociologist. Even as late as 1899 we find Simmel complaining to Durkheim's collaborator Célestin Bouglé that 'it is in fact somewhat painful to me to find that I am only recognised abroad as a sociologist – whereas I am indeed a philosopher, I see philosophy as my life-task and engage in sociology really only as a subsidiary discipline'. [11] Simmel's somewhat disarming remark should not obscure the fact that he was to be recognized long after his death as a major sociologist rather than as a philosopher.

There was, however, another dimension of philosophy which is certainly evident in Simmel's early writings but which assumes greater significance in his mature years, namely the philosophy of art. Indeed, one of his unfulfilled intentions was to produce in his later years a major philosophy of art. Nonetheless, his early studies of music, Dante, Michelangelo, Böcklin, Stefan George, Rodin and others and his later major works on *Kant and Goethe* (1906), *Rembrandt* (1916) and the posthumous collection *On the Philosophy of Art* (1922) testify to a significant aesthetic dimension in Simmel's work. As with his contributions to psychology and philosophy so his aesthetics permeates his sociological work in a variety of ways. In his later writings some of these dimensions merge into a much broader sphere with which Simmel was not only preoccupied but with which he himself identified: a philosophy of culture. Even this intellectual project does not do justice to the breadth of Simmel's concerns. His contemporaries recognized in him the capacity to philosophize on any subject matter and to give it his own individual stamp. As one contemporary comments, 'Simmel "simmelifies" everything he comes into contact with'. This unique capacity may well have been one reason why his academic career remained relatively unsuccessful as far as his academic status was concerned.

Aside from a bizarre attempt on Simmel's life in 1886 [12] – which would surely count as what he himself termed one of 'the fortuitous fragments of reality' – there were more concrete impediments to the progress of Simmel's academic career. Between 1890 and 1900 Simmel produced a number of substantial works as well as a growing number of important articles, some of which were to make up sections of his *Sociology*. The substantive works commenced with *On Social Differentiation* (1890) and was followed by *Problems of the Philosophy of History* (1892), *Introduction to Moral Science* (1892–93) and *The Philosophy of Money* (1900). Parts of these works and several key essays were already translated into Russian, French, Italian and English by 1900. Nonetheless, Simmel spent a remarkably long fifteen years from 1885 to 1900 as a *Privatdozent* which meant that his university salary was dependent upon student fees. Why was this the case?

One compelling reason was, of course, the prevailing anti-Semitism in German universities and especially in Prussia. No doubt some of his colleagues were also jealous of his popularity. By the end of the 1890s Simmel was lecturing in the largest lecture theatre in Berlin University. In 1898 he wrote to Heinrich Rickert that he was

> rather proud of the fact that I have over 70 students in a private seminar on social psychology. This is a lot for such a remote and unpractical area . . . I am also satisfied with the major logic lecture since, in competition with the Ordinarius Professor and at a very inconvenient time, I still have over 80 students. [13]

Indeed, in a course titled 'On Pessimism' in the winter semester of 1894/95 Simmel attracted 269 students. He was also one of the first to permit women as 'guest students' to his lectures long before they were allowed to enter Prussian universities as full students in 1908. Furthermore, he was attracting the wrong kind of students 'from the Eastern countries', especially Russia and Poland. Later it was even said that 'Simmel is a focal point of revolutionary and anti-German aspirations'. However, aside from the conservative rhetoric which emerged on every occasion that Simmel sought academic promotion, there was another reason why he might have been unfavourably viewed by the university authorities. At least until the mid-1890s, Simmel was associated with socialist circles both inside and outside the university, a fact that in these years of anti-socialist legislation would not have gone unnoticed amongst those in authority at 'His Majesty's intellectual regiment of the guards', as the scientist du Bois Reymond characterized Berlin University.

Finally, despite Simmel's subsequent protestations that he was really a philosopher, he had already become identified with the social sciences and with sociology in particular. Before 1918 there were no chairs of sociology at German universities and the social sciences were viewed with considerable suspicion by the authorities. Landmann, in the light of Simmel's popularity amongst students, aptly concludes with regard to his lack of academic advancement that

> The fact that the faculty hesitated for such a long time until they put forward his promotion may have lain in the fact that Simmel was not popular with his closest and most esteemed faculty colleague Dilthey; further, the anti-Semitism of Roethes, one of the most powerful figures in the faculty, jealousy because of his high student numbers, mistrust of the then new discipline of sociology which he supported and opposition to his unorthodox manner in general may all have played a part. [14]

However, in 1898 the faculty did finally seek to promote Simmel to *Extraordinarius* – which would still not permit him to have doctoral candidates. The faculty requests of 1898 (which was unsuccessful) and 1900 (which did succeed) to the minister of education are instructive for the light they throw upon both Simmel's orientation in the social sciences and the common view of sociology. In the faculty request of 1898, signed by Wilhelm Dilthey, Friedrich Paulsen the philosopher, the economists Gustav Schmoller and Adolf Wagner and others, Simmel's position is characterized as follows:

> His standpoint is Spencer's theory of evolution. The task that he has set himself in *so-called sociology* in particular lies in the analysis of sociological forms, dominant processes and structures which are produced and are effective in society. In this respect, his efforts are similar to those in *Völkerpsychologie*. Thus he pursues the effectiveness of the principle of energy-saving in the psychological sphere, he analyses the process of social differentiation psychologically, he deals with the psychological side of such social facts as competition or money. In his most comprehensive work too, the two-volume introduction to moral philosophy, he is inclined to focus upon a sociological and psychological derivation of the basic elements of moral consciousness. [15]

This view of Simmel certainly confirms the extent to which his contemporaries saw sociology and psychology as closely linked in his works of this period. In 1900 the faculty were even more cautious about the role of sociology and expressed serious reservations as to its status since,

> this area of study, like no other, is certainly a hotbed of pseudo-science [*ein Tummelplatz der Halbwissenschaft*]. But precisely because Dr. Simmel has extracted a nexus of useful investigations from the indeterminate collective concept of sociology and has worked upon it with scientific exactitude, he has distinguished himself from other sociologists. [16]

This application was successful and Simmel was granted the title of *Extraordinarius* in the following year.

But is this view of Simmel's sociological task borne out by his own intentions and work in the decade down to 1900? Certainly his first sociological work *On Social Differentiation* sought to deal not merely with the substantive issues of social differentiation and group cohesion but also to provide a grounding for sociology in the first chapter. However, although the book's major reviewer, Ferdinand Tönnies, found many 'psychological comments of great sensitivity' he concluded that 'the introductory chapter, concerned with the methods of the social sciences, does not seem to me to be the strongest one'. [17] But Simmel had more success with his article 'The Problem of Sociology' (1894) – later, in a revised form, the basis for the first chapter of his *Sociology*. [18] So confident was Simmel that he sent an offprint to Althoff the Prussian minister of education explaining not merely that 'sociology is gaining more and more ground in the universities' but that he himself had 'contrived to substitute a new and sharply demarcated complex of specific tasks for the hitherto lack of clarity and confusion surrounding the concept of sociology'. [19] In a similar vein, he explained to Bouglé in 1894 that partly as a result of 'the uncertain and unclear state in which sociology still finds itself', 'I am devoting myself totally to sociological studies and in the foreseeable future will not enter any other area again especially that of moral philosophy'. In the following year, Simmel recommends Bouglé to study 'The Problem of Sociology', 'upon which I myself lay the greatest value and which contains my work programme (and the essential part of my teaching programme)'. He also relates that he is now an 'advising editor' of the newly founded *American Journal of Sociology* (in which between 1896 and 1910 no fewer than nine pieces of his work were translated), as well as indicating to Bouglé that he is working on a psychology of money which he hopes to finish in the near future.

In fact, *The Philosophy of Money* did not appear until 1900, although an increasing number of contributory essays and sections did appear between 1889 (when his original paper 'On the Psychology of Money' was published) and 1900. Simmel did not find the construction of such a monumental 'philosophy' – which contains a wealth of sociological material – an easy task. Writing to Rickert in 1896, Simmel anticipates that 'In the course of the decade I hope to present you with a "Theory of Relativism" ... In the meantime, other things have been commenced.' In 1898 Simmel complains to Rickert of his difficulties in developing a theory of value (and relativism) since he can 'only maintain my relativism if it is capable, as it were, of solving all the problems that are presented by absolutist theories'. Later in the same year Simmel was still speaking of 'the difficulties in the theory of value' since 'I am groaning over and doubting my theory of value. Even the most elementary point up to now provides me with insurmountable difficulties.' [20] However, *The Philosophy of Money* 'which strives to be a philosophy of the whole of historical and social life' did appear in 1900 and was very favourably received.

Nonetheless, these difficulties did not prevent him from producing a considerable number of articles in the 1890s after having already completed the first version of his *Problems of the History of Philosophy* in 1892 and his monumental *Introduction to Moral Science* (1892/93). These include articles on the growing women's movement, trade union rights, socialized medicine and militarism within the political sphere, and in sociology articles upon the sociology of the family, the method of social science, the sociology of religion, sociological aesthetics, and the long essay 'The Self-Preservation of the Social Group' (1898). [21] This does not take into account his essays on philosophy, the dozen or so pieces that were to form part of *The Philosophy of Money*, the essays on literature and art or the many aphorisms and poems some of which, from 1897 onwards, were published in the Munich *Jugendstil* journal *Jugend*. Simmel's earlier interest in psychology was also maintained in reviews of Gustav le Bon, Tarde and essays on the psychology of fashion and the theory of the will. Not content with this, Simmel also intimated to Bouglé in 1899 that he was working on a comprehensive sociology, though he suggested somewhat ominously that with regard to sociology, 'when I have at last fulfilled my obligation to it, namely that I publish a comprehensive sociology – which indeed will occur in the course of the next few years – I shall probably never again come back to it'.

This somewhat ambiguous stance in relation to sociology is confirmed by a letter to Rickert in 1901 in which Simmel indicates his varied interests:

> I wanted to start a very comprehensive sociology (an obligation with which I am not very sympathetic but which is unavoidable) when a second edition of my 'Moral Philosophy' became necessary. This means a completely new book, a completely new foundation . . . On the other hand, for some time now, my major interest has been in the philosophy of art and I am burning to bring together my ideas upon it. [22]

Not only did the second edition of his *Moral Science* not appear; the work on the philosophy of art did not appear either. Simmel did however fulfil his 'obligation' to sociology by continuing to teach the subject every year until 1908 and to publish most of the essays that go to make up the *Sociology*. Together with two earlier essays, Simmel had already published versions of eight of the ten chapters of the *Sociology* by the time it appeared in 1908.

Between 1900 and 1908 Simmel had also extended and deepened his philosophical interests. He published a collection of lectures on *Kant* (1904) and a completely revised second edition of *Problems of the Philosophy of History* (1905) as well as *Kant and Goethe* (1906), *Religion* (1906) and *Schopenhauer and Nietzsche* (1907). Of particular interest here is the new edition of the volume on the philosophy of history designed to overcome 'the naive realism of the historian' and 'psychologism' in historical method. It proved to be a significant source for the development of Max Weber's own methodology of the social sciences. [23]

If Simmel turned away more sharply from sociology after his *Sociology* was published in 1908, then that same year was also a turning point as far as his career prospects were concerned. In that year Simmel was considered for the second chair of philosophy at Heidelberg University. The philosophy faculty expressed themselves as follows for Simmel:

> In his fiftieth year, and in the middle generation of con-
> temporary academic teachers of philosophy Simmel is
> decidedly the most unique figure. One cannot locate him
> in any of the general currents; he has always gone his own
> way . . .
>
> There is no doubt that Simmel, with his extensive and
> many-sided knowledge and with his penetrating intellec-
> tual energy, if anyone were capable of doing so, could
> raise sociology from the state of empirical data collection
> and general reflections to the rank of a genuine philosophi-
> cal discipline. If he can be secured for Heidelberg, then the
> social sciences as a whole and in all their branches . . .
> would find such a comprehensive representation as exists
> nowhere else. [24]

This positive report on Simmel's candidature contrasts sharply with that of Schäfer whose report to the minister of education for Baden speaks of Simmel as 'an Israelite through and through, in his exter-nal appearance, in his bearing and in his mode of thought' who has gained his reputation largely as a sociologist. After dismissing Simmel's sociological achievements, Schäfer sees it as 'a dangerous error to wish to put "society" in the place of the state and the church as the authoritative organ of human co-existence'. [25] In the event, the chair remained unfilled for a year and was then offered to Ernst Troeltsch.

One of Simmel's supporters for the Heidelberg chair was Max Weber who lamented that Simmel 'remains deprived of the "official" recognition that would come from conferring the rank of *Ordinarius* which he more than deserved well over a decade and a half ago'. [26] Had Simmel been successful, the combination of Weber and Simmel working on sociology in Heidelberg would have been formidable. As it was, Weber increasingly took up sociology as Simmel tended to move further away from it. This is indicated by Simmel's active participation in a new journal *Logos* which was to publish several of Simmel's philosophical pieces. Its main orientation, which fitted in with Simmel's interests, was with the philosophy of culture. Affirming to Weber his active commitment to the journal, Simmel explains why he has 'refused and still refuse the presidency of the Sociological Association: neither my time *nor my inclination* or my knowledge is sufficient in order to really do justice to it'. [27] Nonetheless, Simmel did give the opening address to the first German Sociological Congress in Frankfurt in 1910 on 'The Sociology of Sociability'. But this did not indicate the continuing commitment to sociology that Simmel had shown before 1900. Instead, the direction of Simmel's later work seems to confirm Troeltsch's comment that 'in later years, when I brought him round to sociological questions, he rejected discussion of them; these things "no longer interested him"'. [28]

Typical of his post-1908 writings, and containing some of the best of Simmel's essays, is his collection *Philosophical Culture* (1911), whose first edition of 10,000 copies was sold out within six weeks. Many of the essays contained within it, on 'fashion' or 'the adventure' for example, are replete with sociological insights that are embedded in a distinctive mode of philosophizing on modern culture. But in the remainder of his time in Berlin, Simmel offered courses on sociology only in the winter semesters of 1909/10 and 1911/12. His intellectual output lay more decidedly in the spheres of philosophy, literature and art.

Meanwhile, Simmel's academic career failed to advance. In 1910 he was recommended for a chair of philosophy at the small Prussian University of Greifswald but was turned down. In the following year he did obtain an honorary doctorate of politics from Freiburg University in recognition of his work 'as founder of the science of sociology' and for his research on 'the psychology of money'. In 1914, however, at the age of 56, he obtained a chair of philosophy at Strasbourg University. It is clear that Simmel would have preferred to remain in Berlin and only accepted the Strasbourg offer very reluctantly. At the time he wrote, 'if I accept it . . . it will not be with a light heart. For the influence upon our philosophical culture which I can exercise in Berlin will not be achieved so easily elsewhere'. [29] Simmel's departure from Berlin was accompanied by newspaper articles castigating the Berlin faculty and one was even entitled 'Berlin without Simmel'.

Simmel spent four years at Strasbourg University from 1914 until his death in 1918. At the end of his first summer semester in 1914 war was declared and, to the surprise of many and to the disgust of some (such as his erstwhile students Ernst Bloch and Georg Lukács), Simmel declared himself wholeheartedly for the war though not to the extent of many of his colleagues who remained committed to the 'Ideas of 1914'. In fact, his enthusiasm waned as the war progressed. In his correspondence of this period it is not difficult to detect a disillusionment with his move to Strasbourg. Amongst his faculty colleagues he detected 'some interesting minds but the faculty as a whole a half-witted bunch'. With the student body much reduced and increasingly atypical as a result of the war, Simmel quite early sought to leave Strasbourg for Heidelberg in 1915 after the death of Wilhelm Windelband and Emil Lask. Simmel was, however, once more unsuccessful in obtaining either of the vacant chairs of philosophy.

Nonetheless, in the Strasbourg years Simmel remained intellectually productive, though not in the direction of sociology. He taught sociology only twice in the winter semesters of 1914/15 and 1917/18 and then only in one-hour classes and his last sociological work and only one of this period, the brief book *Basic Questions of Sociology*, was published in 1917. In the meantime, Simmel had again turned his attention to the philosophy of history and published a number of essays which were to constitute part of the revised editions of his *Problems of the Philosophy of History* which he never completed. [30] However, his study of Rembrandt appeared in 1916, his wartime essays *The War and Intellectual Decisions* in 1917, *The Conflict in Modern Culture* and his *Interpretation of Life* both in 1918.

Despite this still impressive intellectual output, Simmel was increasingly both mentally and physically exhausted. His years in Strasbourg and the pressure of the war – he confessed to a friend in 1918 – 'have had the effect of ageing me twice or three times what is normal (I was 60 years old some weeks ago). The whole external life is very quiet and runs almost monotonously'. [31] In September of that same year after serious illness Simmel died of liver cancer.

2.2 SIMMEL AND HIS CONTEMPORARIES: THE BERLIN MILIEU

Simmel himself expressed his affinity with Berlin in the following manner: 'Berlin's development from a city to a metropolis in the years around and after the turn of the century coincides with my own strongest and broadest development'. [32] A reviewer said of *The Philosophy of Money* (1900) that it 'could only be written in these times and in Berlin'. This is also the immediate context for one of Simmel's most famous essays 'The Metropolis and Mental Life' (1903). But a city is a somewhat abstract location unless the particular social perspective from which the work emerges is specified. Though Simmel was the author of an essay entitled 'The Intersection of Social Circles' he was not equally at home in all of them.

Little is known of Simmel's early years as a student and *Privatdozent* at Berlin University. At the time of completion of his doctorate, he was already acquainted amongst his fellow students with a future editor of the *Vossischer Zeitung*, the most eminent Berlin newspaper to which Simmel frequently contributed, and a future psychologist with close contact with Stanley Hall the American psychologist (with whom Simmel also corresponded). [33] In the academic world, Lazarus and Steinthal were sufficiently impressed with Simmel's work to publish several of his pieces in their important journal for *Völkerpsychologie*. It is quite probable that Simmel's early academic career was assisted by Gustav Schmoller, the economist, to whose seminar Simmel had contributed in the summer semester of 1889.

It was, however, another economist, Ignaz Jastrow – later Simmel's neighbour, editor of the left-liberal journal *Soziale Praxis*, and one of his closest friends – who belonged to a different social circle in the early 1890s with whom Simmel had close contacts. Recent evidence suggests that Simmel was closely associated with socialist circles in the first half of the 1890s at least. This is confirmed by publications in socialist journals – even in the socialist party's newspaper *Vorwärts* – on a variety of topics that included trade union rights and socialized medicine. Simmel also participated in the 'Social Science Student Association' which, as at many other German universities, had been established early in the decade.

Simmel probably participated in one of their working groups on social psychology and gave a lecture on 'The Psychology of Socialism' (Max Weber also gave a lecture to the same group on 'The Agrarian Worker Question'). Such activity would be unremarkable for a sociologist were it not for the historical context of Imperial Germany and especially the anti-socialist legislation of the period. The same university authorities who disbanded the student association in Berlin in 1895 were also aware of the activities of its contributors. They knew that behind that association stood 'socialist academics' and 'nihilists' with their 'Jewish slyness and fawning ways' who were undermining the German university tradition. [34]

Simmel seems to have distanced himself from socialist circles in the course of the decade without abandoning his view that socialism was the most significant social movement of the period. But if he moved away from socialist circles, Simmel was not without other alternative forms of intellectual sociability. In the previous decade he had already met Sabine Graef – later Sabine Lepsius – who was to introduce Simmel into the circle around the poet Stefan George. In the second half of the 1880s again in Sabine Graef's house he met his future wife Gertrud Kinel whom he married in July 1890. Again, within this same circle he met the writer Paul Ernst (later a close friend of Georg Lukács) who had also written on socialist themes in his early period of work.

But perhaps most typical of all for the author of a piece on 'The Sociology of Sociability' is Simmel's own 'salon' in his home, a location which perhaps persuaded Leopold von Wiese when reviewing Simmel's *Sociology* to refer to it as 'a sociology for the literary salon'. Though more typical of Simmel's life after the turn of the century they certainly commenced earlier since even in 1895 he was writing to Bouglé of 'the really distinguished Berlin circles' which 'for a stranger are only always accessible through a happy coincidence'. One of the frequent participants in Simmel's salon and a close friend, Margaret Susman, captures the atmosphere in the following way:

> The receptions in the Simmel household, the weekly *jours*, were conceived entirely in the spirit of their common culture. They were a sociological creation in miniature: that of a sociability whose significance was the culturation of the highest individuals. Here conversation took on a form . . . which floated in an atmosphere of intellectuality, affability and tact, detached from the ultimate burden of the

personal element. Simmel certainly obtained the masterly chapter . . . on sociability from the experience of this select society. Only exceptional people, distinguished by intellect or even by beauty, took part in these social events. [35]

This same atmosphere was also present in his private seminars, again held at home. As one of the participants, Edith Landmann relates – of a seminar on aesthetics in 1901 – the participants

read out their papers, yet I did not have the impression that Simmel exhibited great interest in them; his interest seemed rather in holding forth upon his own new aesthetic reflections . . . in small circles of people . . . One evening there appeared amongst the few late guests to the *jour* a grand figure dressed in black who had obviously not expected to meet the other guests and before whom one immediately took one's leave. It was George. [36]

Other members of the Stefan George circle also appeared as Elly Heuss-Knapp related in 1906:

At the Simmels I have recently met Lou Andreas Salomé . . . With them it is exquisite . . . They have a small enclosed cultural world with few friends, a pure nervous culture. One does not speak of those things that are topical in Berlin but about the particular rhetoric of the Dauphiné French against the French from the north or about other things of which no one else knows anything. [37]

Although Simmel was not formally a member of the Stefan George circle he did stand very close to this intellectual and cultural grouping and, according to one contemporary, sought to imitate the charismatic poet in posture and dress. Simmel's views on contemporary culture – as they appear in *The Philosophy of Money* and elsewhere – may well have influenced the George circle's own programme for elitist cultural renewal.

Yet the network of intellectual, social and artistic connections around Simmel extended far beyond the Stefan George circle. As Landmann has suggested of the cultural milieu prior to the First World War,

Together with Dilthey, Husserl and Bergson, Simmel is one of the most striking representatives of this period that perhaps did not find such a worldly and clear expression as in him. In Simmel . . . one could feel the pulse-beat of the

times most forcefully. His audience at the University of
Berlin was the largest and most select. He had connections
not only with the foremost philosophers and academics of
his time, with Bergson, Troeltsch and Max Weber, but
also with artists and poets, with Rodin, George and Rilke.
He was the centre of the intellectual elite. [38]

Not surprisingly, then, traces of his work are to be found not only in
that of some of his students such as Ernst Bloch, Georg Lukács and
Karl Mannheim but friends such as Martin Buber or more indirectly Martin Heidegger. And this is only the beginnings of a much
longer list of those who owed much to Simmel's diverse endeavours.

2.3　THE TRANSITION TO MODERNITY IN SIMMEL'S WORK

If Simmel's own prognostication that he would leave behind no
intellectual heirs – and there is no Simmelian school of sociology or
philosophy – is only partly borne out by the facts, then there is at
least one area in which Simmel's talent was universally recognized
by his contemporaries, namely in the analysis of the present. It has
been said that 'Simmel's alert, critical mind not only allowed the
contemporary cultural currents to pass through it but also, simultaneously, as a sociologist and philosopher of culture, to question
their content. In so doing, he "elevated the social reality of the *present*
into scientific consciousness"'. [39] In this respect at least, his
sociology extended far beyond 'a sociology for aesthetes' or 'for the
literary salon'. Simmel's social theory not merely analyses the permanent or even 'eternal' 'forms of sociation'; it is, too, a science of
the present.

But whilst it is true that many of Simmel's contemporaries were
also concerned with the nature and distinctiveness of modern society
and the problems of the transition to modern capitalist society, he
himself had a different interest in the present. It was an interest that
was neither documentary nor historical. In other words, Simmel's
account of modernity is not often grounded in a historical investigation of the important changes in German society around the turn of
the century. In this respect, his analysis has little in common with
that of his contemporaries such as Werner Sombart, Max Weber or
even Ferdinand Tönnies (though some of the latter's analysis in
Gemeinschaft und Gesellschaft does appear in the different context of
The Philosophy of Money). Even Simmel's *Philosophy of Money*, certainly

an important source for his theory of modernity, seldom locates contemporary society in a historical constellation that has any more definite features than that of a mature money economy.

Yet his contemporaries 'scented the instinct for the times' and his 'interpretation of the times from the modernist perspective'. [40] Another suggested that 'it is primarily Simmel's perspective directed so strongly to the present that determines his influence, his preference for the social and ethical questions of our time' that are avoided by many of his colleagues. [41] Yet it must be emphasized that this was no documentary interest in the times. Rather, Simmel's gift lay in capturing the mode of experiencing contemporary reality. On a few occasions, he sought to locate these experiences within a wider social and historical context. More often, however, as in 'The Metropolis and Mental Life' (1903), 'the products of specifically modern life are questioned as to their *inner nature*'. And here no feature of modern everyday life proved insignificant. In this respect, one can detect Simmel's affinities with phenomenology.

Where Simmel does attempt a social and historical location of current tendencies in modern society and especially his own Wilhelmian Germany, he also unwittingly provides us with a location for his own development. In an article which only appeared in English in 1902 titled 'Tendencies in German Life and Thought since 1870', Simmel outlines what for him are the major developments in cultural life. [42] After German unification and the Franco-Prussian war of 1870–71, political and economic forces encouraged the development of 'a practical materialism' and 'the *material* enjoyment of life'. In the economic sphere, this resulted in the primacy of technique, a tendency which also 'infected purely intellectual branches of knowledge: in the historical sciences, as in that of experimental psychology, investigations, essentially worthless and, as regards the ultimate end of all research, most unimportant' were encouraged. But this 'rapid development of external civilization' facilitated by large-scale industrial development 'has assisted the outbreak of the greatest popular movement of the century, namely, the rise of the Social Democrats'. The socialist idea, though embodied in the socialist party as 'the only one that represents unconditionally and exclusively the interests of the labouring classes', also had a wide appeal beyond these social groups, even to 'a type that we find truly unsympathetic and that is gradually vanishing', namely 'parlor socialism – a coquetting with socialist ideals whose realisation would be most unendurable to these very dilettanti'. But Simmel sees the interest in socialism among non-working class groups as having declined once the Social Democrats became 'a reform party on the basis of the existing social order'. Indeed, the interest in social issues he sees as having its basis from another source in part, in the philosophy of Schopenhauer (a major element of Simmel's early philosophy) which was disseminated in the 1860s and 1870s and which embodied the notion that there is no final end in life, only the human will. Hence 'the lack that men felt of a final object, and consequently of an ideal that should dominate the whole of life, was supplied in the eighties by the almost instantaneous rise of the ideal of social justice'. Here Simmel provides the source of what was probably his own interest in socialism, one which is an extension of his theory of the nature of society. He maintains that

> it was seen that it was society, the sum of all social groups, from which we derived every inner and outer good as a loan, that the individual was but the crossing-point of social threads, and that he, by a devotion to the interests of all, merely discharged an obligation of the most fundamental character – by a devotion that has as its primary object the most oppressed and undeveloped portion of society which, nevertheless, through its labor supported the whole. [43]

Yet Simmel discerned 'the rise of an opposite ideal, that of individualism, which about the year 1890 began to compete with the socialist ideal'. Once more, Simmel highlights an associated tendency which is very close to his own in the 1890s, namely amongst those who 'regard socialism as the necessary transition stage to a just and enlightened individualism'. Such an 'enlightened individualism' is embodied in the philosophy of Nietzsche which gained popularity in the 1890s (and is a key to several crucial concepts such as that of 'distance' and 'distinction' in Simmel's own work). However, Nietzsche's ideas were eagerly taken up by many who saw in them 'the justification of an unrestrained egoism, and who considered that they gave an absolute right to develop in the highest degree the personality of the individual in defiance of all social and altruistic claims'. This was particularly attractive to the new German youth movement and to others who, on the basis of a false understanding of Nietzsche's philosophy, sought a false individuality. In contrast to this need for extreme differentiation, in part the result of presumed levelling tendencies in society, Simmel points to a significant demand for equalization in the growing German women's movement, to which he elsewhere devoted much attention. A further tendency discerned by Simmel is the growing centralization of the state and the church and a consequent search by individuals to secure some area 'beyond all the oscillations and fragmentariness of empirical existence', a longing which for them 'assumes an aesthetic character. They seem to find in the artistic conception of things a release from the fragmentary and painful in real life'. This 'passionate aesthetic interest' – and Simmel is writing here at the height of the *art nouveau* movement – results from a 'transcendental impulse' which 'disillusioned by a fragmentary science that is silent as to everything final, and by a social-altruistic activity that neglects the inner, self-centred completion of spiritual development, has sought an outlet for itself in the aesthetic', but in an aesthetic retreat that cannot be a final one.

Simmel's overview of German thought not merely seeks to summarize the various tendencies since 1870 but also indicates his own interests and development. The dialectic of a growing material or objective culture and the increasing difficulty of realizing a genuine individuality in modern society which is present in this overview is a central theme of much of Simmel's mature work; so also is his analysis of modernity in the specific sense of modes of experiencing modern life. Indeed, it can be claimed that Simmel is the first sociologist of modernity in the sense given to it originally by Baudelaire as 'the ephemeral, the fugitive, the contingent' in modern life. The artist of modernity is 'the painter of the passing moment' who captures the newness of the present and is able 'to distil the eternal from the transitory' in city life, fashions, gestures, etc. No sociologist before him had sought to capture the modes of experiencing modern life or the fleeting moments of interaction. Simmel's sociological texts are richly populated with fortuitous fragments of reality, with seemingly superficial phenomena, with a myriad of social vignettes. [44]

Simmel, too, shares with Baudelaire – though in a very different context – the same social experiences that are the foundation for a theory of modernity: 'The most important among them are the experiences of the neurasthenic, of the big-city dweller, and of the customer'. [45] The intense nervousness of metropolitan life is analysed by Simmel in his writings on the city and the money economy. At the very outset of his famous essay on the metropolis, Simmel declares that 'the psychological foundation of the metropolitan personality type is the increase in nervous life, which emerges out of the rapid and unbroken change in external and internal stimuli'. [46]

That same essay, along with many other works, also contains Simmel's analysis of the experiences of modern metropolitan life. Finally, *The Philosophy of Money* is not so much concerned with the consumer as with the whole world of commodity exchange and its effect upon social relationships and forms of sociation.

But if Simmel is the first sociologist of modernity in this sense, then as a sociologist he is faced with the problem of its analysis. How is it possible to capture the fleeting fragmentary social reality of modern life that is always in flux? What is the justification for starting out from 'a fortuitous fragment of reality', from 'each of life's details', from a 'fleeting image of social interaction'? If Simmel's sociology is concerned in this way with contemporary 'forms of sociation' then what we usually understand as a 'formal sociology' could hardly cope with this task. Hence, in order to examine this and other dimensions of Simmel's sociology we have to look in a fresh light at his attempt to ground sociology as an independent discipline.

NOTES AND REFERENCES

[1]   Hans Simmel, 'Auszüge aus den Lebenserinnerungen', in H. Böhringer and K. Gründer (editors), *Ästhetik und Soziologie um die Jahrhundertwende: Georg Simmel*, Frankfurt, Klosterman (1978), pp. 247–8.

[2]   L. Coser, 'Introduction: Georg Simmel', in L. A. Coser (editor), *Georg Simmel*, Englewood Cliffs, N.J., Prentice-Hall (1965), p. 1.

[3]   Hans Simmel, 'Auszüge aus den Lebenserinnerungen', *loc. cit.*, p. 265.

[4]   Cited in M. Landmann, 'Bausteine zur Biographie', in K. Gassen and M. Landmann (editors), *Buch des Dankes an Georg Simmel*, Berlin, Duncker and Humblot (1958), p. 17. This collection is an invaluable source of information on Simmel's career and life.

[5]   M. Landmann, 'Georg Simmel: Konturen seines Denkens', in H. Böhringer and K. Gründer (editors), *Ästhetik und Soziologie um die Jahrhundertwende*, p. 3.

[6]   For the later essay see G. Simmel, 'Uber eine Beziehung der Selektionslehre zur Erkenntnistheorie', *Archiv für systematische Philosophie*, Vol. 1, 1895, pp. 34–45.

[7]   See H. Böhringer, 'Spuren von spekulativem Atomismus in Simmel's formaler Soziologie', in H. Böhringer and K. Grün-

der (editors), *Ästhetik und Soziologie um die Jahrhundertwende*, pp. 105–17. On Simmel's early writings see also K. C. Köhnke, 'Von der Völkerpsychologie zur Soziologie' in H. J. Dahme and O. Rammstedt (editors), *Die Aktualität George Simmels*, Frankfurt, Suhrkamp (1984).

[8]   See Hans Simmel, 'Auszüge aus den Lebenserinnerungen', *loc. cit.* p. 249.

[9]   On Simmel's psychology see my 'Georg Simmel and Social Psychology', *Journal of the History of the Behavioral Sciences*, Vol. 20, 1984.

[10] See Chapter 3.

[11] In a letter of 2.3.1908. See W. Gephart, 'Verlorene und gefundene Briefe Georg Simmel an Célestin Bouglé, Eugen Diederichs, Gabriel Tarde', in H. J. Dahme and O. Rammstedt (editors), *Die Aktualität Georg Simmels*. This is the source of all the letters to Bouglé cited below.

[12] See the note by K. C. Köhnke (translated D. Frisby), 'Murderous Attack on Georg Simmel', *European Journal of Sociology*, Vol. 24, 1983.

[13] Letter to Heinrich Rickert, 19.7.1898, cited in M. Landmann, 'Bausteine zur Biographie', *loc. cit.*, p. 96.

[14] M. Landmann, 'Bausteine zur Biographie', *loc. cit.*, pp. 21–2.

[15] *Ibid.*, pp. 22–3.

[16] *Ibid.*, p. 24.

[17] F. Tönnies, 'Besprechung', *Jahrbücher für Nationalökonomie und Statistik*, Vol. 56, 1891, pp. 269–77, esp. p. 269.

[18] The original appeared as 'Das Problem der Soziologie', *Jahrbuch für Gesetzgebung, Verwaltung und Volkswirtschaft*, Vol. 18, 1894, pp. 271–7. An English translation with a 'Supplementary Note' appeared as 'The Problem of Sociology', *Annals of the American Academy of Politics and Social Science*, Vol. 6, 1895, pp. 52–63. The 1908 revised version (translated K. H. Wolff) is in K. H. Wolff (editor), *Essays on Sociology, Philosophy and Aesthetics by Georg Simmel, et al.*, Columbia, Ohio State University Press (1959), New York, Harper Row (1965) pp. 310–16.

[19] In a letter to Althoff of 3.3.1895. Cited in M. Landmann, 'Bausteine zur Biographie', *loc. cit.*, p. 24.

[20] Letters to Heinrich Rickert of 24.6.1896, 10.5.1898, and 15.8.1898, in K. Gassen and M. Landmann (editors), *Buch des Dankes*, pp. 92, 94, 96.

[21] See 'Die Selbsterhaltung der socialen Gruppe', *Jahrbuch für Gesetzgebung, Verwaltung und Volkswirtschaft*, Volume 22, 1898, pp. 235–86. For an English translation by Albion W. Small,

see 'The Persistence of Social Groups', *American Journal of Sociology*, Vol. 3, pp. 662–98, 829–36, Vol. 4, pp. 35–50. An extended version of this essay appears in G. Simmel, *Soziologie*, 5th edition, Berlin, Dunker and Humblot (1968), pp. 375–459, and remains untranslated.

[22] Letter to Heinrich Rickert of 28.5.1901, in K. Gassen and M. Landmann (editors), *Buch des Dankes*, p. 100.

[23] See G. Simmel, *The Problems of the Philosophy of History* (translated, edited and with introduction by G. Oakes), New York, The Free Press (1977) and Oakes's introduction.

[24] Cited in M. Landmann, 'Bausteine zur Biographie', *loc. cit.*, p. 25.

[25] For the full text of this letter in translation see L. A. Coser, 'The Stranger in the Academy, in L. A. Coser (editor), *Georg Simmel*, pp. 37–9.

[26] M. Weber, 'Georg Simmel as Sociologist' (translated D. Levine), *Social Research*, Vol. 39, 1972, p. 159. This sadly incomplete text is the only extended comment surviving by Weber on Simmel.

[27] Letter to Max Weber of 15.12.1909, in K. Gassen and M. Landmann (editors), *Buch des Dankes*, pp. 129–30. My emphasis.

[28] See E. Troeltsch, 'Der historische Entwicklungsbegriff', *Historische Zeitschrift*, Vol. 124, 1921, p. 423.

[29] Letter to Adolf von Harnack, 3.1.1914, in K. Gassen and M. Landmann (editors), *Buch des Dankes*, p. 82.

[30] These essays have recently appeared in translation. See G. Simmel, *Essays on Interpretation in Social Science* (translated, edited and with introduction by G. Oakes), Manchester, Manchester University Press (1980); Totowa, N.J., Rowman and Littlefield (1980).

[31] Letter to Hermann Keyserling, 25.3.1918, in G. Simmel, *Das individuelle Gesetz* (editor M. Landmann), Frankfurt, Suhrkamp (1968).

[32] Cited in H. Simmel, 'Auszüge aus den Lebenserinnerungen', *loc. cit.*, p. 265.

[33] I owe this information and some of that which follows to the researches of Klaus C. Köhnke.

[34] See E. Schultze, 'Die sozialwissenschaftliche Vereinigung', *Die Zukunft*, Vol. 11, 1895, pp. 466–9.

[35] M. Susman, 'Erinnerungen', in K. Gassen and M. Landmann (editors), *Buch des Dankes*, p. 281.

[36] E. Landmann, 'Erinnerungen', in *ibid.*, p. 210.

[37] Letter to G. F. Knapp, 14.3.1906, in M. Vater (editor), *Bürgerin zweier Welten*, Tübingen (1961), p. 62.

[38] M. Landmann, 'Einleitung' to G. Simmel, *Brücke und Tür*, Stuttgart, K. F. Koehler (1957), p. v.

[39] H. J. Becher, *Georg Simmel*, Stuttgart, Enke, pp. 23–4.

[40] P. Fechter, 'Erinnerungen', in K. Gassen and M. Landmann (editors), *Buch des Dankes*, p. 159.

[41] F. Alafberg, 'Georg Simmel', *Die Grenzboten*, Vol. 70, 1911, p. 188.

[42] G. Simmel, 'Tendencies in German Life and Thought since 1870', *International Monthly*, (N.Y.), Vol. 5, 1902, pp. 93–111, 166–84. It is unfortunate that the German original cannot be traced since the translation is in need of emendation.

[43] *Ibid.*, p. 102.

[44] An earlier version of this argument is to be found in my *Sociological Impressionism: A Reassessment of Georg Simmel's Social Theory*, London, Heinemann (1981). It is more precisely stated in 'Simmels Theorie der Moderne', in H. J. Dahme and O. Rammstedt (editors), *Die Aktualität Georg Simmels*. See also my *Fragments of Modernity: Georg Simmel, Siegfried Kracauer, Walter Benjamin*, London, Heinemann (1985).

[45] W. Benjamin, *Charles Baudelaire: A Lyric Poet in the Era of High capitalism* (translated H. Zohn), London, N.L.B. (1973), p. 106.

[46] There are two English translations of 'Die Grossstädte und das Geistesleben'. The first, by E. Shils, is available in D. Levine (editor), *Georg Simmel on Sociability and Social Forms*, Chicago/London, Chicago University Press (1971), pp. 324–39; the second, by H. Gerth and C. Wright Mills, in K. H. Wolff (editor) *The Sociology of Georg Simmel*, New York, Free Press (1950), pp. 409–74.

3

The Foundation of Sociology

3.1 A NEW CONCEPT OF SOCIOLOGY: FIRST ATTEMPT

In his review of Simmel's *Sociology*, Alfred Vierkandt makes the following ambitious claim:

> If sociology succeeds in developing itself into an autonomous individual science, then its future historian will have to celebrate Simmel as its founder, and even if this process is not completed, his work remains an outstanding, penetrating achievement. He has indeed demarcated an autonomous group of problems for the study of society and thereby demonstrated the possibility and urgent need for a new discipline. His distinction between the form and content of social life elevates him above the encyclopaedic interpretation of sociology. In the same way, he distinguishes himself from those who allow sociology to be identified with the tasks of historical, cultural or social philosophy. For its specific problem is always the interactions and relationships between the individual elements of a group. [1]

If we leave aside for the moment a judgement upon this claim, then we should at least investigate how Simmel arrived at what he himself conceived of as 'a new concept of sociology'. In order to do this it is necessary to return to his early writings so that we may reconstruct systematically and historically Simmel's progress towards this goal.

As Friedrich Tenbruck has pointed out in this connection, any attempt at a realistic assessment of Simmel's contribution to sociology must examine carefully the historical location of his interest in sociology. Simmel's

> sociological period, announced by the themes of several articles in the 1880s, commences with the study *On Social Differentiation* (1890) and reaches its real high point and fulfilment in *The Philosophy of Money* (1900). Between these dates lie a large number of articles which in changed or enlarged forms, in the original formulation or translated, improved, merged with one another, are reworked and finally presented in the collection: *Sociology*. [2]

If we accept this assessment – and it would have to be qualified by some of the articles published after 1900 which make up the *Sociology* – then we should consider Tenbruck's inference that 'Simmel's sociological work is thus confined to a single decade. Hence, he is specifically and in the strict sense not a contemporary of Max Weber. As the latter commenced sociological work, the former had already taken his leave of it'. [3] What is true is that within that decade Simmel had established the basic framework for his sociology. After 1898 he ceased to preface his articles on various aspects of sociology with a justification of the grounds for such a discipline.

If the subtitle of his *On Social Differentiation* – 'Sociological and Psychological Investigations' – indicates an ambiguity as to the content of this work, then this same uncertainty is reflected in the title of its first chapter: 'On the Epistemology of Social Science'. It does not yet indicate a clear commitment to sociology. Nonetheless, it does represent Simmel's first attempt to demarcate sociology as an independent discipline. But before moving on to an analysis of its central arguments, we should briefly consider the context within which Simmel was seeking to establish his particular conception of sociology.

Any attempt to ground sociology anew in the late 1880s in Germany would have to confront the positivist conception of sociology developed by Comte and its extension in Herbert Spencer's evolutionary theory. In Germany, Darwin's evolutionism had already made a major impact on social theory in the biologically and organicist orientated conceptions of sociology such as those of Schäffle and Lilienfeld. Under the influence of developments in statistics, attempts were also made to develop a 'social physics'. But these directions in social theory did not go unchallenged. In his writings of the 1870s and 1880s, Wilhelm Dilthey (also in Berlin University) had already attacked the positivism of Comte and Mill and a Comtean and Spencerian conception of sociology as a 'gigantic dream concept'. In 1883 Dilthey was already speaking of society as the 'play of interactions' or 'the summation of interactions' and, in a passage very close to Simmel's conception of society (though Simmel never acknowledged Dilthey's influence), Dilthey maintained that 'the individual ... is an element in the interactions [*Wechselwirkungen*] of society, a point of intersection of the diverse systems of these interactions who reacts with conscious intention and action upon their effects'. [4] Similarly, Gumplowicz in his *Grundriss der Soziologie* (1885) attacked the overarching concept of society as a fundamental concept of sociology and sought to substitute the study of social groups as its object domain.

In other related areas of social science, attempts were also being made to secure firm foundations for particular disciplines. Since Simmel was attending some of the historical economist Gustav Schmoller's seminars and in the light of the content of his 'On the Psychology of Money' (1889) he was probably acquainted with the methodological dispute, the *Methodenstreit*, in economics from the early 1880s onwards between the historical and theoretical schools of economics. More importantly, Simmel was already schooled in the *Völkerpsychologie* of his teachers Lazarus and Steinthal, as well as the work of Gustav Fechner in the field of psychology and philosophy. A recent study suggests that Fechner's doctrine of logical atomism enabled Simmel to develop a conception of society that did not move either towards 'the hypostatization of a Volksseele' as in much early *Völkerpsychologie* or towards a 'substantive anthropology' as in Spencer's work. [5] Rather, Simmel was able to conceive of society as the interaction of its elements (individuals) rather than as a substance. Similarly, Simmel adopted Fechner's conception of the interaction of elements rather than the operation of forces in one direction, thereby producing a conception of reality whose complexity prevented the development of laws in the positivist sense. This recent study of Simmel's early work concludes that Fechner's simple atomism 'enabled Simmel to move from *Völkerpsychologie* into a sociology that no longer justified its object by a distinctive substance, but rather wished merely to describe the formal relationship of complex elements in a functional constellation'. [6] The other conclusion which may be drawn is that in seeking to establish sociology as an independent discipline, Simmel would necessarily be confronted with the problem of the demarcation of sociology from psychology.

It is within this context that Simmel first sets out to clarify the nature of sociology. 'A newly emergent science' such as sociology seems to be 'an eclectic discipline insofar as the products of other sciences constitute its subject matter'. Seen in this light, sociology provides 'merely a new standpoint for the observation of already known facts'. Hence, sociology cannot be defined in terms of its object of study since 'in the last instance, there is no science whose content emerges out of mere objective facts, but rather always entails their interpretation and ordering according to categories and norms that exist *a priori* for the relevant science'. [7] In other words, there can be no naive positivist grounding of a science of sociology in facts. However, Simmel goes on to argue that sociology cannot merely be grounded in conceptualizations either. Although sociology might ask 'What is a society? What is an individual? How are reciprocal effects of individuals upon each other possible?', it cannot do so on the basis of fixed *a priori* conceptions. Otherwise it 'will fall into the error of the older psychology: one must first have defined the nature of the psyche before one can scientifically recognise psychological phenomena'. [8]

One major reason why *a priori* conceptualizations are inappropriate is that the subject-matter to which they refer, both in psychology and in sociology, is extremely complex. The diversity of 'latent and effective forces' within individuals and society and the 'reciprocal effects' [*gegenseitige Wirkungen*] of individuals and groups upon one another are so great as to make their possible combinations almost infinite and immeasurable. From this Simmel infers that

> if it is the task of sociology to describe the forms of human communal existence and to find the rules according to which he or she is the member of a group, and groups relate to one another, then the complexity of this object has a consequence for our science which places it in an epistemological relationship – which I must extensively ground – to metaphysics and psychology [9]

The two latter disciplines are characterized by the fact that both produce contrary propositions which have the same plausibility, probability and verifiability. For instance, in psychology the general concepts of psychological functions are so general and the 'wealth of nuances' in each psychological function so great that to subsume a complex phenomenon under the same single concept usually leads to a failure to distinguish why different causes produce the same effect. This means, Simmel argues, that 'the establishment of a causal connection between simple psychological concepts ... is always completely one-sided'. In the same way, the sheer complexity of psychological phenomena prevents psychology from arriving at 'any laws in the natural scientific sense ... it is never possible to establish with complete certainty what in fact is indeed the cause of a given effect or the effect of a given cause'. [10]

Similarly, sociology too faces the same problem of the complexity of its object which 'completely prevents its separation into simple parts and its basic forces and relationships'. This also prevents sociology from generating 'laws of social development. Undoubtedly, each element of a society moves according to natural laws. Yet for the whole there exists no law; as in nature, so equally here, there is no higher law above the laws that govern the movement of the smallest parts'. [11] Here we see Simmel attempting to move away from his early Spencerian and Darwinian conception of social reality.

This line of argument also pushes Simmel in the direction of a critique of those conceptions of sociology that take as their starting point an all-embracing concept of society. For Simmel the only genuine reality is the activities of individuals who constitute society:

> If society is merely a ... constellation of individuals who are the actual realities, then the latter and their behaviour also constitutes the real object of science and the concept of society evaporates ... What palpably exists is indeed only individual human beings and their circumstances and activities: therefore, the task can only be to understand them, whereas the essence of society, that emerges purely through an ideal synthesis and is never to be grasped, should not form the object of reflection that is directed towards the investigation of reality. [12]

Simmel here seeks to guard against both a conception of society as an autonomous entity and a thorough-going individualistic foundation for sociology that reduces social reality to isolated atoms.

In order to secure sociology from this latter danger, Simmel has to indicate some object of study that is not merely individuals as such. And here we move towards the core of Simmel's early founda-

tion of sociology. Simmel commences from 'a regulative world principle that everything interacts in some way with everything else, that
between every point in the world and every other force permanently
moving relationships exist'. [13] Following on from the earlier
argument about the complexity of reality, Simmel maintains that we
cannot extract a single element out of this ceaseless interaction and
say that it is the decisive one. Rather, we must assert that what
unites individual elements in some objective form is interaction:
'there exists only one basic factor which provides at least a relative
objectivity of unification: the interaction [*Wechselwirkung*] of the
parts. We characterise any object as unified to the extent to which its
parts stand in a reciprocal dynamic relationship'. [14] Is this how
Simmel conceives of society?

Sociology is concerned with 'empirical atoms, with conceptions,
individuals and groups that function as unities'. It is concerned with
social interactions. Sociology does not therefore take as its starting
point the concept of society since it is

> only the name for the sum of these interactions . . . It is
> therefore not a unified, fixed concept but rather a gradual
> one . . . according to the greater number and cohesion of
> the existing interactions that exist between the given per-
> sons. In this manner, the concept of society completely
> loses its mystical facet that individualistic realism wished
> to see in it. [15]

Society is thus composed of the ceaseless interaction of its individual
elements – groups as well as individuals – which impels Simmel's
sociology towards a concern for social *relationships*, i.e. towards the
study of social interaction.

In his early attempt to ground sociology as an independent
discipline, Simmel first established the regulative principle of the
interaction and inter-relatedness of all phenomena. For sociology
this implied the study not of society as substance but as interaction
of its elements. The more abstract grounding for his regulative principle was already present in his doctoral dissertation (1881) which
criticized Kant's conception of matter:

> If matter emerges out of energies or forces [*Kraften*], then
> one should no longer treat them as purely possible sub-
> stances upon which other energies can exercise their undis-
> turbed interplay; for the product of these energies is no
> finished product, but a continuous process . . . an

emergent entity . . . There exists amongst the energies no difference in their status. [16]

Simmel was later to extend this concept of matter to society itself. Sociology was to examine the interplay of interactions without necessarily giving any of them any logical or societal priority.

3.2 THE PROBLEM OF SOCIOLOGY

What lies between Simmel's first attempt to ground sociology in 1890 and his important essay 'The Problems of Sociology' (1894) is not merely his two-volume *Introduction to Moral Science* (1892/93) but also his *Problems of the Philosophy of History* (1892). As Simmel himself subsequently reflected, he had started out from epistemological and Kantian studies together with historical and social scientific interests:

> The initial result of this was the basic insight (set out in *The Problems of the Philosophy of History*) that "history" signifies the formation [*Formung*] of the events that are objects of immediate experience by means of the *a priori* categories of the scientific intellect just as "nature" signifies the formation of sensually given materials by means of the categories of the understanding.
>
> This separation of the form and content of the historical image, that emerged for me purely epistemologically, was then pursued by me in a methodological principle within a particular discipline. I secured a new concept of sociology in which I separated the forms of sociation [*die Formen der Vergesellschaftung*] from the contents, i.e. the drives, purposes and material content which, only by being taken up by the interactions between individuals, become societal. [17]

This 'new concept of sociology' is outlined in Simmel's essay of 1894 which he himself saw as being so important (1894 was the first year in which he taught a course simply entitled 'Sociology') and which, he wrote, 'contains my work programme'. Indeed, Simmel wrote in 1895: 'I take the small article to be the most fruitful one that I have written'. [18] It is therefore worthy of detailed treatment, especially since, in revised and extended form, it later constituted the first chapter of Simmel's *Sociology*. Some of its content and developments from it also reappear either at the beginning or end of almost every sociological essay Simmel wrote between 1894 and 1898. [19]

Simmel starts out from 'the most significant and momentous progress' in historical and human studies in recent times, namely 'the overthrow of the individualistic perspective'. The replacement of 'individual fates' by 'social forces' and 'collective movements' – the 'real and determining' factors – has ensured that 'the science of human beings has become the science of human society'. [20] However, this tendency can only establish 'a regulative principle for all human sciences'; it cannot be the basis for a 'specific, autonomous science' such as sociology. Rather, it is merely 'a comprehensive name' for the human sciences. Hence,

> Sociology as the history of society and all its contents, i.e. in the sense of an explanation of all events by means of social forces and configurations, is no more a specific science than, for instance, induction. Like the latter – though not in the same formal sense – it is a method of acquiring knowledge, a heuristic principle. [21]

If sociology is to be anything more than 'a mere research tendency that is falsely hypostatized into a science of sociology' it must have a more restricted significance.

What is this more restricted sense of sociology that secures its existence as an independent discipline? Simmel provides an answer by drawing an analogy with psychology to the effect that,

> Just as the differentiation of the specifically psychological from objective matter produces psychology as a science, so a genuine sociology can only deal with what is specifically societal, the form and forms of sociation [*Vergesellschaftung*] as such, as distinct from the particular interests and contents in and through which sociation is realised. [22]

Such interests and contents form the subject matter of other specialized sciences.

Having circumscribed the task of sociology, Simmel is obliged to outline, on the basis of this sociology, what he means by society. In the light of his earlier attempt to ground sociology, his answer is not surprising: 'Society in the broadest sense is indeed to be found wherever several individuals enter into interaction'. Therefore, 'one must recognise sociation of the most diverse levels and types' from the simplest to the most complex. The particular causes and purposes without which no sociation would occur constitute 'the body, the material of the social process'. However,

> The fact that the result of these causes, the pursuance of these goals does in fact call forth an interaction, a sociation amongst its agents, this is the *form* in which this content clothes itself. And the whole existence of a specific science of *society* rests upon the demarcation of the latter by means of scientific abstraction. [23]

These forms of sociation are less diverse than their content since 'the same form, the same type of sociation can enter into the most diverse material'. The constitution of sociology as a discipline thus rests upon

> a realm legitimated by abstraction: that of sociation as such and its forms. These forms develop out of the contact of individuals, relatively independently of the reasons for this contact, and their sum total constitutes, concretely, that entity which is designated by the abstraction: society. [24]

This is what distinguishes Simmel's concept of sociology from earlier theories of society which, on the basis of this abstract concept of society, were able to include within the realm of sociology, for instance, 'any ethnological or pre-historical investigation'. Without denying the value of such research, Simmel maintains that to subsume such studies under the rubric of sociology 'rests upon the faulty distinction between that "society" which is only a collective name arising out of the inability to treat separately individual phenomena and that society which determines the phenomena through specifically social forces'. In other words, there is a failure to distinguish between 'what takes place merely *within* society as a framework and that which really takes place *through* society'. [25] Only the latter constitutes the subject matter of sociology.

Of course, this subject matter presents itself to us in social reality as a fusion of form and content. But, like other sciences, sociology proceeds on the basis of abstraction, in this case the abstraction of the form from the content of social reality. Sociology 'extracts the purely social element from the totality of human history – i.e. what occurs *in* society – for special attention, or, expressed with somewhat paradoxical brevity, it investigates that which in society is "society"'. [26] What does the study of "society" in this second sense consist of? It comprises 'the investigation of the forces, forms and developments of sociation, of the cooperation, association and co-existence of individuals'. This 'should be the sole object of a sociology conceived as a special science'.

If this is the legitimate object of sociology, how should it be investigated? In the light of Simmel's desire to provide the foundations for a strictly demarcated sociological discipline, his answer to this question is surprising:

> The methods according to which the problems of sociation are to be investigated are the same as in all comparative psychological sciences. As a foundation there lie certain psychological presuppositions that belong to them without which no historical science can exist: the phenomena of seeking and giving help, of love and hate, of avarice and the sense of satisfaction in communal existence, the self preservation of individuals . . . and a series of other primary psychological processes must be presupposed in order that one can at all understand how sociation, group formations, relations of individuals to a whole entity, etc., come about. [27]

Certainly these and other psychological phenomena are dealt with by Simmel in his sociological writings. But it also makes all the more important the task of demarcating sociology from psychology, even though sociology in this period was not the only discipline to be grounded in psychological presuppositions as the history of economics demonstrates. Sociology, for Simmel, does not remain content with these psychological presuppositions but through a process of 'abstraction and combination' separates the content and form of social events. It 'treats these forms by means of inductive abstraction from the collective phenomena . . . It is the only science which really seeks to know only society, *sensu strictissimo*'. [28] And in a 'Supplementary Note' to the English translation of 1895, Simmel argues that rather than being a narrow discipline 'as it appeared to a number of my critics' it actually deals with a whole range of forms of sociation from the most general to the most particular. [29]

Simmel also conceives of the possibility at least of this new mode of sociological analysis providing a comprehensive understanding of society. In the opening passage to his article on 'Superiority and Subordination' (1896) Simmel argues that 'if we could exhibit the totality of possible forms of social relationship in their gradations and variations we should have in such [an] exhibit complete knowledge of "society" as such'. [30] But again Simmel guards against a reduction or even 'an approximate reduction' of our knowledge of society to a few simple propositions on the grounds that

Social phenomena are too immeasurably complicated, and the methods of analysis are too incomplete. The consequence is that if sociological forms and names are used with precision they apply only within a relatively contracted circle of manifestations. Long and patient labour will be necessary before we can understand the concrete historical forms of socialisation [sociation, D.F.] as the actual compounds of a few simple fundamental forms of human association. [31]

And even if we are able to discover the 'laws, forms and developments' of sociation then we must also recognise that they determine social reality 'only together with other functions and forces'. [32] This implies that Simmel is not guilty of that form of sociologism which became so common in social theory. But, once more, it raises the necessity of demarcating sociology from the study of these 'other functions and forces', especially where – with considerable ambiguity – Simmel declares sociology's task to be the 'description and determination of *the historico-psychological origin* of those forms in which interactions take place between human beings'. [33] It is to Simmel's demarcation of sociology from psychology and from history that we must now turn.

3.3 THE DEMARCATION OF SOCIOLOGY

3.3.1 From psychology

As someone who had started out from *Völkerpsychologie* before coming to sociology, Simmel was well aware that 'the attempt has been made to reduce all sciences to psychology' – a reference perhaps to Wilhelm Wundt (amongst others). The grounds for this reduction are that the sciences are all the product of the human mind. Simmel rejects this argument as a failure to distinguish between the science of psychology and the functions of the mind.

But as we have seen, Simmel's real demarcation problem arises out of his own inclusion of psychological presuppositions into his foundation of sociology. Certain specific structures within the socio-historical complex must be related back not only to social interactions but also 'psychological states'. [34] Sociology confines itself to the 'immediate psychological significance' of a course of events. But sociology must go beyond this on the basis of its own abstractions. This is necessary since 'if society is to be an autonomous object of an independent science, then it can only be so through the fact that, out of the sum of individual elements that constitute it, a new entity emerges; otherwise all problems of social science would only be those of individual psychology'. [35]

There is another reason why the demarcation of sociology from psychology is necessary for Simmel. The more he concentrated upon small-scale face-to-face interactions, upon 'microscopic-molecular processes within human material' that 'exhibit society, as it were, *statu nascendi*', the more Simmel recognized that 'the delicate, invisible threads that are woven between one person and another' are 'only accessible through psychological microscopy'. [36] Insofar as Simmel also maintains that explanation of the smallest interactions is necessary in order to explain the major constellations of society, he thereby traces his sociological thematic back to psychological variables.

Simmel was conscious of this problem in the first chapter of his *Sociology* in which he admits that such a focus 'seems to make the investigations planned here to be nothing other than chapters of psychology, at best social psychology'. [37] Indeed, he concedes that 'all societal processes and instincts have their seat in minds and that sociation is, as a consequence, a psychical phenomenon'. Further, we should recognize 'psychic motivations – feelings, thoughts, and needs – . . . not merely as bearers of . . . external relations but also as their essence, as what really and solely interest us', and which 'we reconstruct by means of an instinctive or methodical psychology'.

Simmel's attempt to separate sociology and psychology does not rest upon a strong argument. He maintains that 'the scientific treatment of psychic data is not thereby automatically psychological' since the 'one reality' of social scientific study can be considered 'from a number of different viewpoints'. Hence, although 'the givens of sociology are psychological processes whose immediate reality presents itself first of all under psychological categories . . . [they] remain outside the purposes of sociological investigation. It is to this end that we direct our study to the objective reality of sociation'. [38]

In defending Simmel against the charge of establishing a psychologistic foundation for sociology, one recent commentator has suggested with regard to the study of the regularities of human behaviour that

Whilst statistical figures, interpreted social psychologically, bring out qualities of individuals, viewed sociologically they bring out features of interaction, qualities of systems. With this demarcation Simmel sought once more to establish the possibility of an independent sociology, although he knew that in any particular concrete individual study the boundaries between social psychological and sociological analysis are always fluid. He therefore never seriously concerned himself with avoiding social psychological statements in his sociological investigations. [39]

Such arguments did not, of course, prevent some of Simmel's contemporaries from arguing that he provided a psychologistic foundation for sociology. Othmar Spann, for instance, maintained that Simmel's 'psychologistic concept of society' was based on his 'definition of societal interaction as the interaction of *psychological* entities'. Against this, Spann argued that a 'specifically *social* criterion for interaction' could only be derived from an adequate conception of society not grounded in or reduced to psychological entities. [40] Similarly, Max Weber referred to Spann's 'perceptive criticism' of Simmel's sociology prior to the publication of his *Sociology* but qualified this judgement by stating that 'in relation to the earlier work which Spann criticised, Simmel's recently published *Sociology* shows some notable, but not *fundamental*, modifications'. [41] Viewed from a very different perspective, however, the grounding of sociology in some psychological categories may be one reason why Simmel's sociology has proved attractive not merely to the interactionist tradition but also to social psychology.

3.3.2 From history

In a brief notice of 1895, Simmel suggests that 'sociology might . . . unify the advantages of naturalism and idealism because its object possesses the quality of being accessible to us just as much from the inside – psychologically, through our essential identity with everything human – as from the outside – through statistical, empirical, historical observation'. [42] Having shown that Simmel's sociology has very close connections with psychology, is this equally true for sociology's relationship to history?

As we have seen, Simmel rejects the notion of sociology as 'the history of society' as an inadequate foundation for sociology as a distinctive discipline. It is, however, 'a method of acquiring knowledge, a heuristic principle'. But insofar as sociology is the study of not merely the forces and forms of sociation but also the '*developments of* sociation' it must have a historical component. This historical dimension is a restricted one. As Dahme has argued, this historical dimension does not lead us to a 'historical' sociology:

> Since, according to Simmel, social reality is always to be grasped as a "historical reality", so similarly the actors in social life are to be viewed as historical entities. Simmel draws the unequivocal conclusion from this that a sociology cannot ignore historical developments. Simmel himself always attends to this insight in his sociological investigations, insofar as he seeks to take account of and to analyse historical developments as bringing about the modification of modes of behaviour and changes in social forms. But, in *taking account of historical elements* it is still not necessary for Simmel to *practise sociology as a historical sociology*. [43]

What this implies is that in his particular studies, on fashion for instance, Simmel shows how social formations change over time. In his *Philosophy of Money* it is possible to trace historical variations in forms of exchange and their consequences for social relationships. What is missing, however, is a historical sociology of money relationships. This is an important distinction between the sociologies of Simmel and Max Weber. Simmel's students detected the absence of a systematic historical sociological approach. Karl Mannheim, with reference to Simmel's analysis of the money economy, suggests that though he 'has characterised in many ways the empirically changing objects of the world that are associated with money forms . . . yet in so doing he has abstracted, in a completely unhistorical manner, the capitalistic money form from its capitalistic background and imputed the characteristic structural change to "money as such"'. [44] Simmel is aware of historical variations in forms of sociation but he seldom ever subjects them to a systematic historical analysis. As a result, the reader is often left with the impression that his works are filled with historical instances and examples. As Siegfried Kracauer said of Simmel's analyses of forms of sociation, 'none of them live in historical time'. [45]

But perhaps there is a reason for this retreat from systematic historical analysis that relates to Simmel's attempt to establish sociology as a distinctive science. Simmel consistently seeks to guard against the reduction of sociology to a philosophy of history and any assertion of the existence of historical laws. Sociology conceived as a philosophy of history was being propagated in Germany by such theorists as Paul Barth. The existence of historical laws was asserted by various groups within German Marxism. Simmel insists that sociology must be strictly demarcated from the philosophy of history which seeks 'to subsume historical facts in their totality, both external and psychological, under "general concepts"' whereas sociology should confine itself 'completely within the course of events and their immediate psychological significance'. [46] And in the same context, Simmel adds – on the basis of his own arguments in *The Problems of the Philosophy of History* – that 'there is certainly no longer any doubt today that "laws of history" are not to be found; for history is, on the one hand, such a hugely complex structure, on the other, such an uncertain and subjectively demarcated section extracted from cosmic events, that no unified formula for its development as a totality can be given'. [47] In rejecting sociology as a philosophy of history and historical laws (as also laws of society), Simmel maintains that sociology may itself provide a further contribution to the 'separation of the totality of historical events' insofar as it 'extracts the function of sociation and its countless forms and developments as a special field'. [48]

Thus, despite Simmel's protestation that 'if one attempts to understand . . . aspects of the present time, this can be achieved only through history, i.e. by knowing and understanding the past', [49] Simmel's sociology does not move in the direction of a historical sociology. History is one of those perspectives from which the totality of reality can be viewed but never fully grasped.

3.4 THE QUESTION OF METHOD

It should be evident that Simmel's attempt to ground sociology as an independent science does not rest upon the discovery of a new object for sociological investigation. Rather, 'Simmel's sociology is . . . based on no *new material object* but on a *formal object*, a new "mode of observation", a "standpoint", an "abstraction"'. [50] But since Simmel, unlike Durkheim or Weber, wrote no treatise on this 'method' and regarded preoccupation with methodological issues as a form of fetishism, Becher's judgement is more appropriate, namely that 'expressions such as "mode of observation", "viewpoint", "standpoint", "research tendency" would be more accurate here. This would also correspond with Simmel's perspectivism. The concept of "method", taken in its strict sense, is false'. [51] Bearing in

mind this important qualification, it is nonetheless possible to outline the basic elements of Simmel's attempt to provide 'a new and
sharply demarcated complex of specific tasks' for sociology.

As we have seen, Simmel starts out in 1890 from 'a regulative
world principle that everything interacts in some way with everything else'. This implies that relationships between things are in
permanent flux; 'between every point in the world and every other
force permanently moving relationships exist'. [52] Indeed, trans-
ferring this principle to the study of social reality, Kracauer detected
in Simmel's work a 'core principle' of 'the fundamental inter-
relatedness [*Wesenszusammengehörigkeit*] of the most diverse
phenomena'. [53] In his sociological work, this enabled Simmel to
start out from any point within the totality of social life and arrive at
any other. But it is worth noting here that this first regulative principle itself rests upon a 'general tendency of modern thought, with
its dissolving of substances into functions, the fixed and permanent
in the flux of restless development – an intellectual tendency that
certainly stands in interaction with the practical movements' of the
period. [54] Its substantive foundation therefore rests in social reality itself and in his *Philosophy of Money* we can see its social
origins. In terms of Simmel's approach to sociology, however, what
is important is that this first principle already points to a feature of
the world that preoccupies Simmel, namely the relationships that
exist between the most diverse and seemingly unconnected
phenomena. We might add a further corollary here to the effect that
Simmel's key concepts that define his sociology are all relational
concepts: interaction [*Wechselwirkung*] and sociation [*Vergesellschaftung*]. Even the notion of form too can only be seen in relation to
content.

There is a second 'regulative principle for all the human sciences' (1894) that does not yet indicate the role of sociology but
which it must nonetheless presuppose. This is that 'social forces,
collective movements' are 'the real and determining' factors in
social life rather than individual fates. There are also two further
assumptions which Simmel makes in his early writings that are
significant for his delineation of sociology. The first, to which he
often refers, is that the world – including the social world and the
individuals in it – is an extremely complex and differentiated
phenomenon. Simmel always returns to this premise as an argument
against historical laws or laws of social development that seeks to
encompass their particular object in its totality. And, to anticipate
Simmel's conception of sociology proper, there is a second important

premise that sociology in its concern with the social interactions of individuals must take account of a whole range of 'psychological presuppositions' upon which its own generalizations in part rest.

In his first attempt to ground sociology, Simmel applies the concept of interaction or reciprocal effect to social life and indicates that its basis lies in the interaction or reciprocal relationship between its elements. These elements are conscious individuals or groups of individuals who interact with one another for a variety of motives, purposes and interests. This is the source of the psychological propositions which Simmel acknowledges in his social theory.

However, in order to discover and elucidate the general features of human interaction, Simmel maintains that the investigator must proceed, as in all other sciences, on the basis of a methodical abstraction. For Simmel this constitutes the separation of the form from the content of social interactions, the forms by which individuals and groups of individuals come to be members of society. Sociology's task is therefore the investigation of the forms of being part of society, namely the forms of sociation [*Vergesellschaftung*]. Hence, as Becher has argued, 'Simmel does *not* start out from the isolated individual, *not* from society and also not from the opposition between individual and society, although this opposition greatly interested him'. [55] In starting out from social interactions, Simmel also removes the content of that interaction by a process of abstraction. His problem is therefore that of locating 'the sociality of interaction in the *consciousness* of those interacting' without at the same time hypostatizing or psychologizing the concept of social interaction. Participants in social interaction consciously interact with one another, though Simmel recognizes that interaction also takes place between, say, individuals and supra-personal social forms such as the state and that interactions can be institutionalized in rules. In other words, there is

> no interaction in itself, in its abstract conception . . . rather always a whole wealth of diverse types and forms of interactions. This is what Simmel implies by the concept of form. Sociation is interaction. Interaction always presents itself in a particular form. Hence, society is always a formed society or it does not exist. [56]

Society exists 'where a number of people enter into interaction and form a temporary or permanent unity'. [57]

As Tenbruck has argued, Simmel decisively goes beyond

Dilthey's use of the concept of interaction 'in that he defines the *forms* of interaction as the object of sociology'. This 'formed nature of social action does not lie uppermost in individual actions and their comparison but in the stable structure of relationships'. [58] Even though the sociologist must abstract the forms of sociation from social reality, this does not imply that Simmel was pleading 'for the establishment of categories of a high degree of abstractedness'. [59] Nor is the distinction between form and content, essential to the abstraction of forms of sociation, a 'pure abstraction, insofar as – just like his concept of society – it possesses a *fundamentum in re*'. [60] All this should suggest that Simmel is not concerned to develop either an abstract classification of social forms or an endless typification and taxonomy of social interactions, as formal sociology has so often been identified with. Simmel's sociology is not grounded in a deductive procedure. As he himself often insists, in the study of human sociation 'we will . . . recognise *the forms and laws of sociation* in such a way that we combine social phenomena of the most diverse contents and in fact, *explore inductively* what is nonetheless common to all of them'. [61] Thus, on the basis of this inductive procedure, we abstract these forms of sociation from a variety of social phenomena. Such forms, as Tenbruck suggests, 'represent a specific "layer" of reality. Although they cannot – and are not meant to – account for interaction itself, they are operative in it; they account for its patterns'. [62] Interaction itself for Simmel has its origins in individual motives, interests, etc. This is also where the 'psychological presuppositions' of the analysis of interaction are relevant.

But Simmel is not merely interested in the forms of simple individual interactions. The study of 'sociation of the most diverse levels and types' must include not merely face-to-face interactions but also the investigation of those social relations that have become crystallized in supra-individual forms. These 'objective structures present themselves in the most diverse types of phenomena: as specific organs of the division of labour, as cohesive symbols, as timelessly valid norms'. [63] Such processes often 'appear as products and functions of an impersonal structure' and 'confront the individual as something objective, split off from the conditions of personal life'. [64] But when we speak of such processes as if they were autonomous entities, we ignore the fact that they are 'merely the complex of infinite mechanical interactions of the smallest parts of organic bodies'. [65] In other words, we ignore the fact that 'the interaction between individuals is the starting point of all social formations'. [66] Ultimately then, Simmel assumes that more complex social formations are extensions of simpler interactions between individuals.

It should follow from this that those who see in Simmel's work a formal sociology that is increasingly divorced and abstracted from social reality ignore the increasing refinement of his foundation of sociology as his work progressed. As Dahme has argued, Simmel – at least from 1894 onwards – perhaps unwittingly anticipated this charge insofar as, and in contrast to the form–content division, he increasingly

> places more emphasis upon the *interactional and reciprocal character of social relationships*. The interaction that is typical of social life is now characterised by him as *sociation*. Social interactions are now no longer conceived merely as abstract determinations of form and function, but rather are made more precise so that they are bound up with concrete agents of the process of sociation. Processes of sociation can only be dealt with in terms of individuals, groups or social structures. [67]

The object of sociology, lying in social agents of sociation, thus becomes empirically accessible.

Since Simmel's guidelines to empirical sociological research are never systematically presented and are few and far between, it seems reasonable to examine his procedure within the context of his substantive works. However, some brief indication of the direction of Simmel's work can be given here.

In his essay of 1894 on 'The Problem of Sociology', Simmel does intimate two directions which sociological research can take. One is to follow 'the longitudinal direction of individual development' in such a way that the development of a social institution is rendered sociological 'insofar as social forms – super- and subordination, the formation of an objective community compared with the mere sum of individuals, the growth of subdivisions, the modification of the social form by quantitative changes in the group – appear in complex phenomena and are extractable from them'. A second direction is 'to draw a cross-section through individual developments' in order to extract what is common to all of them: inductively derived 'social constellations as such'. They might comprise 'those most general relationships and their transformations which are called forth by constant individual similarities and differences of individuals in the formation of any association, or . . . the special forms of association that are to be found in the sociations either within a specific sphere – economic, religious, domestic, social, political – or within a specific period'. [68] In indicating the content of longitudinal and cross-sectional analysis, Simmel was also intimating some of the areas which his own sociological research had either already taken up or was about to embark upon.

In an important essay on 'Sociological Aesthetics' (1896), Simmel also hints that his sociological project is no orthodox empirical sociology. There he announces that,

> For us the essence of aesthetic observation and interpretation lies in the fact that the typical is to be found in what is unique, the law-like in what is fortuitous, the essence and significance of things in the superficial and transitory . . . Every point conceals the possibility of being released into absolute aesthetic significance. To the adequately trained eye, the *total* beauty, the *total* meaning of the world as a whole radiates from every single point. [69]

Translated into Simmel's sociology, this implies that his sociological investigations will not merely be confined to 'structures of a higher order' but also to 'the delicate, invisible threads' that bind individuals together, to the 'fortuitous fragment of social reality' whose investigation produces a 'deeper and more accurate' understanding of society than does 'the mere treatment of major, completely supra-individual total structures'. [70] Simmel's sociology is therefore also concerned with human interaction at mealtimes, in public transport, in written communications etc. Even the monumental *Philosophy of Money* is held together, Simmel announces, by 'the possibility . . . of finding in each of life's details the totality of its meaning'. [71] In order to indicate the breadth of Simmel's sociological project we must therefore turn to his substantive works.

NOTES AND REFERENCES

[1] A. Vierkandt, 'Neue Gesamtdarstellungen der Soziologie', *Zeitschrift für Politik*, Vol. 2, 1909, pp. 305–10, esp. p. 308.

[2] F. H. Tenbruck, 'Georg Simmel (1858–1918)', *Kölner Zeitschrift für Soziologie*, Vol. 10, 1958, p. 592.

[3] *Ibid.*, p. 593.

[4] W. Dilthey, *Einleitung in die Geisteswissenschaften*, 2nd edition, Leipzig/Berlin, Teubner (1923), p. 37.

[5] H. Böhringer, 'Spuren von spekulativen Atomismus in Sim-

mels formaler Soziologie', in H. Böhringer and K. Gründer (editors), *Ästhetik und Soziologie um die Jahrhundertwende: Georg Simmel*, Frankfurt, Kolosterman (1978), p. 116.

[6] *Ibid.*, p. 114.
[7] G. Simmel, 'Einleitung. Zur Erkenntnistheorie der Sozialwissenschaft', in *Über soziale Differenzierung*, p. 3.
[8] *Ibid.*
[9] *Ibid.*, p. 4.
[10] *Ibid.*, p. 7.
[11] *Ibid.*, p. 9.
[12] *Ibid.*, p. 10.
[13] *Ibid.*, p. 13.
[14] *Ibid.*, pp. 12–13.
[15] *Ibid.*, p. 15.
[16] G. Simmel, *Das Wesen der Materie nach Kant's Physischer Monadologie*, Berlin, Norddeutschen Buchdruckerei (1881), p. 19.
[17] G. Simmel, 'Anfang einer unvollendeten Selbstdarstellung', in K. Gassen and M. Landmann (editors), *Buch des Dankes an Georg Simmel*, Berlin, Duncker and Humblot (1958), p. 9.
[18] Letter to C. Bouglé of 27.11.1895, in W. Gephart, 'Verlorene und gefunde Briefe Georg Simmels', in H. J. Dahme and O. Rammsted (editors), *Georg Simmel und die Moderne*, Frankfurt, Suhrkamp (1984).
[19] See, for instance, G. Simmel, 'Superiority and Subordination as Subject-Matter of Sociology', *American Journal of Sociology*, Vol. 2, 1896, pp. 167–89, 392–415.
[20] G. Simmel, 'Das Problem der Soziologie', *Jahrbuch für Gesetzgebung, Verwaltung und Volkswirtschaft*, Vol. 18, 1894, pp. 271–277, esp. p. 271. For the English translation see G. Simmel, 'The Problem of Sociology', *Annals of the American Academy of Political and Social Science*, Vol. 6, 1895, pp. 412–23. All page references are to the German original which I have translated.
[21] *Ibid.*, p. 272.
[22] *Ibid.*
[23] *Ibid.*, p. 273.
[24] *Ibid.*
[25] *Ibid.*, p. 274.
[26] *Ibid.*, p. 275.
[27] *Ibid.*, pp. 275–6.
[28] G. Simmel, 'The Problem of Sociology', *loc. cit.*, pp. 421–2.

[29]   *Ibid.*, p. 422.

[30]   G. Simmel, 'Superiority and Subordination', p. 168.

[31]   *Ibid.*

[32]   *Ibid.*, p. 415.

[33]   *Ibid.*, p. 167.

[34]   G. Simmel, 'Das Problem der Soziologie', p. 276.

[35]   G. Simmel, 'Zur Methodik der Socialwissenschaft', *Jahrbuch für Gesetzgebung, Verwaltung and Volkswirtschaft*, vol. 20, 1896, pp. 227–37, esp. p. 232.

[36]   G. Simmel, 'Soziologie der Sinne', *Die Neue Rundschau*, Vol. 18, 1907, pp. 1025–36, esp. p. 1026.

[37]   G. Simmel, 'The Problem of Sociology', in K. H. Wolff (editor), *Essays on Sociology, Philosophy and Aesthetics by Georg Simmel, et al.*, Columbia, Ohio State University Press (1959), New York, Harper Row (1965), pp. 329–30.

[38]   *Ibid.*, pp. 322–3.

[39]   H. J. Dahme, *Soziologie als exakte Wissenschaft*, Stuttgart, Enke (1981), p. 403.

[40]   O. Spann, *Wirtschaft und Gesellschaft*, Dresden (1907); reprinted in O. Spann, *Frühe Schriften in Auswahl*, Grax (1974), esp. pp. 223–60.

[41]   M. Weber, 'Georg Simmel as Sociologist', *Social Research*, Vol. 39, 1972, pp. 155–63, esp. n. 5, p. 162. My emphasis.

[42]   G. Simmel, 'Bernès, Marcel: Les deux directions de la Sociologie contemporaine', *Jahrbuch für Gesetzgebung, Verwaltung und Volkswirtschaft*, Vol. 19, 1985, p. 327.

[43]   H. J. Dahme, *Soziologie als exakte Wissenschaft*, p. 394.

[44]   K. Mannheim, 'Eine soziologische Theorie der Kultur und ihrer Erkennbarkeit', manuscript, p. 9. Now in K. Mannheim, *Structures of Thinking*, London/Boston, Routledge (1981).

[45]   S. Kracauer, *Georg Simmel*, ms., p. 92.

[46]   G. Simmel, 'Das Problem der Soziologie', p. 276.

[47]   *Ibid.*, p. 277.

[48]   *Ibid.*

[49]   G. Simmel, *The Philosophy of Money* (Translated T. Bottomore and D. Frisby), London/Boston, Routledge (1978), p. 112.

[50]   M. Steinhoff, 'Die Form als soziologische Grundkategorie bei Georg Simmel', *Kölner Vierteljahreshefte für Soziologie*, Vol. 4, 1924/25, pp. 215–59, esp. pp. 228–9.

[51]   H.-J. Becher, *Georg Simmel. Die Grundlagen seiner Soziologie*, Stuttgart, Enke (1971), p. 14.

[52] G. Simmel, *Über sociale Differenzierung*, p. 13.

[53] S. Kracauer, 'George Simmel', *Logos*, Vol. 9, 1920, pp. 307–38, esp. p. 314.

[54] G. Simmel, *Einleitung in die Moralphilosophie*, Berlin, Hertz (1892–1893), Vol. 2, pp. 359–60.

[55] H.-J. Becher, *Georg Simmel*, pp. 30–1.

[56] *Ibid.*, p. 51.

[57] *Ibid.*, p. 52.

[58] F. H. Tenbruck, 'George Simmel (1858–1918)', p. 597.

[59] F. H. Tenbruck, 'Formal Sociology', in K. H. Wolff (editor), *Essays on Sociology, Philosophy and Aesthetics by Georg Simmel, et al.*, p. 75.

[60] M. Steinhoff, 'Die Form als soziologische Kategorie bei Georg Simmel', p. 231.

[61] G. Simmel, 'Die Selbsterhaltung der sozialen Gruppe', *Jahrbuch für Gesetzgebung, Verwaltung und Volkswirtschaft*, Vol. 22 (1898), p. 236. My emphasis.

[62] F. H. Tenbruck, 'Formal Sociology', p. 85.

[63] M. Steinhoff, 'Die Form als soziologische Kategorie bei Georg Simmel', p. 250.

[64] G. Simmel, 'Die Selbsterhaltung der sozialen Gruppe', p. 238.

[65] *Ibid.*, p. 239.

[66] G. Simmel, *The Philosophy of Money*, p. 174.

[67] H. J. Dahme, *Soziologie als exakte Wissenschaft*, p. 370.

[68] G. Simmel, 'Das Problem der Soziologie', p. 276.

[69] G. Simmel, 'Soziologische Aesthetik', *Die Zukunft*, Vol. 17, 1896, pp. 204–16, esp. p. 206. There is an English translation in K. P. Etzkorn (editor and translator), Georg Simmel, *The Conflict in Modern Culture and Other Essays*, New York, Teachers College Press (1968), pp. 68–80.

[70] G. Simmel, 'Soziologie der Sinne', p. 1025.

[71] G. Simmel, *The Philosophy of Money*, p. 55.

4

The Works

A consideration of the works of an author who has twenty-five volumes and over three hundred essays, reviews and other pieces to his name would be a formidable task. Even when the focus of such a study is narrowed down to Simmel's 'sociological' works the problems remain. Despite his early attempt to demarcate a set of specific tasks for sociology and to ground it as an independent discipline, he himself continued to make contributions to the discipline in essays that would today probably not be considered sociological in their content. This is particularly true of those essays that are devoted to, or are instances of, his later attempt to develop a philosophy of culture. In the light of these difficulties, it is necessary to concentrate upon Simmel's major contributions to sociology. Aside from brief discussions of his early orientations – important because they are often neglected – the following analysis concentrates upon three key texts: *On Social Differentiation* (1890), *The Philosophy of Money* (1900), and *Sociology* (1908). Where necessary other material is also referred to in the text.

The analysis of Simmel's major sociological works proceeds chronologically. Since this was the procedure in the previous chapter on his attempt to ground sociology it is logical to adopt a similar course here. But there is a more compelling reason for emphasizing the chronological development of Simmel's substantive sociology.

The reception of Simmel's sociology has suffered from a lack of any sense of chronological development. The absence of translations of many of his major works has meant that he is often recognized to be the author of stimulating essays but lacking in any comprehensive conception of sociology. Hence it has been argued, with considerable justification, that American sociology responded to Simmel's work as if to a collection of 'enclosed miniature theories' of aspects of social life rather than seeing specific themes and modes of analysis in his work as part of a totality. [1] This is in part the result of an empiricist sociological tradition that gravitates towards sociological traditions and authors in search of fruitful, testable hypotheses rather than a contextual understanding of them.

4.1   EARLY ORIENTATIONS: THE UNKNOWN SIMMEL

Partly as a result of the lack of materials available and partly because the young Simmel seems so far removed from our conception of him as to render him inaccessible, Simmel's early work has received scant attention. [2] Though this is not the place to remedy this defect, since substantive research has hardly commenced, it is nonetheless useful to indicate at least three neglected interests that are manifested in various ways in Simmel's early work: in *Völkerpsychologie*, in evolutionary theory but, above all, in Herbert Spencer's work and in socialism. All three proved to be significant either in the development of his methodology or his substantive sociology. And none of them at first sight seem to be typical of our conception of Simmel's interests in his mature works.

4.1.1   Simmel and 'Völkerpsychologie'
If we start out from Simmel's retrospective judgement that Heyman Steinthal and Moritz Lazarus were his two most significant teachers, then it is not surprising that his early interests should be in the direction of *Völkerpsychologie*. As we have seen, Simmel's interest in psychology runs parallel with and influences his development of a sociological perspective both at a methodological and substantive level. But what was the probable attraction of *Völkerpsychologie* for the young Simmel?

In their 'Introductory Thoughts on *Völkerpsychologie*' (1860) [3], Lazarus and Steinthal presented a programme for their version of psychology which went far beyond existing individual psychology. Some aspects of this programme – also to be found in Lazarus's *The Life of the Soul* (third edition 1883) [4], especially 'On the Relationship of Individuals to the Totality' – formed the starting point for Simmel's early work as themes which he took up and sought to go beyond. Amongst the most important features of their programme for Simmel were the concern for society and culture and the relationship between the 'objective mind' and the individual.

For Lazarus and Steinthal, 'psychology teaches us that human beings are thoroughly and according to their essence societal; i.e. that they are determined by social life'. [5] Human beings are characterized by the common features they have with contemporary fellow individuals and by their consciousness. But the individual does not live with all his or her fellow contemporaries and predecessors to the same extent: 'within the large circle of society, smaller circles are formed . . . These circles, however, to not stand side by side but intersect and affect one another in many ways. Thus, within society there emerges a highly varied . . . relationship of connection and separation [*Absonderung*].' [6] Thus, the object of *Völkerpsychologie* is 'the psychology of societal human beings or human society'. However, this does not mean that society is a 'mere *sum* of all individual minds'. The unity of a plurality of individuals lies in the '*content and the form* or mode of their *activity*'. [7] However, what Lazarus and Steinthal have in mind here is not so much social interaction as a *Volksgeist*: 'that which is common to the inner activity of all individuals'.

Individuals interacting with one another create their culture as an *objektive Geist*. For Lazarus and Steinthal, this process was conceived

> in a more or less dialectical fashion. Thus the individuals whose common activity created the objective reality of cultural forms were themselves to be seen as the product of these forms . . . "Wherever several people live together it is a necessary result of their companionship that there develops an objective mental content which then becomes the content, norm and organ of their further subjective activity" (Lazarus). Social attitudes and cognitive forms are objective insofar as they have a characteristic and durable social distribution, but they exist only through the activity of individual subjects. [8]

In precisely the same manner, Simmel designated culture as 'that which the mind had deposited in language, morals, institutions, art and, last but not least, technology too. Culture is *objective Geist* in the sense in which he had become acquainted with it from Moritz Lazarus'. [9] Simmel's conception of the tragedy of culture is not only present here. It is also formulated in Simmel's review of Steinthal's volume on ethics as early as 1886, where Simmel maintains, however, not merely that the objective mind only has such content as is given to it by historical development but also that the power and effect of ideas is totally independent of their justice and their relationship to ideals. Such an argument foreshadows Simmel's rejection of all idealist ethics in his *Introduction to Moral Philosophy*. The most concrete formulation of the dialectic of human culture is to be found in *The Philosophy of Money*.

4.1.2 Simmel and Herbert Spencer

Like many of his generation, the young Simmel was also impressed by developments in the natural sciences and their implications for philosophy, the social sciences and social change in general. In part this emerged out of his studies in Berlin under such figures as the physicist and physiologist Helmholz. The move towards materialism was undoubtedly further stimulated by the highly influential work of Friedrich A. Lange's *History of Materialism* (1866, by 1908 reprinted seven times) which, amongst other themes, pleaded for a materialist psychology. Of particular significance was the German reception of Darwin's evolutionism, the influence of which is to be found not only in Simmel's pragmatic theory of truth but also in his rejected dissertation on the origins of music which takes as its starting point one of Darwin's theses in *The Descent of Man*. As has been recently suggested, another possible source for this first publication by Simmel is Herbert Spencer's 'Origin and Function of Music' (1857). [10] But Spencer's influence on the young Simmel is more apparent from the German translation in 1875 of Spencer's *First Principles* (1862).

This work contains a number of basic themes that are later taken up in Simmel's work. As well as asserting the relativity of all knowledge as a result of conceiving of the reality of the world in relational terms – 'we think in relations. This is truly the form of all thought' [11] – Spencer develops his own theory of evolution. A constituent feature of evolution is 'a change from the homogeneous to the heterogeneous ... from the indefinite to the definite'. [12] Alongside this process is an increase in complexity as organisms develop. At a later stage in Spencer's argument this evolutionary tendency forms the basis for his theory of differentiation. But before moving on to the principles of differentiation, Spencer introduces a series of other principles that, in a modified form, appear in Simmel's early works. The theory of evolution requires that the world is in continuous motion impelled by a persistent force. This motion is evident in society too as the rhythms of social life. Further, this motion is impelled by forces or energy, a conception which Simmel takes up in his early theory of interaction as the exchange of energies. Indeed, as we shall see, Simmel relates the process of differentiation to his own principle of energy saving in the last chapter of his *On Social Differentiation*.

It is, of course, Spencer's theory of differentiation that Simmel takes as his starting point here. For Spencer, differentiation is a universal process through which social systems are integrated within a division of labour. At the most general level, it involves 'the transformation of an indefinite, incoherent homogeneity into a definite coherent heterogeneity', the 'metamorphosis of an indeterminate uniformity into a determinate multiformity'. [13] For Simmel, as we shall see, this is translated in the social sphere into the development of heterogeneous spheres of homogeneous elements out of apparently homogeneous spheres of heterogeneous elements. These heterogeneous elements interact with one another on the basis of exchanges of energy.

It has been suggested that in his early works Simmel does indeed operate with concepts very similar to those of Spencer. One recent commentator suggests with regard to Spencer's attempted general synthesis of the findings of diverse individual disciplines that

> His central categories are therefore concepts such as force, matter, motion, space and time. Similarly, Simmel works centrally with such physical concepts and conceptions, as for instance with that of energy and of motion. For Simmel all objects of knowledge are to be conceived as relational entities. The relations that exist between elements are therefore energetic exchange relations of attraction or repulsion. [14]

How far this is true must be assessed after examining Simmel's early key work *On Social Differentiation*. More questionable is whether Simmel was still operating with the same kind of conception a decade later in his *The Philosophy of Money*, where, it has been argued, the concept of energy had become an 'ethereal pale fluid'. [15]

4.1.3 Simmel and socialism

The reader of *The Philosophy of Money* will also be confronted not merely with many references to socialism but also a critique of Marx's labour theory of value. But Simmel's ambiguous attitude towards socialism had already been in evidence over a decade earlier. Furthermore, since we usually assume that Simmel was *the* sociologist of his period who was committed to analysing the problems of the development of human individuality, it may come as a surprise to learn that in the early 1890s at least Simmel stood very close to socialist circles. He even contributed brief articles to the main socialist journals such as *Vorwärts* and *Die Neue Zeit*.

Simmel's earliest references to socialism are to be found in his review of his teacher Steinthal's volume on ethics in 1886. [16] There Simmel is critical of Steinthal's optimistic and idealistic socialism on two grounds. First, that Steinthal's plan for the wages of labour to reflect their social usefulness and to be seen as pure 'inner value' fails to take account of the fact that the most menial labour lacks this inner value that mental labour possesses. Second, that Steinthal's argument that socialism will lead to the unhindered development of culture ignores the fact that all culture only arises on the basis of a minority whose work is unconstrained and without responsibility for the production of cultural goods. Such arguments – and the second is reminiscent of another major influence on Simmel: Friedrich Nietzsche – recur in the wider context of *The Philosophy of Money* over a decade later. They also indicate that Simmel's path to socialism was not that of the idealist socialism of the neo-Kantian tradition. As one recent commentator suggests:

> Georg Simmel draws exactly contrary conclusions from Steinthal's socialism: after his fundamental critique of all basic ethical concepts, he will find his way to social democracy and socialist positions precisely because these ideal notions were untenable and the problems and grievances of the real world required active intervention. [17]

Indeed, only a few years after this early review was written Simmel was identifying himself with the socialist movement of his day and discussing some of its practical problems.

It is only possible to indicate here some of Simmel's socialist interests and arguments in the early 1890s. In 1892, in a socialist journal, Simmel was reviewing the relevance of Gerhardt Hauptmann's play 'The Weaver' for 'our social movement', a play whose novelty lay in the fact that 'not the fate of individual human beings but that of whole classes forms the content of the action'. In this play 'the struggle against romantic individualism, of whose extension over the field of real and material interests every line of this journal relates, has won its first victory in the sphere of "pure form"'. [18] In another brief article in the same journal, Simmel inveighs against 'the impression which one has as if our legislation, just as it is legislation in favour of the wealthy, should also be a legislation in favour of the morally and aesthetically minded'. [19]

On occasion Simmel also expressed his own general position with regard to socialism, as in a review of a book by his close friend Jastrow.

> Jastrow's main standpoint . . . indicates unmistakably the two characteristics of socialism: the striving towards the equalisation of economic circumstances and, as a means towards it, the organisation of social processes through their centralisation . . . The book . . . is evidence for the view which the reviewer has already developed in other contexts: that in the present situation all the progress in the public sphere lies in the direction of socialism; it so proceeds *as if* it wishes to terminate in the socialist state . . . If social development moves along in a zigzag line, it is a most common error to assume that the direction of that part of it upon which one finds oneself is to be taken as the definitive one and that the ideal of the total development will proceed via its direct extension. [20]

However, not only does Simmel argue here against the naive evolutionary socialism of sections of the Second International, he goes on to question the nature of state socialism on the grounds that

> If one understands 'the state' namely in its present sense, that means as a class determined organisation, in which the one class legally or substantively dominates the other, then state socialism as such, as long as one is serious about the latter part of the phrase, is a *contradicto in adjecto*, an association of words that is just as meaningless as, for instance, a round square. [21]

Taken at its face value, these most explicit statements by Simmel on socialism should cast a new light on his subsequent critique of socialism insofar as it becomes necessary to question whether that critique is of state socialism or socialism as such.

As a brief indication of Simmel's position on substantive issues we may take his articles on free trades unions, social medicine and the German women's movement. Writing in the context of the protracted French miners' strike of 1892 and a draft law permitting an employer to dismiss an employee because of trade union membership, Simmel argues that 'the raising of the standard of living is not only the worker's individual right but also his social duty: he *may* not only struggle for it, he *should* struggle for it'. Simmel goes on to argue – in a manner reminiscent of Durkheim – that 'the more the erroneous nature of the individualistic world-view is recognised, the more deeply one examines the close interaction of all social elements which connect each individual's action with some kind of consequences for the totality'. [22]

In the more specific context of a review of a study on 'Social Medicine' (1897), [23] we find Simmel arguing for state intervention in preventive medicine and health care as against 'individual therapy or case work' on the grounds that 'an individual's problem and its solution rest on society and with the kinds of social action taken'. This implies that 'we have to influence general conditions if we are to provide for the common good of all individuals'. At a more general but explicitly political level, Simmel seems to suggest that individual reforms cannot be restricted but demand a 'more basic reform of the social structure'. However, Simmel stops short of a revolutionary transformation, even though he does

> concede the interdependence of the parts of society. Such interdependence seems logically to exclude the perfection of society by means of reforming its units. This difficulty can be resolved by acknowledging that while it is not possible to achieve ideal conditions for an individual without also achieving them for all individuals, one can work towards such an ideal in stages . . . And this is a far safer and more achievable path than that advocated by revolutionaries who share our ends but not our means. [24]

In other words, Simmel here favours social reformism as a political strategy.

Simmel had already adopted a similar position in his article on 'The Women's Congress and Social Democracy' (1896) [25] in which he highlighted the split between the bourgeois and social democratic wings of the women's movement in order to show that 'the question of socialism is the "secret king" of all specific social questions'. Again rejecting the then official social democratic position of 'internal revolution', Simmel maintains that one does not necessarily have to abandon 'the complete transcendence of class distinctions and the private ownership of property'. Rather, one can assert that 'the first and most urgent task of the times' is the abolition of poverty whilst not believing in 'the radical means of revolutionary transformation of the total social system as, for instance, in a sudden miracle from heaven'. Ultimately, then, Simmel favours the 'more sober tendency towards – relatively – slowly advancing evolution that ... allows the radical transformation of the total situation to develop as the sum of improved individual elements'.

Simmel's socialist standpoint in these years, however, is combined with a rejection of historical materialism as a philosophy of history. This follows from his *Problems of the Philosophy of History* (1892) in which both historical laws and the concept of historical necessity are decisively rejected – a standpoint which again distances Simmel from the orthodoxy of the Second International. In itself it does not indicate a rejection of socialism as such. But viewed as a form of social organization, Simmel appears already sceptical of socialism's tendency 'towards the complete rationalisation of life, towards its direction by means of a highly unified principle'. [26] This gives socialism an aesthetic appeal because whereas a complex capitalist society is composed of 'heterogeneous interests and irreconcilable tendencies', the image of a harmonious and symmetrical socialist society 'requires a minimum of intellectual effort. This fact in its aesthetic significance would seem to figure decisively in the intellectual appeal of socialism.' [27] Hence by 1896 when this was written, Simmel seems to have already begun to distance himself from his earlier socialist position, a process which continued and found its fullest expression in his *Philosophy of Money*.

4.2   'ON SOCIAL DIFFERENTIATION' (1890)

In the years around 1890 there appeared a whole series of works on the division of labour and social differentiation. In 1889 Gustav Schmoller published an essay on 'The Facts of the Division of Labour' and in the following year an essay on 'The Nature of the Division of Labour and the Formation of Classes'. Schmoller's essays prompted a reply by Karl Bücher in 1892 on 'The Division of Labour and the Formation of Social Classes'. [28] Both were taken up to a varying extent in editions of Emile Durkheim's *The Division of*

Labour in Society (1893). In 1890 Simmel published his *On Social Differentiation* – as a volume in a series edited by Schmoller – which received a brief mention in the second edition of Durkheim's study. There Durkheim remarks that for Simmel 'it is not a question of the division of labour specifically but of the process of individuation in general'. [29] Aside from a possible comparison of Durkheim and Simmel on social differentiation, what is significant about this context is that although Simmel knew of Schmoller's work he did not display any great interest in the division of labour until his *Philosophy of Money*. Perhaps more surprisingly Simmel did not in any obvious manner take up the treatment of differentiation that is to be found in Ferdinand Tönnies's *Gemeinschaft und Gesellschaft* (1887). Rather, what interested Simmel was specifically the processes of social differentiation and the development of human individuation – two central themes and conceptualizations in his sociological work in succeeding decades.

But as most contemporary reviewers remarked, Simmel did not provide a systematic treatment of the development of social differentiation either. One review suggested that 'one misses a genuine historical observation' of the phenomenon. Another saw that in Simmel's study 'its individual parts follow more in succession than in connection with one another'. Indeed, Simmel's subtitle 'Sociological and Psychological Studies', best describes this work which, aside from the introductory chapter dealt with earlier on the foundations of social science, in fact considers aspects of social differentiation that are not obviously connected with one another.

4.2.1 Aspects of social differentiation

In the introductory epistemological chapter of this study, Simmel already announces his basic interest in differentiation. In the context of the relationship between the general and the particular, Simmel raises the issues of how to conceptualize the relationship between the social group and the individual. Our dependency upon society and the social group seems so thorough and continuous that it is difficult to conceive of individuality except in contrast to something or someone else:

> *A human being is basically a differentiating entity* [*ein Unterschiedswesen*]. Just as we never perceive the absolute amount of a stimulus but only its distinction from the previous state of feelings, so too our interest attaches not to these contents of life that always and everywhere exist but

to those through which each is distinguished from every other . . . For all practical interests, all that defines our position in the world, all utilization of other human beings rests upon these distinctions between one human being and another, whereas the common ground on the basis of which this transpires is a constant factor. [30]

Hence Simmel's interest in differentiation starts out from a vantage point almost diametrically opposed to that of his contemporary Durkheim for whom the social group is the central focus. This Simmel makes explicit when he argues that

In contrast to the movements of the whole group, which offered itself to sociological thought as its primary object, the following investigations will basically indicate the position and fate of the individual, how on the basis of interaction with others it serves to combine the individual with others into a social whole. [31]

What then follows in Simmel's study is five forms of social relationship that indicate not merely the relationship between the individual and the social group but also the process of social differentiation. They comprise: the study of collective responsibility as it progresses through various stages of social differentiation; the relationships of dependency which exist between the quantitative (i.e. extensive) enlargement of the social group and the development of individuality; the internal and intensive creation of a social whole in a particular social level; the pattern of relationships arising out of the intersection of social circles; and finally the differentiation of individuals and groups on the basis of the utilization and development of energy.

At first sight, there may appear to be little connection between these five aspects of differentiation. Certainly each chapter is characterized by a wealth of propositions and instances without their necessarily being held together by a guiding argument. But nonetheless, at a more abstract level, the overall development of the themes taken as a whole does cohere. The first chapter of collective responsibility is concerned with what the individual gives over to the group. The second chapter offers the reverse instance of the group (in particular its enlargement) facilitating the development of the individual. The third chapter on social levels looks at the internal dynamics of the group from within a particular social level. The fourth chapter on the intersection of social circles looks at social groups and levels externally insofar as they come into contact with one another. Finally, the chapter on energy saving looks at the advantages of differentiation: 'a saving of energy'.

Simmel commences his discussion of collective responsibility with the example of responsibility for criminal acts in primitive society in which, since the individual criminal act is seen as the responsibility of the whole collectivity, e.g. clan, family, etc., the problem of restitution is difficult to solve. Simmel maintains that a lack of differentiation in primitive societies is indicated here both objectively in the fusion of the individual and the collectivity such that the deeds of the individual are seen as the deeds of the collectivity and subjectively in the inability of those passing judgement to distinguish the individual from the group. In the primitive collectivity, the principle of heredity operates in favour of the similarity of individuals and the principle of adaptation in favour of the variability of individuals. The former predominates over the latter. It is worth noting in passing here that not only does Simmel take up this issue again in his *Philosophy of Money* but also that it provides a central argument for Durkheim's *Division of Labour in Society*.

However, Simmel moves in a different direction to Durkheim. Operating with a distinction between primitive and more complex collectivities, between small and large groupings, Simmel seeks to show how group ties are progressively loosened, thereby permitting the greater development of individuality. He maintains that we feel closely bound to a group when only a few ties bind us to it but where nonetheless these affect all directions of our actions and emotions. Hence, the simpler those forces are which encompass the individual, the closer and more solidaristic is the connection between the individual and the group. The individual in the small group is bound to it as to an organism – an analogy that is in constant use in this study of differentiation and is applied to individuals and social totalities. However, when speaking of the group as an organism and its 'life forces' – power of resistance, healing power, self-preservation – Simmel maintains that such forces do not exist outside the parts of the organism but are the collective expression of the interaction of its parts – 'the immeasurable fineness and interlinking of these interactions'.

In primitive social circumstances, the differentiation of individual forces and activities is still incomplete and can lead to the emergence of sharp divisions of obligations. But where the individual places him- or herself in the service of the group then the interests of the group become the interests of the individual, even to the extent of the individual's nature being merged with the group. Hence, where conflict between groups breaks out the individual does not face an opponent as a specific person but rather as 'a mere member of the hostile group'. And here Simmel moves on to a central dimension of interaction to which he often returns, namely the significance of the third party or third element. He seeks to show how 'the common relation to a third element brings about and enforces collective solidarity'. This is the reason why 'the immeasurable socializing effect of religion rests fundamentally upon the communality of relationship to the highest principle'. The importance of the third element is thus, for Simmel, that it creates communality out of seriality.

Simmel goes on to show how collective responsibility and the position of the individual change with an increase in social and individual differentiation. Where greater differentiation exists, and where the individual personality is more developed and individual drives and capacities are differentiated from one another, the more an element of the individual and the less the total individual becomes responsible for actions. And where the social group to which the individual belongs is enlarged the individual as such is able to secure greater moral freedom, 'the purely quantitative enlargement of the group is merely the most obvious instance of the moral unburdening of the individual'. In modern society, this can take a form which seems to be a regression to an earlier form of collective responsibility, namely, 'to make society responsible for the individual's guilt'. Hence, 'to the extent that the earlier individualistic world-view is replaced by the historical-sociological one, which sees in the individual merely a point of intersection of social threads, collective guilt must take the place of individual guilt'.

But there are other consequences of the enlargement of the social group within which the individual acts. In an argument reminiscent of eighteenth-century moral philosophy, Simmel maintains that 'in the simple relationships of a small group the individual is able to achieve by relatively simple means . . . his egoistic or altruistic goals. The larger his social circle becomes the more indirect routes he requires for this' since many things are required which 'are far away from our present sphere of power'. In other words, 'the larger the social circle is, in fact the more developed the economic relationships are, the more often must I serve the interests of others if I wish them to serve my own'. The implication Simmel draws from this is that the enlargement of the social circle leads to more collective moral action without us consciously working towards it. Collectivistic measures, too, lead to moral action on the part of individuals. Even egoistic goals are only achievable 'in the socially prescribed forms'. As an instance of this, Simmel cites the joint stock company which transfers individual debt to society and regulates individual speculation.

Simmel views the preceding arguments in the chapter as confirmation of the sociological standpoint which he wishes to develop. Our knowledge of the individual's dependency on social forms teaches us that

> every person stands at the cross point of countless social threads so that each of his or her actions must have the most diverse social effects; within the social group no corn seed falls, as it were, upon the fields that is not tended by the uninterrupted interactions with the living generation with respect to the present, the influence of its activity upon inherited material but with respect to the future. The confinement of the individual to him or herself ceases just as much *a parte ante* as *a parte post*, so that the sociological standpoint both increase his or her liberation and burdening and thus proves to be a genuine cultural principle. [32]

In the following chapter, on the basis of this 'cultural principle, Simmel proceeds to demonstrate the relationship between the expansion of the social group and the development of individuality.

'As is well known', Simmel commences, 'competition develops the specialisation of the individual.' At the level of the social group, however, competition between two groups produces similarities between them. But is competition the only process that produces individuation? For Simmel differentiation and individuation act together in the sense that 'differentiation and individualisation loosen the tie with the next person in order to weave a new – real and ideal – tie with those more distant'. The close or tight social circle is weakened by individualization of its participants and by its extension and connection with more remote individuals. Thus, 'where the circle is enlarged within which we act and within which our interests are expressed so more space is created for the development of our individuality'. In terms of the relationship between the group and the individual, this can be expressed as 'a universal norm': where the group is more distinctive its members are more similar and, conversely, where the group is 'colourless' its individual elements possess a greater distinctiveness. This implies that the individual and the group exist in permanent interaction with one another such that neither pole of individuality or collectivity is ever complete: 'the circle of social interests lie concentrically around us: the tighter they enclose us the smaller they must be. But the human being is never merely a collective entity any more than it is ever a merely individual entity'. This is an important argument against a sociologistic reduction of the individual to a purely social essence, and is a precondition for the development of any role theory.

However, what interests Simmel here is the way in which larger social groups permit greater differentiation and more distinctive life styles. The positive evaluation of individuality also possesses a distinctive social location in that 'a strong development of individuality and a strong positive evaluation of individuality often goes together with cosmopolitan convictions' where 'devotion to a narrowly bounded social group hinders both'. But this development that leads from the narrow social group to greater individualism and increased socialization need not imply that both elements are realized to the same extent. Indeed, Simmel emphasizes that 'what is at issue here is not a metaphysical harmony or a natural law that with inner necessity binds a quantity of the one with a corresponding quantity of the other, but rather the whole relationship may only exist as a very general comprehensive expression for the result of very complex and modifiable historical conditions'. The force of this important qualification lies in the direction of a negation of any conception of Simmel's sociology as a naturalistic 'geometry' of social life.

Viewed historically, the more the individual comes to the centre of the social stage the more the development of the human being as such with universal qualities and moral obligations emerges. Such universal obligations to humanity – the perfection of the individual personality, self-preservation etc. – always clash with the interests of the small social circle. Hence, viewed subjectively, the sense of individuality develops more with the enlargement of the social group. All this points towards a 'relationship of reciprocity between individualisation and generalisation' in concrete social developments. For instance, the differentiation of individual elements of a group is necessary for the latter's enlargement since otherwise the unity of the whole would disappear: 'Where a large totality is formed, there are to be found together so many tendencies, drives and interests that the unity of the whole, its very existence would be threatened if the differentiation of the objectively diverse elements were not divided amongst different persons, institutions or groups'. What this indicates is Simmel's reluctance to see any one-way process in social life. It implies that although the proposition that the enlargement of the group leads to the development of individuality, we should not lose sight of the fact that the differentiation of its individual elements is, in turn, necessary for group enlargement itself.

Having examined the relationship between individual differentiation and group development, Simmel moves on to what he terms 'the social level' – the process by which individuals develop common attributes within a particular social level. He commences from the general proposition that

> The similarity with others is indeed both as a fact and a tendency of no less importance than the difference between them and both, in the most diverse forms, are the major principles of all external and internal development, so that the cultural history of humanity can be interpreted as the history of the struggle and attempted reconciliation between them. [33]

In individual action, however, it is the differences between individuals that is important, almost as if the individual gains significance only in relation to others.

What we seek to differentiate in society is that which is rare and new from that which is old and handed down to us. In terms of social level, this provided Simmel with a contrast between the individual and the mass. In a manner reminiscent of Nietzsche, Simmel examines the mass of society, oscillating between a merely quantitative mass and a conception of the mass as 'the masses'. For Simmel, the masses only take up the simplest, most unambiguous conceptions of the world, be they religious or political. Where the member of a group stands in a very low position within it, then what he or she has in common with it is very great. An undeveloped social level is therefore dominated by 'a lack of individual differentiation'. What all members of a group have in common can only be the possession of those who have least. Therefore, any levelling process only takes place downwards. And whoever wishes to have any effect upon the masses must resort to them 'not by means of theoretical convictions but basically only by appeal to their feelings . . . For feeling, compared with thought, is undoubtedly phylogenetically the lower stage . . . for indeed, the mass as such is undifferentiated.' This is why in a crowd we experience a heightening of our impressions and feelings. Here, in the crowd, 'the purest interaction takes place; each individual produces his contribution to the total sentiment that affects him with an amount in which his own contribution is hidden from him'.

Still within the context of collective sentiments within the mass, Simmel considers briefly for the first time – though this becomes a central theme in his later characterization of modern, money-orientated metropolitan society – 'collective nervosity' and sympathy. The 'increase in nervous life' that is brought about by sociation is correlated with the multitude of impressions and stimuli that are present in larger and more differentiated social circles. At a more general level, we respond collectively, emotionally and often physically to stimuli when we are in a group of people, as in listening to music or at the theatre. This is in part due to the power of imitation – 'one of the lower intellectual functions' – which is of the greatest importance in social relationships. A great many of our activities 'are directed to imitation of already existing forms'. But 'the growing striving for differentiation has indeed created a form which possesses all the advantages of imitation and social dependency whilst at the same time possessing the attraction of highly changeable differentiation: fashion'. Indeed, fashion rather than imitation became one of these social forms of differentiation which Simmel returned to on many subsequent occasions.

For the moment, these reflections on the mass lead Simmel to one of 'the most adventurous sociological ideas':

> The actions of a society, compared to those of the individual, possess an unswerving accuracy and expediency. The individual is pushed hither and thither by contradictory impressions, impulses and thoughts and his mind offers at each moment a multitude of possibilities for action, between which he not always knows how to choose with objective accuracy or even merely with subjective certainty. In contrast, the social group is indeed clear who it holds to be its friend and who its enemy. [34]

Although such a reflection might lead one to maintain that the movement of the mass accords with a natural law, this is not so. Since nature has no purpose we cannot characterize its path through a relationship as a long or short one. Rather, the difference between the individual and the mass with regard to action lies in the latter's more highly differentiated goals and the ever-increasing links in the teleological chain of means. And here, once more, Simmel merely touches upon what was to be a central issue of his *Philosophy of Money*, namely how a seemingly central entity such as money affects the teleological chain of means to given ends.

But to return to the apparent objectivity of mass activity, Simmel maintains that the emergence of objective entities in a large group comes about as a result of the fusion of subjective conceptions, even a 'condensation of individuals'. The larger the social circle, the more interests interact with one another as if the generality makes no errors compared to the individual. Further, the permanent inter-action of social relations gives the individual a sense of security. This can also be achieved by adherence to the dogmatism of a religion.

Finally, Simmel turns to the relationship between the significance of social levels and differentiation in the economic sphere. The offer of the same goods where there is limited demand produces competition between producers and suppliers to offer their com-modities at least in a different form. To take another example, in the process of specialization of tasks we find that the differentiation of individuals leads to an increase in social levels. But there is also the possibility that precisely the diversity and differentiation of modes of activity have created strata of workers as self-conscious totalities – all this without the mention of the role of trades unions! At the level of collective entities, Simmel maintains that the principle of energy saving impels individuals and groups to give over many of their activities to a greater collectivity. Socialism, too, seeks to maximize the individual and collective levels: 'the equality of individuals is only to be achieved through the absence of competition, the latter however is only to be achieved by the centralisation of all the economy by the state'. Simmel does not view the demand for the equalization of levels as necessarily absolutely conflicting with dif-ferentiation on the grounds that the striving for a higher level of existence can only take place via differentiation as a means to that end. Simmel sees in socialism no difference in interest between its demand for equality and that of higher classes to maintain inequal-ity. Socialism is based for Simmel here on a psychological drive, 'in the drive for increasing happiness'. Since this is an unending pro-cess, the process of differentiation would continue under socialism.

The persistence of social levels and social differentiation is the precondition for the succeeding chapter of Simmel's study: 'The Intersection of Social Circles'. [35] With the development of human sociation, we move towards 'associative relationships of homogene-ous elements of heterogeneous circles'. Indeed, 'the number of dif-ferent circles to which the individual belongs is in fact one of the yardsticks of culture'. In the modern world, each individual partici-pates in the course of his or her biographical development in more and more diverse social circles from the parental family to diffuse circles such as nationality as well as all those associated with work and leisure. Some of these may be co-ordinated, one with another.

This membership of diverse social circles has important consequences. For instance, the individual personality 'will be more closely defined if the majority of the defining spheres are contiguous rather than concentric'. In other words, where the various group membership is separate and not overlapping a wide variety of possibilities is open to the individual. Secondly, there exists a 'vast scope for individual differentiation' wherever 'the same person may occupy quite different relative positions with various spheres'. This means that the individual may occupy a high position in one social sphere and a low one in another. Thirdly, 'membership of a large variety of spheres with widely varying proportions of competition and co-operation provides incalculable scope for individual permutations'. In contrast to competition and co-operation, Simmel provides a final consequence of the plurality of social circles that arises out of conflicting social circles and is most common in 'a highly diversified culture with an intense political life'. There we have 'the intersection of incompatible spheres which often arises when an individual or group is governed by contrary interests and hence belongs simultaneously to opposing factions'.

Does this intersection of social spheres leave the individual personality more vulnerable compared with earlier social forms? Simmel maintains that the individual's identity is preserved

> by the *combination* of groups which can be different in each individual case. Advanced culture increasingly enlarges the social sphere to which we belong . . . but at the same time it makes the individual increasingly self-dependent and deprives him of much of the support and advantage of a close-knit sphere. But the formation of spheres and associations as meeting-points for any number of people with common interests and goals compensates for this personal isolation resulting from the rejection of the constriction of earlier ways of life. [36]

Hence, in the modern world, there are other groups outside the family which may also possess a close-knit structure. How far this is the case 'can be measured by whether and to what extent they have evolved a particular sense of "honour", which ensures 'desirable behaviour on the part of their members'. Such groups do not require external compulsion to achieve this aim. Thus, where external, centralised constraint (e.g. political, religious) is minimal, 'the association of homogeneous elements from heterogeneous spheres' can take place.

In the context of the division of labour and wider social circles, differentiation takes a number of forms:

> Differentiation and division of labour are, to begin with, quantitative . . . spheres of activity are distributed in such a way that different individuals or groups are allocated different spheres, but each sphere comprises a number of qualitatively distinct aspects. But later the different aspects are differentiated out of all these spheres and re-organised in new, qualitatively unified spheres of activity. [37]

In the field of public administration, for example, areas are initially separated out *spatially*. At a later stage of development, administration is differentiated on a *functional* basis. Without making the distinction an obvious one, Simmel also refers to differentiation according to *purpose* where, in the context of the example of the supply of raw materials for a wide variety of goods, Simmel argues that what they have in common is that 'they all serve a *single purpose*, the *terminus ad quem*; whereas division of labour is usually determined by a single *terminus a quo*, viz. the methods of manufacture'. The recognition of this distinction does not, however, lead Simmel to take up the crucial importance of the distinction between the division of labour in society and in manufacture as does Marx in key chapters of the first volume of *Capital*.

Nonetheless, Simmel does indicate a number of further consequences of the division of labour. One is the creation of 'a common social consciousness' and 'solidarity' amongst wage-earners arising out of their 'identical relationship to capital' despite their varied individual work locations. For Simmel the primary significance of this process lies in its relationship to differentiation: 'First the differentiation of labour creates its various spheres, then a more abstract consciousness rediscovers their common element and unifies this element in a new social sphere'.

But prior to a more advanced division of labour, Simmel points to two important contrary instances. The first, formulated somewhat obtusely, refers to the hitherto indistinct role of women. Whereas it is only recently that 'large numbers of women have joined forces to agitate for social and political rights or to make collective arrangements for economic support and other purposes which concern only women as such' this was due to the fact that in the past their activities were too similar for a 'general concept' to come into being. In a second example – one which plays a central role in Durkheim's *Division of Labour in Society* – Simmel cites the medieval guild which 'controlled the entire personality' and way of life. Here a single interest governed other spheres of life. In contrast, 'with the increasing differentiation of occupations, the individual was bound to realise that difference of occupation was compatible with the closest similarity in other aspects of life, and that the latter must therefore be substantially independent of occupation'.

Finally, still within the context of the division of labour, Simmel for the first time formulates a theory of the 'rational objectivity' of culture which is not only dealt with in much greater detail in his *Philosophy of Money* but which subsequently constitutes the first seeds of his thesis of 'the tragedy of culture' developed more fully in succeeding decades. As 'a peculiar manifestation of cultural life', Simmel cites the fact that 'meaningful, profoundly significant institutions and modes of life are replaced by others which *per se* appear utterly mechanical, external and mindless'. Individual elements themselves no longer embody higher ideals (e.g. the modern soldier cannot compare with the medieval knight, or the machine worker with the craftsman). Since the world is now too complex, its individual elements can no longer embody a higher unifying concept:

> On the other hand, the differentiation which separates out the intellectual element of an activity has the widespread effect that the mechanical and intellectual aspects come to exist separately. For example, a woman working at an embroidering machine is engaged in a much more mindless activity than an embroideress; the intellectual element of the activity has been taken over by the machine and objectified in it. Thus social institutions, gradations, and associations can become more mechanical and external and yet serve the progress of culture. [38]

In this way Simmel ignores the historical specificity of the separation of intellectual and manual labour, subsumes it under a general theory of differentiation and then universalizes it subsequently into a theory of a modern culture.

In the light of the discussion of social differentiation in the previous chapters of this study, the final chapter on 'Differentiation and the Principle of Energy Saving' introduces a theme – namely the principle of energy saving – which is seldom encountered in discussions of differentiation. As so often in his early work, Simmel commences with an organicist argument in announcing his principle of energy saving: 'All upward development in the series of organisms can be regarded as dominant by the tendency to save energy . . . Any being is more complete to the extent that it achieves the same end with a smaller amount of energy'. Simmel detects 'three obstacles to purposive activity by avoiding which energy is saved: friction, indirectness and the superfluous co-ordination of means. Indirectness is in consecutive form what co-ordination of means is in concurrent form'. In this context, differentiation's evolutionary advantage lies in its saving energy. Though Simmel views the energy saving principle as applicable to all spheres, including intellectual processes, what is important here is its sociological significance. For instance, Simmel posits a relationship between energy consumption and differentiation in what he terms the 'quantitative' division of labour, i.e. where one person or group does more work than another. Here, 'slavery and the capitalist economy demonstrate the cultural value of this quantitative division of labour. Its conversion to a qualitative division began with the differentiation of physical and mental activity', since the latter 'achieves greater effects with less expenditure of energy' – though it should be made explicit here that Simmel does not see the separation of mental and manual labour as an absolute division. Announcing the theme of his next major work, Simmel draws an analogy between thought and money:

> Thought interposes itself between mechanical activities just as money does between real economic values and processes: concentrating, mediating, removing obstacles. Money also came into being out of a process of differentiation. The exchange value of things, a quality or function they acquire in addition to their other properties, had to be detached from them and made independent in people's minds before this quality, which is common to the most disparate things, could be integrated in one overriding concept and symbol. [39]

But there are many counter-instances where energy is lost 'where the division of labour has not yet allocated a special area to everyone and competition is unleashed by conflicting claims to the same undivided area'. This also applies to differentiation of energies within the individual (which might easily cancel one another out) as well as to differentiation in society as a whole. Conversely, there is a danger of 'excessive individualisation and division of labour', where 'one-sided exertion weakens the very organ it was intended to strengthen, because it affects the constitution of the entire organism'. It is worth noting in passing, that this is a central theme of

Durkheim's argument on excessive individualism, though Durkheim does not draw the same conclusions for the saving of energy. Simmel, however, seeks to show how the original process of centralization in the legal, religious and military spheres which is energy saving in his sense, often provokes a counter-tendency which results in power or individual faith reverting back to the individual. A further possibility is a move away from concurrent differentiation within the group (e.g. leaders and followers) to consecutive differentiation within the individual's life.

All this suggests a basic contradiction which Simmel acknowledges. It arises from the fact that

> differentiation of the social group is evidently directly opposed to that of the individual. The former requires that the individual must be as specialised as possible, that some single task must absorb all his energies . . . The differentiation of the individual, by contrast, entails precisely the rejection of specialisation. It breaks down the interwoven capacities of will and thought and develops each of them into an independent quality. [40]

In a crucial qualification to this contradiction, Simmel insists that this apparent incompatibility is not absolute but limited to the fact that the process of differentiation is not unilinear but calls forth resistance by individuals and counter-tendencies. However, with increasing differentiation and individual diversification, what Simmel terms the 'problematic character' is produced. Individuals experience the contradictions between consecutive and concurrent differentiation, between specialization and self-development.

Conflict will also arise in a different sense from concurrent differentiation in which latent energies are taken into account. The possession of capital, especially money capital, is regarded by Simmel as latent differentiation since 'its essence is that it can be used to produce an unlimited diversity of effects'. Indeed, not only does the origin of money lie in the differentiation of economic life but the individual's ownership of it 'is the opportunity for any economic differentiation. Money is thus the most thoroughgoing form of potential concurrent differentiation'.

Viewing money and capital in this way and in the light of the principle of energy saving, Simmel approaches 'the struggle between capital and labour'. Simmel's argument runs as follows:

> Capital is objectified saving of energy, in the dual sense that previously created energy is stored up rather than

immediately consumed, and that future effects are achieved with this all-embracing, all-purpose instrument. Money is clearly the instrument whose use entails less loss of energy through friction than any other. It is produced from work and differentiation, and it is converted into work and differentiation without anything being lost in the process of conversion. But consequently it also necessitates the separate existence of work and differentiation; for otherwise it is simply the general without the particular, function devoid of raw materials, a meaningless word. Thus, simultaneous differentiation, in the sense that we have attributed to capital, necessarily implies consecutive differentiation. [41]

On the basis of this argument, Simmel maintains that it is illusory to look for a permanent, stable relationship between the current differentiation of labour and the latent differentiation of capital. Rejecting some socialist attempts to secure some such constant relationship, Simmel argues that a 'volatile balance' exists between the two. In conclusion, Simmel maintains that the complexity of the relationship between capital and labour 'will not be achieved by direct extrapolation under the illusion that the one is directly determined by the other, but rather by returning to the original processes of differentiation of which both capital and labour are merely different combinations or stages of development'. In other words, and quite unequivocally, social and individual differentiation is the starting point for the study of 'such universal and complex structures' as exist in society.

4.2.2 The significance of social differentiation

The importance of *On Social Differentiation* for the development of Simmel's social theory lies in the fact that in 1890 he had already sketched out many of the theories to which he was later to devote more attention. Two of the chapters – on the intersection of social circles and the enlargement of the group – were sufficiently significant for Simmel's conception of sociology to be incorporated in a revised form in his *Sociology* in 1908. The discussion of money was later to be vastly extended in his *Philosophy of Money* in 1900. In more general terms, the variable relationship between social differentiation and individuation is dealt with in a whole variety of Simmel's later works. Simmel's theory of conflict is also already contained in the study of differentiation. At the level of the development of modern society, Simmel's study contains his first statement of the problem of the separation of subjective and objective culture that is subsequently expanded into a theory of cultural alienation.

Simmel's contemporaries, however, were less impressed. Some, like the historian Friedrich Meinecke, saw Simmel's study as 'a perceptive but completely one-sided attempt to explain a series of historical processes by means of a mechanical, atomistic mode of observation'. [42] Certainly, the logical atomism from which Simmel later distanced himself is very much in evidence in this work. But more damning is Tönnies's verdict that 'the book is intelligent but from the study-room of the big city dweller'. [43] What Tönnies had in mind is the abstract distance which Simmel maintained when discussing important social issues such as the relationship between capital and labour. In more general terms Tönnies maintained Simmel's 'observations bear their weakness in their strength; subtle logic, mathematical deductions. What is distinctive about the elementary forces and motifs comes too little to the fore.' [44]

But what his contemporaries could not see was the significance of social differentiation for Simmel's sociological programme. A precondition for social interaction is individual differentiation. In Simmel's early formulation of sociology's task as the study of social interaction, individual and social differentiation must be presupposed. What Simmel had not developed in 1890 was his further delineation of sociology as the study of forms of sociation. Whereas Simmel conceived of interaction in his early work as the interaction of two elements (e.g. self and other), as a dualistic form, the study of social differentiation also contains an alternative that, it has been argued, is crucial for his sociology, namely the 'third' element. Its significance is as follows:

> According to Simmel's analyses, the "third" appears as the genuine sociating element of interactions. Whereas the constellation of two – and in a rudimentary form also a constellation of one – represents merely the beginning of sociation, the figure three or more than three first establishes those more differentiated and more complex forms of interactions upon the analysis of which Simmel basically concentrates. [45]

The analysis moves not merely in the direction of social types – the third person as mediator – but also the significance of the 'third' for forms of domination or the transformation of economic exchange relationships by means of money. Such analyses are often only sketched out in Simmel's early study of differentiation but they constitute the seeds of subsequent elaborations.

More problematic is Simmel's attempt to explain social differentiation in a quasi-physicalistic manner by means of his principle of energy saving. Whereas the attempt at explanation is at least an advance over earlier theories of differentiation which, as in Spencer's evolutionary model, merely saw differentiation as a universal process of development in both the natural and social world, it is interesting to note that the principle is not further developed in his later work. Instead it recurs in a much muted form and not explicitly in his *Philosophy of Money*.

Finally, in the light of the then contemporary discussion of the division of labour, Simmel's assertion of the primacy of social differentiation is significant. If for Durkheim the division of labour was the prime concern, Simmel did not move on from the study of social differentiation to the division of labour and then on to the problems of social class formation. Capital and labour or social classes as such are for Simmel merely particular combinations of social differentiation. Not surprisingly, Simmel's analysis of social differentiation in his next major work moved in the direction of the study of the ultimate mediator of differentiation: money.

4.3 'THE PHILOSOPHY OF MONEY' (1900)

The origins of perhaps Simmel's most systematic work in social theory reach back to the time when he was a young lecturer. The economist Gustav Schmoller relates that 'on the 20th May 1889, Dr. Simmel delivered a paper on the "Psychology of Money" in my political science seminar . . . It was the germ of . . . *The Philosophy of Money*'. [46] That original paper already outlined some of the themes that were to appear eleven years later in Simmel's major work on the subject. As we have seen, some account of the relationship between money and social differentiation was provided in Simmel's *On Social Differentiation*. In the intervening eleven years down to 1900 Simmel published a whole range of essays that were to be taken up in the major study. Somewhat optimistically, Simmel related to Bouglé in the summer of 1895 that 'at the moment 1 am working on a "Psychology of Money" which will hopefully be completed in the next few years'. By 1899 the title had changed to *The Philosophy of Money*, a work which 'strives to be a philosophy of the whole of historical and social life'. [47]

When it appeared in 1900 it was greated with wide acclaim. Some saw it as 'a philosophy of the times' (Karl Joël). Others saw it as 'the keystone of his social psychological investigations and is a document of the relativistic interpretation of existence which one can characterise as Simmel's world view' (Paul Altmann). Max Weber later praised the analysis of the spirit of capitalism it contained as 'simply brilliant'. George Herbert Mead praised it as containing 'an enormous wealth of psychological illustrations' and as a work which 'demonstrates . . . the value of approaching economic science from the philosophic standpoint'. Franz Eulenburg praised it as 'Simmel's most mature and complete work' whose wide-ranging content 'expresses itself in the intersecting and overlapping spinning of threads between the apparently most external and inessential things and the inner substance of life'. [48]

Some reviewers saw fit to compare *The Philosophy of Money* with other major works in social theory. Schmoller, for instance, maintained that

> Just as Durkheim provides a sociological-philosophical treatment of the division of labour, so Simmel seeks to provide a similar treatment of money or, one could almost say, of modern economic forms as a whole. For he extends far beyond money, he assembles everything that he has to say about the modern economy around money as the centre of these phenomena. The problem which he seeks to solve is . . . really the question as to what money and the money economy have made of the thoughts, feelings and intentions of individuals, of societal constellations of social, legal and economic institutions. His theme is the retroactive effect of the most important institution of the modern economy – money – upon all the sides of life, of culture. [49]

This comparison between Simmel's study of money and Durkheim's study of the division of labour could also be extended, as we have seen, to Simmel's work on social differentiation. In his review of *The Philosophy of Money*, however, Durkheim himself did not make such a comparison. Indeed, whilst praising Simmel's 'treatise on social philosophy' and its 'ingenious ideas' and fund of 'curious relationships', Durkheim questioned both the analysis of types of money and the logic of Simmel's argument as being too replete with 'illegitimate speculation'. [50]

An even more fruitful comparison, however, was made by

Rudolf Goldscheid when he suggested that *The Philosophy of Money*

> forms a very interesting correlate to Marx's *Capital*. Marx
> could very well have said that not a single line of his inves-
> tigations was meant to be psychological. And in fact some
> passages of *The Philosophy of Money* read like a translation of
> Marx's economic discussions into the language of psychol-
> ogy. Yet one would do Simmel's book a great disservice if
> one merely treated it as such a translation. Just as *The
> Philosophy of Money* could undoubtedly not have been writ-
> ten if it had not been preceded by Marx's *Capital*, so it is
> equally important to emphasise that Simmel's book con-
> tains a supplementation of Marx's life work such as has
> hitherto not existed in social science, even in attempts at
> such. In any case, *The Philosophy of Money* is written too
> much in the spirit of philosophical meditation. [51]

Elsewhere, Goldscheid points to 'a multitude of very interesting
parallels between Marx's theory of capitalism and Simmel's theories
concerning the relativism of money . . . In my opinion, it is an error
of Simmel's book that it confronts Marx too little'. [52]

What this brief survey of the reception to Simmel's study suggests is that his contemporaries saw it as an important work in social
theory that could not be confined to a single discipline – be it
economics, the philosophy of economic life, psychology or sociology.
Even if we agree with one reviewer that it is 'at once metaphysical,
economic and sociological . . . metaphysical in its methods,
economic in many of the elements of its contents, and sociological in
the larger framework of human relations in which the whole finds its
setting', [53] then this statement too seems hardly to do justice to
Simmel's intentions. Therefore, before we examine the 'sociological'
dimensions of *The Philosophy of Money*, it is essential to attend carefully to Simmel's methodological presuppositions and aims in this
work.

4.3.1 Methodological presuppositions

Simmel announces in the preface to his *Philosophy of Money* [54] that
the 'analytical part' of his study 'relates money to the conditions that
determine its essence and the meaning of its existence'. Hence, the
first three chapters should outline the preconditions for the
emergence of a money economy – a theory of value and money's
'preconditions in non-economic concepts and facts'. The 'synthetic
part' – the last three chapters – is where 'the historical phenomenon

of money . . . is studied . . . in its effects upon the inner world – upon the vitality of individuals, upon the linking of their fates, upon culture in general'. In other words, the synthetic part should analyse the actual historical nature of social relations transformed by money or 'its consequences for non-economic values and relationships'. But Simmel did not merely choose to study money as an empirical entity. For Simmel it has a deeper significance as 'the symbol of the essential forms of movement within this world'. Therefore, we cannot grasp the object of study merely as a particular historical empirical object. This Simmel makes quite explicit when he states that 'the unity of these investigations does not lie . . . in an assertion about a particular content of knowledge . . . but rather in *the possibility* – which must be demonstrated – *of finding in each of life's details the totality of its meaning*'. The possibility of some naive accumulation of empirical knowledge of an object such as money is ruled out from the very outset since such knowledge always remains incomplete: the 'ever-fragmentary contents of positive knowledge' must be 'augmented by definitive concepts into a world picture and . . . be related to the totality of life'. Money, like other phenomena, can never be grasped from a single science since 'the very standpoint of a single science . . . never exhausts the totality of reality'. And this applies in the context of a study of money to economics too. Simmel asserts that 'not a single line of these investigations is meant to be a statement about economics'. Those economic phenomena 'which economics views from *one* standpoint, are here viewed from another'.

But what then is Simmel's intention? From what standpoint is money viewed? Money, Simmel states, 'is simply a means, a material or an example for the presentation of relations that exist between the most superficial, "realistic" and fortuitous phenomena and . . . the most profound currents of individual life and history'. Hence, Simmel's intention is 'to derive from the surface level of economic affairs a guideline that leads to the ultimate values and things of importance in all that is human'. His starting point, in other words, is 'what is apparently most superficial and insubstantial'. But his analysis does not remain at this phenomenal level. Rather, Simmel seeks to penetrate 'the inner substance of life', 'the essential forms of movements'. Does this mean that Simmel is intent upon providing a 'philosophy' of money? Even here Simmel qualifies his aim. Rather than merely a philosophical approach to money, he seems to suggest an aesthetic one since whereas the problem philosophy sets itself is 'nothing less than the totality of being', art in contrast 'sets itself a single, narrowly defined problem every time: a person, a landscape, a mood'. In keeping with this aesthetic aim, Simmel declares that he will seek 'to regard the problem as restricted and small in order to do justice to it by extending it to the totality and the highest level of generality'.

What this implies, methodologically, is that we are justified – in philosophy too – in starting out from the insignificant details of social reality, from its 'fortuitous fragments' since they hold the key to the understanding of social reality as a whole. And bearing in mind Simmel's 'regulative principle' already affirmed a decade earlier that everything interacts with everything else, there exists no privileged starting point for sociological analysis. But money does have an advantage as a starting point for Simmel because it symbolizes an extension of the first principle, namely the fundamental inter-relatedness of social reality.

There is, however, another methodological intention which Simmel boldly asserts, namely

> to construct a new storey beneath historical materialism such that *the explanatory value of the incorporation of economic life into the causes of intellectual culture is preserved,* while these economic forms themselves are recognised to be *the result of more profound valuations and currents of psychological or even metaphysical preconditions* . . . Every interpretation of an ideal structure by means of an economic structure must lead to the demand that the latter in turn be understood from more ideal depths, while for these depths themselves the general economic base has to be sought, and so on indefinitely. [55]

This ambitious aim seems to retain a dialectical intention to recognize the insights of historical materialism whilst at the same time going beyond them to more profound layers of human existence. Whilst it is true that Simmel is opposed to all monocausal theories – which is how he interprets historical materialism – the question as to whether his own relativistic or relationistic alternative is a success must remain an open one.

4.3.2 Exchange as a crucial instance of interaction and sociation

Simmel's aim in the first part of *The Philosophy of Money* is to 'present the preconditions that, situated in the mental states, in social relations and in the logical structure of reality and values, give money its meaning and its practical position'. And just as his study is not meant to be an economic one or even solely a philosophical one so too this aim is not historical either. Despite the frequent use of historical examples, it does not examine the 'preconditions' for a money economy in terms of 'the origin of money'. What Simmel does put forward is a largely subjectivist theory of value and a conception of the economy as a system of exchange. This is the context within which Simmel emphasizes the importance of exchange relations in society and the implicit rudiments of a sociology of money. Simmel's economic presuppositions are therefore significant for our understanding of his social theory of the money economy.

Simmel starts out from a subjectivist theory of value that accords with that of contemporary marginal utility theorists such as Carl Menger. [56] A subjectivist theory of value views the economy from the perspective of the individual's demand for goods which means for Simmel that 'the world of value is my demand'. Hence, where the economy as a whole is viewed from the demand side, the emphasis is upon consumption. But Simmel also conceives of the economy as grounded in the exchange of goods, of use values that are subsequently consumed by individuals. The economy is grounded in exchange not production. The latter is very narrowly defined as when Simmel speaks of 'the exchange with nature which we call production'. In keeping with this obfuscation of the social nature of production, Simmel declares that 'exchange is just as productive and value-creating as is production itself' or that 'exchange, i.e. the economy, is the source of economic values'. Since Simmel maintains that 'it is of great importance to reduce the economic process to *what really happens in the mind of each economic subject*', there exists no difference between exchange in a subsistence and a market economy, nor between the exchange of goods or land and the same 'subjective process of sacrifice and gain in the individual mind' occurs in both instances. Therefore, 'economic objects have no significance except directly or indirectly in our consumption and in the exchange that occurs between them'. It also follows from this that the economy is 'a special case of the general form of exchange'.

But it is not merely the economy that is grounded ultimately in exchange. Exchange is also a crucial instance of human sociation. Not only is exchange 'a sociological phenomenon *sui generis*', it is also 'the purest and most developed kind of interaction which shapes human life'. Indeed, social interaction is itself an exchange insofar as 'every interaction has to be regarded as an exchange'. It is worth noting in passing that this conception of social interaction is already to be found in Simmel's earlier study of social differentiation where interaction is viewed as the reciprocal exchange of energies. And here too in *The Philosophy of Money* the emphasis is upon exchange, though it is now given a much wider referent: 'Every interaction has to be regarded as an exchange: every conversation, every affection (even if it is rejected), every game, every glance at another person'. What is involved in such interactions is 'always personal energy'. In the economic realm this takes the form of 'an exchange of sacrifices'. Indeed, 'the interchange between sacrifice and acquisition within the individual is the basic presupposition and, as it were, the essential substance of exchange between two people'. At the societal level, exchange is 'an original form and function of social life'. If exchange is one of the most basic forms of social existence, what is the implication for Simmel's concept of society which, from the very outset of his sociological investigations, he was at pains not to reify?

The process of exchange in fact enables Simmel to clarify and deepen his conception of society which, in his early writings, had remained a somewhat problematic notion. Simmel now explicitly points to the relevance of exchange for society. Society is

> a structure that transcends the individual, but that is not abstract. Historical life thus escapes the alternative of taking place either in individuals or in abstract generalities. Society is the universal which, at the same time, is concretely alive. From this arises the unique significance that exchange, as the economic-historical realisation of the relativity of things, has for society; exchange raises the specific object and its significance for the individual above its singularity, not into the sphere of abstraction, but into that of lively interaction. [57]

Thus, the universality of exchange relationships and constant reciprocal interaction avoids both the reification of society and its atomistic conception as a mere sum of individuals. Society is not a reified entity since 'the unity of the social organism . . . signifies only the forces of attraction and cohesion amongst its individual members'.

In exchange relations, Simmel found a concrete constellation of interactions that themselves embodied what he intended by the notion of sociation. Not only is it the case that 'the interaction between individuals is the starting point of all social formations' but the exchange of possessions

> is obviously one of the purest and most primitive forms of

human sociation; not in the sense that "society" already
existed and then brought about acts of exchange but, on
the contrary, that exchange is one of the functions that
creates an inner bond between human beings – a society in
place of a mere collection of individuals. [58]

In this respect, then, 'society . . . is only the synthesis or the general
term for the totality of . . . specific interactions'. It is composed of
these interactions. It is possible that any one of these interactions
can disappear without society disintegrating. But 'if all interaction
ceases there is no longer any society'. Amongst the crucial forms of
interaction, exchange is not merely 'a form of sociation'; it is also
'the purest sociological occurrence, the most complete form of interaction'.

But how does this sociological occurrence, this important relationship manifest itself? It is symbolized in a remarkable entity:
money. This is because money 'represents pure interaction in its
purest form; it makes comprehensible the most abstract concept; it is
an individual thing whose essential significance is to reach beyond
individualities'. It is 'the pure form of exchangeability' in the
developed economy. Hence 'the function of exchange, as a direct
interaction between individuals, becomes crystallized in the form of
money as an independent structure'. It belongs to the category of
'reified social functions' that seem to exist over and above the individual. In keeping with Simmel's earlier epistemological position
that sought to substitute function for substance, relations for things
themselves, Simmel found in money an entity which, in society,
expresses this substitution since 'money is the reification of exchange
among people, the embodiment of a pure function'.

In turn, however, this pure form of the exchange relationship,
this 'pure function' is only possible on the basis of a distinctively
human trait – trust:

Without the general trust that people have in each other,
society itself would disintegrate, for very few relationships
are based entirely upon what is known with certainty
about another person, and very few relationships would
endure if trust were not as strong as, or stronger than,
rational proof or personal observation. [59]

And here a precondition for exchange relationships itself becomes
the precondition for the continuation of society, very much in the
manner of the eighteenth-century Scottish moralists.

Yet the attraction that money has as an object of study for a sociologist concerned to demonstrate that society rests upon social interaction and forms of sociation is not merely that money embodies the motif of society as a network of interrelationships, as a labyrinth. The social relationships that constitute society not only exist in space as a web, labyrinth or network. They also exist in time as fleeting relationships, as permanent relationships, as a constellation of relationships in flux. Money embodies this social reality that is in 'constant motion'. There exists, for Simmel, 'no more striking symbol of the completely dynamic character of the world than money . . . the vehicle for a movement in which everything else that is not in motion is completely extinguished. It is, as it were, an *actus purus*.' Yet in representing 'abstract economic value in general' it also embodies the permanency of relationships: 'in its content it is the most stable, since it stands at the point of indifference and balance between all other phenomena in the world'. It is the spider that spins society's web.

By taking up the phenomenon of the exchange relationship and its embodiment in money, Simmel was able not only to give substance to his earlier discussion of the intersecting and interlocking nature of social relationships but also to pull together a wide variety of diverse relationships within a totality that was absent in his earlier writings. This was seen by one of Simmel's most perceptive students Siegfried Kracauer, who argued that Simmel came closest to capturing the totality of modern life in *The Philosophy of Money* than in any of his other works. Nowhere else did Simmel provide

> such a comprehensive picture of the interconnectedness and entanglement of phenomena. He clearly extracts their essence in order to melt it down once more into a multitude of connections . . . and reveals the many common meetings that reside within them. Amongst these phenomena belong, for instance, exchange, ownership, greed, extravagance, cynicism, individual freedom, the style of life, culture, the value of the personality, etc. [60]

What holds them all together, according to Kracauer, is a 'unifying core conception', namely that 'from any point of the totality one can arrive at any other; each phenomenon bears and supports the other, there is nothing absolute that exists unconnected to other phenomena and that possesses validity in and for itself'. On the basis of this unifying conception and in the light of Simmel's emphasis upon exchange as a crucial instance of sociation, was he also in a position to sketch out at least the rudiments of a sociology of money relationships?

4.3.3 Towards a sociology of money

To some extent, Simmel's analysis of the consequences of the development of a mature money economy follows on from his earlier deliberations on social differentiation by taking up such themes as the relationship between differentiation and individual freedom within the context of a money economy, the intersection of social circles as facilitated by money transactions, etc. But now, more obviously than in his earlier writings, there is a dialectical turn in the mode or presentation of his argument. The processes that lie behind money's transformation of social relations are usually conceived quasi-dialectically. At an abstract level, we are presented with positive and negative features of a money economy, with general (universal) and particular (historically specific to a modern, implicitly capitalist, money economy) features. At a more concrete level, we have such processes as an ends–means dialectic of purposive human action, increasing differentiation that is accompanied by increasing homogeneity (levelling) and indifference, the relationship between personal and impersonal social ties, exchange as the linking up of social relations and exchange as creating distance, the transformation of qualities into quantities, and so on. We also have a more concrete presentation of social types and psychological states as indicative of social processes.

Simmel already commences his analysis of the effects of money upon social relationships in the first part of *The Philosophy of Money* where, in the third chapter, he takes up the consequences of monetary relationships for purposive human action. In so doing, he returns to a theme which had preoccupied him in his earlier essay on the psychology of money (1889), namely the relationship between means and ends in human activity. There Simmel had been fascinated by 'the, in itself, merely indifferent means' to human ends which had itself become an end of human action. Money infected those caught within its network with its own indifference and 'colourlessness'. Its seeming neutrality rendered it 'the common point of intersection of different series of ends'.

In *The Philosophy of Money*, and on the basis of a theory of purposive social action which emphasizes the lengthening of the teleological chain of connections by the addition of more and more means or instruments (including institutions) for achieving a given end, Simmel shows how money not only lengthens the teleological chain between the individual and his or her ends but also brings about the realization of otherwise impossible goals. In relation to these ends or purposes, however, money is totally indifferent. It is 'the purest reification of means ... a pure instrument', which 'embodies and sublimates the practical relation of man to the objects of his will, his power and his impotence'. By virtue of its universality and total lack of content, money has a totally unrestricted relationship to ends.

But as the economy develops temporally and spatially, money as a means can also become an absolute end. The extent to which this takes place 'depends on the major transformation of economic interest from primitive production to industrial enterprise', from consumption to production. In extreme and contrary instances such as extravagance and ascetic poverty, 'money takes on the character of an independent interest beyond its role as a mere intermediary'. Both can develop in the early stages of the development of a money economy. In contrast, Simmel also analyses 'two processes that are almost endemic to the heights of a money culture – cynicism and a blasé attitude'. In the case of cynicism, nurtured in 'those places with high turnovers', money can 'reduce the highest as well as the lowest values equally to one value form and thereby ... place them on the same level, regardless of their diverse kinds and amounts'. Cynicism is thus born out of an indifference to the evaluation of things whereas the blasé attitude arises out of indifference to the nature of things themselves. The decisive element here is not 'the devaluation of things as such, but indifference to their specific qualities ... Whoever has become possessed by the fact that the same amount of money can procure all the possibilities that life has to offer must also become blasé'. The blasé attitude, which regards all things as being of 'an equally dull and grey hue', seeks to compensate for this in 'the craving for excitement, for extreme impressions, for the greatest speed in its change' that is manifested in 'the modern preference for "stimulation" as such'.

Still within the context of the teleology of means and ends, Simmel examines a far-reaching feature of money in a developed economy – one that comes to the fore in much Marxist discussion of money – namely, the transformation of the quality of money into its quantity. This arises out of the fact that 'since money is nothing but the indifferent means for concrete and infinitely varied purposes, its quantity is its only important determinant as far as we are concerned'. Since money has no regard for personal and other qualitative differences, it 'moves from one personality to the other without any internal resistance, so that the relations and situations that pertain to it can easily and adequately adjust to any change'.

But if money is indifferent to personal qualities and differentiation, what role does it play in the development of individual freedom? Simmel examines this issue in terms of the historical development of individual worker's duties and freedoms, from a slave economy in which the person is totally obligated, through feudalism in which the person is obliged to provide labour services or a part of what they produce, to a capitalist economy where the person receives money payment in exchange for the use of labour power. What particularly interests Simmel in the early transformation of feudalism is the commutation of labour services or payment in kind into money payments thereby creating a greater degree of personal freedom. At first sight, however, the money economy seems to create new dependencies, especially upon third persons, not as persons but as representatives of functions. Here personal dependencies are exchanged for impersonal ones. This creates a further important result that the personalities of those we are dependent upon become irrelevant. Its origin lies in 'the modern division of labour' which 'permits the number of dependencies to increase just as it causes personalities to disappear behind their functions, because only one side of them operates, at the expense of all those others whose composition would make up a personality'. The total realization of this tendency, Simmel argues, would be found in 'extreme state socialism'. Under a capitalist money economy, there exists wide differentiation in the sphere of private interests. This is facilitated by money which both 'makes possible the plurality of economic dependencies through its infinite flexibility and durability' and is also 'conducive to the removal of the personal element from human relationships through its indifferent and objective nature'. Yet this depersonalization of human relationships should not lead us to imagine that individual freedom is synonymous with total independence from other individuals since 'individual freedom is not a pure inner condition of an isolated subject' but rather 'freedom in a social sense . . . is a relationship between human beings'. Money's role in this process is ambiguous since 'it makes possible relationships between people but leaves them personally undisturbed; it is the exact measure of material achievements, but is very inadequate for the particular and the personal'.

In terms of the possession of material goods too, Simmel maintains that money gives its owner a greater freedom than does the possession of land or capital which carry with them a whole range of personal duties. Furthermore, money facilitates the differentiation of property and person in a manner unknown in feudal and earlier social formations. For instance, money makes possible a spatial separation of the individual and his or her possessions (e.g. through share-holding, land-leasing, etc.) whilst at the same time bridging the distance between the two. More importantly, Simmel maintains that the differentiation brought about by money also affects labour relations which also become increasingly impersonal. Whereas contractual labour hiring suggests that the working person is hired, 'in reality, the person as a total, unlimited complex of labour power is hired'. Similarly, the manager, too, produces for an impersonal market of 'totally unknown and indifferent consumers'. This is, in turn, part of a much wider process of the differentiation between the individual and what he or she produces.

Equally significant is the fact that this general process of differentiation also takes place within the individual in the form of 'an atomisation of the individual person': 'Whereas in the period prior to the emergence of a money economy, the individual was directly dependent upon his group and the exchange of services united everyone closely with the whole of society, today everyone carries around within him, in a condensed latent form, his claim to the achievements of others'. In contrast, money also facilitates the possibility of participating in a wide range of associations without any personal involvement or commitment. In other words, money possesses not merely a 'disintegrating and isolating effect' but also under certain historical conditions a 'unifying effect' to the extent that, having destroyed a whole series of relationships between people, it also establishes relationships between elements that otherwise would have no connection whatsoever.

If, on balance, Simmel views the development of a money economy as bringing about greater individual freedom, does this imply the same positive role for money in relation to human values and qualities? What happens when we reduce personal values and attributes to a money equivalent? Simmel indicates how the process by which an individual's life is given a price which must be paid when that person is killed (e.g. Anglo-Saxon *Wergild*) and the whole notion that one can compensate for a person's death, wounding or injury by money payment is threatened once human beings come to be valued as unique entities. This new valuation Simmel sees as arising out of Christianity and as rendering expiation for murder by money payment inappropriate. But in the case of lesser crimes and with the development of a mature money economy, money fines become more widely used.

Of greater interest is Simmel's account of the way in which the status of women changes in relation to money. In the case of marriage by purchase, Simmel suggests three stages of development: the exchange of women under a barter agreement, the recognition of the 'use value' of women (marriage by purchase) and finally the substitution of the dowry for direct purchase which Simmel relates to the division of labour in domestic production. Payment for sexual relations outside marriage, however, graphically illustrates the close relationship between prostitution and money. As Simmel puts it (echoing Moses Hess and the young Marx),

> We experience in the nature of money itself something of the essence of prostitution. The indifference as to its use, the lack of attachment to any individual because it is unrelated to any of them, the objectivity inherent in money as a mere means which excludes any emotional relationship – all this produces an ominous analogy between money and prostitution. [61]

Simmel goes on to argue that marrying for money can, from one viewpoint, also be seen as 'a variation on prostitution'. In modern society, he also points to advertisements for a marriage partner as often revealing that 'the financial status of both parties is the real, though sometimes disguised, centre of interest'.

Yet another instance of the purchase of a person by monetary means is provided by bribery, an instance which reveals other features of money in that

> Money, more than any other form of value, makes possible the secrecy, invisibility and silence of exchange ... money's formlessness and abstractness makes it possible to invest it in the most varied and most remote values and thereby to remove it completely from the gaze of neighbours. Its anonymity and colourlessness does not reveal the source from which it came. [62]

Whereas money is thus the most appropriate means for bribery, it is most inappropriate in the case of individual distinction or excellence. Anything that is valued as distinctive comes to be devalued through the levelling process of money purchase. This Simmel also seeks to assert in the context of a critique of the labour theory of value which centres around the distinction between mental and manual labour, between complex and simple labour. Although Simmel acknowledges the labour theory of value to be 'at least philosophically, the most interesting theory', he goes on to argue that mental effort involves an unpaid contribution to what is produced that cannot be reduced to either simple labour power or money wages. This renders manual labour inappropriate as the unit of measuring labour. Simmel maintains that socialists must therefore find another unit of labour which can encompass all forms of labour power – an argument that still finds resonance today in discussions of the problem of complex labour within a labour theory of value.

4.3.4 A theory of cultural alienation

The Philosophy of Money contains not merely an account of the positive and negative consequences of the money economy, but also a theory of cultural alienation which, at first sight, seems remarkably close to that of the young Marx. In this respect, Simmel's theory of alienation seems to anticipate the discussion of alienation in Marx's *Paris Manuscripts* (not discovered until the early 1930s) and some aspects of Georg Lukács' theory of reification (in the central chapter of *History and Class Consciousness*, published in 1923). [63]

In the last chapter of *The Philosophy of Money* – which would stand in its own right as one of the first sociological analyses of the modes of experiencing modernity – Simmel sets the stage for a theory of alienation within the context of modern cultural developments. Money, Simmel says, is 'the reification of the pure relationship between things as expressed in their economic motion'. Money creates a spectral objectivity which stands over against individuals as a natural entity:

> since money measures all objects with merciless objectivity, and since its standards of value so measured determines their relationship, a web of objective and personal aspects of life emerges which is similar to the natural cosmos with its continuous cohesion and strict causality. This web is held together by the all-pervasive money value, just as nature is held together by the energy that gives life to everything. [64]

This supra-individual world as a culture of things confronts the individual as something alien even though 'in the last analysis, it is not objects but people who carry on these processes, and the relations between objects are really relations between people'. This 'objectivity of human interaction . . . finds its highest expression in purely monetary economic interests'. It is also manifested in the intellectualization and functionalization of relationships. And here

Simmel draws a series of parallels between intellectualization, rationalization (including the legal system) and 'calculating exactness of modern times' and the development of a mature money economy that – along with the earlier work of Tönnies – surely anticipates some aspects of Max Weber's subsequent examination of the process of rationalization as well as Lukács's later analysis of reification. For instance, Simmel asserts that 'one may characterise the intellectual functions that are used at present in coping with the world and in regulating both individual and social relations as *calculative* functions. Their calculative ideal is to conceive of the world as a huge arithmetical problem.'

Within this reified objective culture and the reified world of monetary relationships, each individual's opportunity for creativity and development becomes increasingly restricted. This 'preponderance of objective over subjective culture' is manifested in the enigmatic relationship between 'social life and its products on the one hand and the fragmentary life-contents of individuals on the other'. Simmel sets himself the task of discovering 'the concrete, effective causes' of this widening separation of subjective and objective culture in modern society and finds its origins in 'the division of labour within production as well as consumption'.

At this point, Simmel provides an account of the division of labour and specialization which at times echoes that of Marx, though with significantly different emphases. In the modern production process, 'the product is completed at the expense of the development of the producer' whose total personality 'becomes stunted because of the diversion of energies . . . indispensably for the harmonious growth of the self'. Individual workers cannot recognize themselves in what they produce since the meaning of the latter is derived solely 'from its relationship with products of a different origin', namely other commodities. What is produced is merely a fragment that lacks the concrete definition 'that can be easily perceived in a product of labour that is wholly the work of a *single* person'.

The worker's alienation is also reinforced by 'the separation of the worker from the means of production' since whereas the capitalist's function is 'to acquire, organise and allocate the means of production, these means acquire a very different objectivity for the worker than for those who work with their own materials'. This process is further reinforced by the fact that 'work itself is separated from the worker' wherever 'labour power has become a commodity'. Under these circumstances, 'labour now shares the same character, mode of valuation and fate with all other commodities'. But rather than engage in a historically specific analysis of this process, Simmel reduces it to merely 'one side of the far-reaching process of differentiation'.

This process of the separation of the worker from the means of production is even more apparent in the case of automatic machine production which is

> the result of a highly advanced breakdown and specialisation of materials and energies, akin to the character of a highly developed state administration ... In that the machine becomes a totality and carries out a growing proportion of the work itself, it confronts the worker as an autonomous power. [65]

But machine production is also imbued with another characteristic. It is the embodiment of objectified knowledge ('objective mind') that is far greater than that of the individual producer.

However, not merely the production process but also the product itself confronts its producer as an alien object since 'the product of labour in the capitalist era is an object with a decidedly autonomous character, with its own laws of motion and a character alien to the producing subject' and is 'most forcefully illustrated where the worker is compelled to buy his own product'. But individual workers are also confronted with a greatly increased range of possible items of consumption. Here the process at work is one of levelling of quality and price: more impersonal objects are better suited for more people and the object must be produced cheaply enough to satisfy the widest possible demand.

Here, Simmel contrasts custom production with mass production. Whereas the former 'gave the consumer a personal relationship to the commodity', in the latter case the commodity is something external and autonomous to the consumer. Not only does the division of labour destroy custom production, 'the subjective aura of the product also disappears in relation to the consumer because the commodity is now produced independently of him'. In more general terms, the individual becomes estranged not only from the wider cultural milieux but also from the more intimate aspects of daily life. There are three reasons for this. The first is the dramatic increase in the sheer quantity of commodities available, what Simmel refers to as 'concurrent differentiation', and which reaches its peak in the five cents store and the slot machine. The second is 'consecutive differentiation' of commodities as manifested in fashions. The third is the plurality of styles that confront the individual as objective entities.

It must be emphasized that the context within which this analysis of the alienating effects of the division of labour is located is the widening gap between subjective and objective culture. A decade later Simmel was to speak of this increasing separation of subjective and objective culture not merely in terms of a 'crisis of culture', or even as a 'tragedy of culture', but also as the 'pathology of culture'. In so doing Simmel elevated what he earlier saw as possibly historically specific into the realm of an eternal tragedy of culture that was inevitable in all developed societies. Thus, in his essay on 'The Concept and Tragedy of Culture', [66] Simmel maintains that 'the "fetishism" which Marx assigned to economic commodities represents only a special case of this general fate of contents of culture', which although created by human beings, follow their own 'immanent logic of development' and are impelled by 'cultural' necessities. Indeed, the whole theory of the increasing separation of subjective and objective culture and later the tragedy of culture – which requires Simmel to postulate a new mode of individuality that is not totally incorporated into this tragic fate – raises the question as to whether, in such a theory of cultural alienation the concept of society disappears altogether, and whether society becomes synonymous with culture.

4.3.5   The importance of Simmel's 'Philosophy of Money'

Any attempt to summarize even some of the central themes of Simmel's *Philosophy of Money* cannot do justice to the wealth of material it contains and, in contrast with many other works, the systematic nature of its analysis. Much more obviously than in his other writings, Simmel is able to develop a comprehensive theory of society on the basis of his analysis of money relationships. It is also a remarkable attempt to develop a social theory of modernity from an unusual standpoint. On the one hand, it is true that

> the work belongs alongside the group of those fundamental attempts which almost simultaneously economists such as Sombart and Max Weber, students of religion such as Troeltsch and others have undertaken to interpret the "spirit of capitalism" as a common rejection of historical materialism. [67]

On the other hand, however, its mode of presentation and often its content did prove attractive to those seeking a way into a Marxism that was not bounded by a rigid base-superstructure framework. But, more important, there is something distinctive about Simmel's theory of modernity: it is not specifically or directly concerned with the process of industrialization and the development of industrial capitalism. Simmel approaches its consequences indirectly through the money economy. In other words, its central focus lies in the analysis of exchange relationships and not production relations. This means that when we are reading Simmel's account of the money economy, the fact that this mature money economy is a capitalist economy often remains implicit. If, especially in the second part of the work, it is read as a phenomenology of commodity exchange in a capitalist society, then it does indeed read 'like a translation of Marx's economic discussion into the language of psychology'.

Viewed from a different perspective, *The Philosophy of Money* testifies to the centrality of the process of social differentiation as a theme in his work – one that was already announced a decade earlier. But the emphasis upon an exchange economy whose crucial mediating mechanism is money transactions also enables Simmel to push forward his social analysis into other spheres. One important instance is the metropolis whose analysis presupposes exchange in its widest sense and an exchange economy. Other instances might be Simmel's analyses of competition, trust, individuality, the stranger and so on. Hence, rather than viewing each of Simmel's major works in social theory as discrete entities we can also see them as building upon one another. A sociology that is grounded in interaction and forms of sociation has no thematic boundaries. But if interaction is a central focus then the sociologist is likely to take up some themes rather than others. Money as pure interaction may well be an obvious choice.

4.4 'SOCIOLOGY' (1908)

When Simmel's *Sociology* appeared in 1908, it marked the culmination of many years preoccupation with sociology as an independent discipline. Writing to Bouglé early in 1908, Simmel refers to his *Sociology* 'which is finally finished after the work on it was extended over fifteen years'. In fact, the work incorporates material Simmel had published as early as 1888. In the intervening twenty years, Simmel certainly devoted much of his attention to sociology, especially from 1894 onwards. In 1895 he spoke of his 'plan to write an epistemology of the social sciences' which never appeared (though the brief essay 'How is Society Possible?' in his *Soziologie* would form part of his project). More concretely in 1896 Simmel described his essay on super- and subordination as 'a chapter of my prospective sociology'. But then in 1899 Simmel suggested that once he had fulfilled his duty to sociology by publishing a comprehensive sociology he would probably never return to it again. In 1901 he confided to Rickert that this comprehensive sociology was 'an obligation with which I am not very sympathetic'. Nonetheless, Simmel was then working on the essays that came to constitute his *Sociology*. For instance in 1902, Simmel prefaced his article on 'The Quantitative Determination of the Group' with the comment that it constitutes 'a chapter of a *Sociology* to be published by me in the future'. By 1908 Simmel had already published versions of all the main chapters of his *Sociology* and most of the important 'excursions' that go to make up the whole work. One interesting exception is 'Excursus on the Problem: How is Society Possible?'.

The reasons for this brief outline of the development of this major sociological work are twofold. First, the volume does not exist in complete translation in English. This might give the reader the impression that those essays that have been translated merely form part of a *collection of essays*. Second, Simmel's contemporaries and subsequent generations of German sociologists have displayed an ambiguous attitude to the *Sociology*. On the one hand, those who were convinced that Simmel's sociology as a whole has a coherence that is derived from his method could see his *Sociology* as a volume that illustrates the application of that method to a wide variety of areas of social reality. On the other, those who wished to maintain that Simmel's sociological work centres around a number of central themes and problematics were faced with the problem of accounting for the apparent diversity of themes with which the reader of his *Sociology* is confronted. Here the question arises as to whether this major work – in the critical German edition it comprises 863 pages – does indeed possess a structure or central thematic. Such issues are worthy of re-examination, especially since the problem of cohesiveness is so often raised not merely in relation to Simmel's *Sociology* but to the whole of his sociological enterprise.

4.4.1 The structure of the text

As a preliminary step towards an investigation of the nature and possible structure of Simmel's *Sociology* it is necessary to outline the actual contents of the work. The dates in parentheses signify the date of publication of earlier versions or parts of the chapters ([E] denotes English translation available).

SOCIOLOGY

Investigations of the Forms of Sociation

Foreword

1. The Problem of Sociology (1894; 1894 French; 1895 English; 1899 Italian)   [E]
    Excursus on the Problem: How is Society Possible?   [E]
2. The Quantitative Determination of the Group (1895 French; 1902 English)   [E]
3. Super- and Subordination (1896/97 English; 1907; 1907)   [E]
    Excursus on Out-voting   [E]
4. Conflict (1903; 1904 English; 1905; 1908)   [E]
5. The Secret and the Secret Society (1906 English; 1906)   [E]
    Excursus on Adornment (1908)   [E]
    Excursus on Written Communication (1908)   [E]
6. The intersection of Social Circles (1890)   [E]
7. The Poor (1906)   [E]
    Excursus on the Negativity of Collective Modes of Behaviour
8. The Self-preservation of the Social Group (1896/97 French; 1898; 1898 English)
    Excursus on Hereditary Office
    Excursus on Social Psychology (1908)   [E]
    Excursus on Faithfulness and Gratitude (1907)   [E]
9. Space and the Spatial Structures of Society (1903; 1903)   [E]
    Excursus on the Social Boundary
    Excursus on the Sociology of the Senses (1907)   [E, in part]
    Excursus on the Stranger (1900 *Philosophy of Money*)   [E]

10. The Enlargement of the Group and the
     Development of Individuality (1888;
     1890)   [E, in part]
     Excursus on Nobility (1907)   [E]
     Excursus on the Analogy between
     Individual-Psychological and Sociologi-
     cal Circumstances

This outline certainly lends credence to the view that Simmel's
Sociology is a collection of essays that are held together – if by anything at all – by the opening chapter and its appended note.
Simmel's 'Preface', a mere half page, is itself unable to perform this
task. Yet it does indicate how Simmel advised the reader to treat this
text. Simmel suggests that

> if the manner in which the investigation connects
> phenomena finds no model for its formula in any domain of
> the recognised disciplines – then, clearly, the determina-
> tion of its place within the system of the sciences, the dis-
> cussion of its method and potential fruitfulness, is a new
> task itself, which requires its solution not in a preface, but
> as the first part of the very investigation.
>   This is the situation of the present attempt at giving
> the fluctuating concept of sociology an unambiguous con-
> tent, dominated by one, methodologically certain,
> problem-idea. The request to the reader to hold on, unin-
> terruptedly, to this one method of asking questions, as it is
> developed in the first chapter (since otherwise these pages
> might impress him as an accumulation of unrelated facts
> and reflections) – this request is the only matter which
> must be mentioned at the start of this book. [68]

Similarly, at the very end of the book in a note to Simmel's own
inadequate index, he returns to this same request. The chapters, he
argues are

> relatively *independent* contributions to the total problem.
> The ultimate intention and the methodological structure of
> these studies required their arrangement under few central
> concepts but, at the same time, required greater latitude in
> regard to the particular questions treated under their
> heads. [69]

Commenting on these requests, Wolff suggests that its chapters 'might be likened to connected nets which must be opened by those who want to know what they contain'.

If we return to Simmel's early statements on the nature of his sociology, then we can find further support for the view that Simmel conceived of his sociology as cohering around a new methodical vantage point rather than a new content. In 1896 Simmel declares that 'it is indeed a difficult task to educate students into the *sociological viewpoint* upon which everything depends . . . Once one has this viewpoint from the outset, then sociological facts too are not so very difficult to find'. [70] Such a statement seems to confirm Simmel's intention in his *Sociology*. But perhaps Simmel's early reflections also provide a clue to the *content* of his *Sociology*. In 1894 in 'The Problem of Sociology', Simmel declared 'the sole object' of sociology to be 'the investigation of the forces, forms and developments of sociation, of individual co-operation, association and co-existence'. In the following year in a supplementary note to the same article Simmel outlines the kind of problems which his sociology will deal with. They include examination of 'the formation, rules and development of parties in general', 'the formation and importance of competition, treated purely as a reciprocal action among men', 'the importance . . . of a common meal-time for the cohesion of individuals', 'the differences in socialisations [sociations D.F.] which are connected with variations in the number of associates', 'the importance of the "non-partisan" in the conflict of members (*Genossen*); the "poor" as organic members of societies; the representation of bodies through individuals; the *primus inter pares* and the *tertius gaudens*'. [71] In fact in 1895 when this programme was drawn up Simmel had not written in any depth on any of these themes. But they all form part of his *Sociology* some thirteen years later. Unfortunately, such a list of topics fails to provide the basis for its thematic coherence.

Indeed most contemporary reviewers were also hard pressed to detect a thematic coherence. Leopold von Wiese, for example, suggested that the book as a whole lacked any synthetic intention, that its contents read better as discrete essays and that 'out of the countless studies of diverse forms of sociation there emerges no unified theory of the forms of sociation'. [72] Thomas Masaryk also argued that Simmel's book contains 'several very good and valuable studies, but sociology as a whole and as a system is not contained in the book'. [73] Eleutheropulos lamented that 'at best what it contains is a collection of sociological essays'. David Koigen maintained that 'the whole . . . is shaped through "counterpoint" . . . The forms of sociation run free and parallel to one another, both burdened and enriched by thousands of "episodes".' [74] Only Alfred Vierkandt defended the book's structure as 'a series of variations upon the theme: "what is the task of sociology?"', as concerned with 'three groups of questions' – the nature and diverse types of social forms and relations whose 'characteristic qualities' are described and analysed; 'the causes which bring about and maintain these phenomena'; and 'the effect that they produce'. Vierkandt argues that Simmel is primarily concerned with the first of these tasks whereas 'the question of the causal connection, especially the effects of these relations, is to some extent of secondary significance'. [75] But even Vierkandt's defence of Simmel hardly exposes the structure of his *Sociology*.

In a sense, many reviewers overlooked what Simmel himself acknowledged in his *Sociology*, namely his stress upon 'the wholly fragmentary, incomplete character of this book' whose problems 'doubtless present an haphazard character'. Yet, Simmel continues,

> if this character should strike one as a defect, this would only go to prove that I have not been able to clarify the fundamental idea of the present volume. For according to this idea, nothing more can be attempted than to establish the beginning and the direction of an infinitely long road – the pretension of any systematic and definitive complete-ness would be, at least, a self-illusion. [76]

It seems as if Simmel himself is acknowledging that his *Sociology* possesses no structural cohesiveness.

But beyond the initial statement of sociology's 'problem' and the three sociological '*a priori*'s of society (in 'How is Society Poss-ible?'), is there any way in which the subsequent problems that Simmel deals with can be at least ordered, grouped together or made more cohesive? One possibility is to look for central principles in Simmel's sociological work as a whole and then examine how far they are applicable to the *Sociology*. Donald Levine [77] has argued that although the results of Simmel's sociological enquiries consti-tute 'a series of discrete analyses' which 'do not lend themselves to being integrated through a single interpretative scheme', there do exist 'four basic presuppositions' which 'underlie all of Simmel's analyses of culture, society and personality. These may be identified as the principles of form, reciprocity, distance and dualism.' When applied to Simmel's sociology they highlight his preoccupation with the 'determinate identity structure and meaning' of contents of social life that are structured in social forms; 'the degree of reciprocity among individuals or groups'; the fact that 'all social forms are defined to some extent in terms of the dimension of interpersonal distance'; and the specific sociological dualism of, for instance, 'publicity and privacy, conformity and individuation, antagonism and solidarity, compliance and rebelliousness, freedom and constraint'. All these principles are indeed exemplified throughout most of the concrete analyses in Simmel's *Sociology*.

A not dissimilar search for guiding principles is suggested by Renate Mayntz [78] who argues that Simmel's '*Soziologie* . . . really does possess a surprising – if partly implicit – internal coherence' on the basis of 'very general, abstract structural principles' operative in forms of sociation. Those which Simmel himself explicitly referred to are

> the relation of superordination–subordination; the relation of antagonism (conflict); the division of labour or relation of functional interdependence; the ingroup–outgroup relation and the related principle of party formation; the principle of representation; the principles of spatial and temporal structuring; and the quantitative dimension. Other structural principles are implied in Simmel's writings, such as the dependence–autonomy dimension, which plays such a crucial role in his analysis of group membership and individuality. [79]

The author continues by suggesting that Simmel's aim was 'not the causal explanation of these social forms but the analysis of their . . . *objective meaning* which is something distinct from their psychologically explained genesis'. This led Simmel to examine 'their essential characteristics and range of empirical variation, on the one hand, and . . . their consequences on the other'. Elsewhere in his *Sociology*, Simmel focused 'on a specific type of group (e.g. secret societies) or class of persons (e.g. the stranger, the poor man, the aristocrat) . . . to show how they are characterised and determined by a unique constellation of several of these structural principles'. Sometimes a longitudinal analysis which links his sociology to his theory of social development is employed as where he deals with 'specific structural principles (e.g. conflict), special types of relationship, such as marriage, or special types of groups, such as secret societies'. [80] In this respect, Simmel was seeking to analyse social forms in the terms he had outlined over a decade earlier.

More recently, another attempt to discover the structural principles of Simmel's sociological work has been undertaken by Birgitta

Nedelmann [81] which draws on the earlier work of Levine and Mayntz. Nedelmann detects five structural principles 'applied by Simmel' in his study of forms of interaction. The first is the 'heuristic strategy of *contrasting*' 'the degree, permanency or stability of socia- tion' in order to reveal 'the sociating element in specific forms of interaction' such as domination and subordination. The second principle is that of *number* both in the sense of few or many partici- pants in interaction and in the sense of highlighting the significance of third parties or simply 'the third' element of interaction. A further principle is that of *space* not merely in the sense of social space (and Simmel was the first to write explicitly on this theme) but also in highlighting the significance of social types such as 'the wanderer' or 'the stranger' who combine both nearness and distance, as well as the wider process of social demarcation of groups. Fourthly, Simmel applies the structural principle of *dualism* as in the aspects of coer- cion and freedom in domination and subordination. Finally, Simmel insists upon the fundamentally *'dynamic* character if interactions' which leads him to analyse these processes of transformation that exist within existing forms of interaction. As is implicit in the rela- tional character of Simmel's key concepts, his interest lies in social processes rather than reified structures or institutions.

Yet it must be emphasized that Simmel does not commence his *Sociology* with an account of such principles as are highlighted by Levine, Mayntz or Nedelmann. Rather, it is possible to show that Simmel applies them in his various analyses of forms of sociations and that we can recognize them in his analysis. If we return to the actual content of Simmel's *Sociology* it is possible to see a more limited number of themes than is indicated by the chapter titles and supplementary excursions. There are two further issues involved here. First, do the essays follow on from one another or are they interlinked in any way? Second, do the supplements or excursions relate to their main themes? As we have seen, Simmel did have some conception of the kind of issues he wished to deal with in a 'com- prehensive sociology' as early as 1894–95, though what was offered in 1908 was hardly such a comprehensive work as possibly originally planned.

With regard to the central themes, Simmel suggests that the reader hold on to the guiding problematic of the first chapter on how sociology as an independent science is possible (and, one can add, how society itself is possible). With respect to the latter, one should bear in mind that Simmel's sociological answer to this question is in terms of the processes of sociation of individuals in groups and not in terms of an overarching conception of society. In the light of the possible guiding principles outlined above, Simmel commences with the general issues of mass or quantity of individuals in a social group and how changes in group size affect both the individual and the group. With some degree of licence, we can see this theme as an aspect of a horizontal morphology of social groups. Simmel then moves on to the vertical morphology, as it were, with his discussion of domination and subordination, not merely as a problem of social hierarchy but as the interaction of dominant and subordinate members of a group or groups. The appended note on outvoting is a supplementary dimension of subordination. The next theme, already presupposing the existence of social groups, deals with the *external* dynamic and internal consequences of group relations, namely the varieties of conflict, including competition and all-out struggle. In the following chapter, Simmel takes up a different aspect of group and individual relations that centres around our knowledge or lack of knowledge of other individuals and groups ('The Secret and the Secret Society'). The two appended notes on adornment and written communication both, at the most general level, examine aspects of our knowledge of others (perhaps in contrast to the central theme of non-communication with others by members of secret societies). This is followed by the theme of intersecting social circles (the English translation is somewhat inappropriately titled 'The Web of Group Affiliations') which takes up the external and internal consequences of multiple interactions in a variety of settings. Whereas the central focus is the individual's participation in a variety of social groups, the following theme, 'The Poor', examines, amongst other things, how a group comes to be defined as different from other groups and, to some extent, excluded from a variety of social circles. The appended note on the negative aspects of collective action might fit within this general rubric. The eighth chapter on the self-preservation of social groups examines how any group is able to maintain itself over time. Two of the appended notes can also be incorporated into this theme. Viewed from above, as it were, hereditary office is one instance of groups of individuals perpetuating their existence, whilst, viewed from below, the social group requires for its continuation faithfulness and gratitude. What cannot be incorporated into the general theme is the note on social psychology which might more appropriately be placed with the opening chapter on demarcating sociology as an independent discipline. The following section on 'Space and the Spatial Structures of Society' deals not merely with a formal precondition for sociation – social space – but also the general issue of social distance. In this context, the three appendices on social demarcation, the sociology of the senses and the stranger all take up different dimensions of social distance. The final chapter – and here the argument has to be stretched – takes up the spatial and physical extension of the group (i.e. its enlargement) and the consequences for the development of human individuality. The appendix on the nobility refers to a social group that cannot be extended indefinitely without losing its identity. The second note on the analogy between individual psychological and sociological circumstances deals more generally with individual and group processes viewed from two apparently different perspectives.

However inadequate such an outline may be, it does give some support for the view that Simmel's procedure is not entirely an arbitary one. Simmel does seek to incorporate not merely some of the formal preconditions for sociation (number, space) but also a very wide variety of basic forms of human interaction and sociation in his *Sociology*. Partly as a result of the absence of translations, not all these basic aspects of interaction have been taken up in the succeeding sociological literature. Some attention has been given to quantitative characteristics of groups (notably in dyadic and triadic analyses), to the development of a sociology of conflict, to the development of social network analysis, to the study of secret societies and social distance and to empirical applications of social types such as the stranger. None of these has been fully developed and not all these areas of research can be traced back merely to an impetus derived from studying Simmel's *Sociology*. There are, of course, other more general aspects of Simmel's sociological analysis incorporated in this work which have received considerable treatment such as role and reference group theory.

Any attempt to deal with or even summarize the themes outlined and developed in Simmel's *Sociology* would prove an impossible task within the present context. What is more appropriate is a brief examination of some of Simmel's 'investigations of the forms of sociation' as the author subtitles this work.

4.4.2 How is society possible?

The manner in which Simmel answered the question as to how sociology as an independent discipline is possible has been dealt with in the third chapter of this study. 'The Problem of Sociology' as the first chapter of Simmel's *Sociology* was to provide the reader with the basic starting point to the rest of his investigations of forms of sociation. It had been outlined on several occasions from 1890 onwards. What is new in the *Sociology* is the posing of the transcendental question 'How is society possible?' [82] – a question which usually receives scant attention in the deliberations of sociologists. This is not posed in strictly Kantian terms as how knowledge of society is possible but is located at the somewhat more substantive level of how society is possible. The transcendental subject in Kant's problematic is replaced by the commitment of empirical human subjects to interaction. Towards the end of his *Sociology*, Simmel somewhat disarmingly states that 'humanity has created sociation as its form of life – which, as it were, was not the only logical possibility; rather, the human species could also have chosen to be unsocial, just as unsocial animal species exist alongside social ones'. [83] In the earlier chapter Simmel examines 'the aprioristic conditions under which society is possible'.

Whereas, in Kantian terms, the unity of nature requires the knowing subject, 'the unity of society needs no observer. It is directly realised by its own elements because those elements are themselves conscious and synthesising units.' The idea of society is mediated through the experience of individuals' forms of sociation which are not themselves 'antecedent causes' of society but 'part of the synthesis to which we give the inclusive name of "society"'. In this way, Simmel seeks to establish a notion of society that is neither a 'real product' nor a 'purely transcendental presupposition of sociological experience'. The answer to the question as to how society is possible is provided by an examination of

> the conditions which reside a priori in the elements themselves [individuals and groups – D.F.], through which they combine, in reality, into the synthesis, society. In a certain sense, the entire content of this book . . . is the beginning of the answer to this question. For it inquires into the processes – those which, ultimately, take place in the individuals themselves – that condition the existence of the individuals as society. [84]

What are these *a priori* conditions of forms of sociation that make society possible?

Unlike the basis of Kant's *a priori* for knowledge of the material world which is grounded in a knowing human subject, the basis for Simmel's *a priori* is not merely the self but also the other as *you*, 'as something independent of our representation' of the existing ego, 'as something that exists with exactly the same autonomy as does our own existence'. This is the fundamental psychologico-epistemological paradigm and problem of sociation'. With this in mind, Simmel outlines three *a priori*s of forms of sociation (the fact that he refers to 'some' of them suggests Simmel posited more) which Uta Gerhardt [85] has succinctly termed the three *a priori*s of 'role', 'individuality' and 'structure'. The first *a priori* is the social mediation of action in the sense that action is always 'social' action. The relations between actors is always the product of social abstractions (a generalized image of the other) since it is impossible either to completely know the other person or to characterize them as an object with fixed properties. The role-governed nature of social existence is indicated not merely by the image of the other but also the knowledge of the structural context within which individual social action takes place. In that we typify other actors, typification mediates between knowledge and action. The second *a priori* of 'individuality' hinges on the concept of the social role as the 'mediation of sociability and sociality' insofar as 'every element of a group is not only a societal part but, in addition, something else'. Simmel thus presupposes that 'life is not completely social'. This implies that there exists a non-sociated being as identity itself (individuality) and, further, that the individual is not merely a bundle of roles. The individual is never totally involved or identified in a social role. As Simmel states it, individual existence is

> the synthesis or simultaneity of two logically contradictory characterisations of man – the characterisation which is based on his function as a member, as a product and a content of society; and the opposing characterisation which is based on his functions as an autonomous being, and which views his life from its own centre and for its own sake. [86]

The third *a priori* of 'structure' rests upon 'the phenomenological structure of society' as

> the sum of the objective existences and actions of its elements and the interrelations among these existences and actions . . . Purely personal and creative aspects of the ego, its impulses and reflexes, have no place in this system . . . The life of society . . . takes its course as if each of its elements were predestined for its particular place in it. [87]

This *a priori* provides the 'possibility' of the individual 'being a member of a society'. To clarify this, Simmel provides 'a small-scale analogy . . . in bureaucracy' which is 'an ideal structure, irrespective of the particular occupants of these positions' whereas in society we must speak of 'a deeply entangled play and counterplay' of functions to which individuals are allocated. As such the third *a priori* is, like the other two, one of the 'ideational, logical presuppositions for the perfect society (which is perhaps never realised in this perfection, however)'. At the individual level Simmel maintains that the relevance of this structural *a priori* is revealed in 'the vocation as the individualisation of the whole in the roles of the human subject'. [88]

Simmel's answer to the question as to how society is possible outlines the possibility for sociation in the interaction of the 'I' and the 'You' through idealized typifications of self and other. In so doing it anticipates the other more well-known grounding for interactionist sociology in the work of George Herbert Mead. It also anticipates elements of Max Weber's ideal type constructs. Finally, if we interpret Simmel's question phenomenologically as 'How is Society *made* possible?', as John O'Neill [89] has attempted, we move towards a phenomenological answer to this question that is only partly made explicit by Simmel himself.

4.4.3 Investigations of the forms of sociation

However, as Simmel indicated, his *Sociology* can be seen as a beginning to the answer to the question 'How is Society Possible?', through the investigation of the various forms which human sociation takes. It would clearly be impossible to summarize Simmel's wide variety of analyses of forms of sociation that are to be found in the *Sociology* and elsewhere. Merely as an indication of the different objects of Simmel's analysis, a limited number have been chosen. As an instance of the 'pure' form of sociation we can cite Simmel's 'Sociology of Sociability' (1910) which does not appear in his *Sociology*. As an instance of the formal preconditions for sociation the neglected essay on 'Space and the Spatial Structures of Society' can be taken. Two of the appendices to this chapter and Simmel's more famous essay on the metropolis are also considered. Such a selection clearly does not do justice to Simmel's sociological work as a whole since it leaves out of account his many studies of seemingly insignificant details of everyday life: mealtimes, letter writing, coquetry, shame, discretion, etc. Nor does it do justice to the much wider group of analyses of the basic forms of human interaction which make up a large part of his *Sociology*: domination, subordination, conflict, competition, etc. We should also not forget that Simmel wrote on the sociology of the family and religion.

4.4.3.1   Sociability

In his opening address to the first German Sociological Association
Congress in 1910, Simmel, 'with his noted suggestive finesse' (Durkheim), examines the sociology of sociability. In the light of his
earlier discussions of the nature of society, the focus upon sociability
gains its significance from the fact that it is 'the *play-form of sociation*'.
Arguing against rationalism's dismissal of sociability as 'empty idle-
ness', Simmel maintains that sociability is also the pure *form* of
sociation itself:

> The political, the economic, the purposive society of any
> sort is, to be sure, always "society". But only the sociable
> gathering is "a society" without further qualification,
> because it alone represents the pure abstract play of form,
> all the specific contents of the one-sided and qualified
> "societies" being dissolved away. [90]

In other words, 'the impulse to sociability distils, as it were, out of
the realities of social life the pure essence of sociation, of the sociating process as a value and as a satisfaction'.

   Though the substance of sociability is made up from 'numerous
fundamental forms of serious relationships', it is a substance that is
'spared the frictional relations of real life'. This enables sociability to
represent 'the pure form, the freeplaying, interacting inter-
dependence of individuals'. In its pure form, sociability possesses
'no ulterior end, no content, and no result outside itself, it is oriented
completely around personalities'. But although the personal traits of
its participants 'determine the character of purely sociable sociation', individuality cannot be emphasized in an excessive manner
since it would destroy sociability itself. This is the basis for the
significance that the sense of 'tact' has for society since 'it guides the
self-regulation of the individual in his personal relations to others
where no external or directly egoistic interests provide regulation'.
Where participants do come to direct their sociation towards definite purposes and contents, sociability ceases to be the guiding principle of sociation and becomes instead 'at most a formalistic and
outwardly instrumental principle'.

   Viewed as a democratic form of sociation, the world of sociability is 'an artificial world, made up of beings who have renounced
both the objective and the purely personal features . . . of life in
order to being about amongst themselves a pure interaction', even
'an ideal sociological world, for in it . . . the pleasure of the
individual is always contingent on the joy of others'. As 'the

abstraction of sociation' it demands the purest form of interaction amongst equals, even in the sense in which each participant '"acts" as though all were equal'. It is a 'sociological play-form' like play itself – part of the 'social game'. But here Simmel extracts the deeper meaning of this instance of the social game when he points out 'that it is played not only *in* a society as its outward bearer but that with its help people actually "play" "society"'.

This social game is played in various spheres of social life. In the sociology of the sexes, for instance, 'eroticism has elaborated a form of play: *coquetry*, which finds in sociability its highest, most playful, and yet its widest realisation'. Hence just as 'sociability plays at the forms of society, so coquetry plays out the forms of eroticism'. At a much more universal level, the social game is played out 'in that most extensive instrument of all human common life, *conversation*'. In sociability 'talking is an end in itself', 'a legitimate end in itself'. As a pure form of mutuality, sociable conversation 'becomes the most adequate fulfilment of a relation, which is, so to speak, nothing but relationship'. A further instance of sociability revealing its aesthetic significance lies in court *etiquette* of, say, the *ancien régime*, in 'forms whose force, definitions, and relations were purely sociable and in no way symbols or functions of the real meanings and intensities of persons and institutions'. In this respect, court etiquette 'became an end in itself; it "etiquetted" no content any longer but had elaborated immanent laws, comparable to those of art, which have validity only from the viewpoint of art'. But to the extent that sociability cuts itself off totally from life, it can easily become a caricature of itself which 'turns from play to empty farce, to a lifeless schematisation proud of its woodenness'. In the *ancien régime*, this rigid form of sociability constituted an escape from an unbearable social reality (an impulse not unknown to 'parties' today) in order that 'the heavily burdened forces of reality are felt only as from a distance, their burden fleeting in a charm'.

Simmel's sociology of sociability illustrates his search for pure forms of sociation and interaction and, in highlighting its positive and negative features, is typical of his mode of analysis. It also takes up briefly themes such as tact and coquetry which are dealt with in detail elsewhere in his work. Finally, it is indicative of his search for the fleeting charm of seemingly insignificant social interactions. But in order to illustrate more fully Simmel's sociological analysis in his *Sociology* we may turn to one of its neglected chapters which, together with its excursions and a set of themes developed more fully elsewhere, demonstrates the way in which he takes up a central theme and analyses it from various perspectives or vantage points.

4.4.3.2   The sociology of space and social distance

The penultimate chapter of Simmel's *Sociology* concerns itself with 'Space and the Spacial Structures of Society'. It also has three excursions on 'The Social Boundary' (omitted here), 'The Sociology of the Senses' and 'The Stranger' all of which reveal different aspects of the spatial dimension of social interaction. Since part of the major chapter also contains a discussion of metropolitan social space, Simmel's famous essay 'The Metropolis and Mental Life' -- which was originally published in the same year (1903) as the original essay version of 'The Sociology of Space' and 'On Spatial Projections of Social Forms' – is also discussed. The essay on the metropolis is added for another reason, namely that many of the themes which Simmel takes up in his *Sociology* are not merely studies of 'forms of sociation' in an abstract or analytical sense but are intimately linked to both his general theory of societal development and his sociology of modernity. The same is also true of the last chapter of his *Sociology* on 'The Enlargement of the Group and the Development of Individuality' which takes up many themes already developed in *The Philosophy of Money*.

Simmel's sociology of space is part of his incomplete study of the formal preconditions for human sociation that would comprise space, time and mass (number). What is largely absent is a sociology of time (though there are fruitful indicators in the last section of *The Philosophy of Money* on the tempo and rhythm of social life, whilst the essay 'The Adventure' (1910, 1911) contains some insights into the phenomenology of time). The whole discussion of the sociology of space and social distance contains a wealth of insights and material much of which has hardly been researched. The outline which follows seeks to show the coherence of at least one section of Simmel's *Sociology* and its wider ramifications.

In itself space remains a form without effect, a form which has to be filled with social and psychological energies. A geographical area, for instance, does not form a large empire. Rather, the activities of its inhabitants create that empire. In other words, and in more general terms, 'interaction amongst human beings – aside from all the other things that it is – is also experienced as the filling in of space'. Even the simplest interactions between two people fills in that which is between them. Simmel adapts Kant's definition of space as 'the possibility of being together' into a sociological theme insofar as 'interaction makes what was previously empty and void into something *for us*, it fills it in insofar as it makes it possible'. Simmel therefore commences by enquiring into the significance that the spatial preconditions of sociation possess for the development of sociation itself. There exist, Simmel maintains, a number of basic qualities of spatial forms which communal life must take into account. They are the exclusiveness of space, its boundaries, the fixing or locating of social forms in space, nearness and distance and, finally, the possibility of moving from place to place.

Each part of space possesses a kind of uniqueness. This is also true where a social form is identified with a particular piece of territory, such as the state, or districts of cities. Whereas the connection between people that is created by the state is closely bound up with a specific territory, the city is significant in that its influence extends far beyond its boundaries. In contrast to the quantitative filling out of space as territory, there is a tendency – whose principle Simmel asserted from his earliest work onwards – to fill out space not quantitatively but functionally as in a medieval city which possesses a number of active guilds or corporations (i.e. separate functions which can exist alongside one another within the same space of the city).

Space can also be broken up into pieces for our practical utilization in which case space becomes a unity that is framed in by boundaries. Indeed frames have a very similar significance for the social group as they do for the work of art. A society also possesses a sharply demarcated existential space such that the extensiveness of space collides with the intensity of social relationships. This may be contrasted with nature for whom the setting of boundaries is arbitrary. And although political, territorial boundaries seem to be merely along geometric lines, any such boundary is a defensive and offensive spatial expression of unified relations between two neighbours. Simmel emphasizes the extent to which the concept of a boundary is extremely important in all relationship between people. The social boundary signifies a quite unique interaction in that each element affects the other insofar as it sets a boundary but without wishing to extend the effects to the other element. This suggests that 'the boundary is not a spatial fact with sociological consequences but a sociological fact that is formed spatially'. In other words 'the sociological boundary signifies a quite unique interaction', in which what is important is the interactions that are woven on each side of the boundary. Another significant factor is the narrowness or breadth of the frame of boundary which is related not to the size of the social group but to the forces of tension that develop within the group (Simmel instances here broad boundaries in oriental empires and narrow boundaries such as the Venetian empire). Yet the significance of the spatial framework or boundary of the social group is not merely political. Simmel points to the relationship between the impulsiveness of crowds in open spaces giving them a sense of freedom, in contrast to the tension of a crowd in an enclosed space. Another example of the non-political boundary is indicated by the indeterminacy of the spatial framework in darkness, in which the narrowness and breadth of the framework merge together and provide scope for fantasy.

In contrast, the third significant spatial feature in social formations is provided by the fixing of social forms in space. And here Simmel points to four possibilities. The first is the existence of a continuum from the completely local binding together of individuals (as in those medieval towns that did not permit its citizens to move beyond their boundaries) to a situation of total freedom. The second is the fixing of a social form at a focal point. The spatial establishment of an object of interest creates specific forms of relationships that group around it. The obvious example is economic transactions, but Simmel points out that there exists a historical development from substantive to functional fixing of a focal point so that economic interactions are not derived from the substantive immobility of a particular place but from the functions connected to the place. The third possibility arises out of otherwise independent elements being brought together around a particular space (for religious groupings their communities centre around churches). Characteristically, Simmel provides the fascinating instance of the rendezvous whose sociological significance 'lies in the tension between the punctuality and fleeting nature of the occurrence on the one hand and its spatio-temporal fixing on the other'. In passing, Simmel notes that the rendezvous also indicates that human memory is stronger on place than on time. The final sociological significance of the fixed point in space lies in the individualizing of place (the naming of houses and subsequently their numbering). Large organizations (e.g. Rome as a focus for the Catholic Church) require a central location or focal point. Within the large organization too, the one who gives orders must also have a fixed, identifiable location.

The fourth significant dimension of social space is the sensory proximity and distance between persons who stand in some relationship to one another. Indeed, Simmel maintains that all social interactions could be graded on some scale of nearness or distance. Along this scale we could find more primitive consciousness that is unable to conceive of its own connection with what is distant from it, the close relationship to one's neighbour in a small town today compared to such relationship in a metropolis where indifference is more common, human relationships across long distances that require a relatively high degree of intellectual development, the proximity of relationships of friendship, the significance of inner distance particularly in modern society, and so on.

It is within the context of this fourth dimension of social space that Simmel inserts his note on the sociology of the senses. Again, Simmel was the first sociologist to take up this important dimension of social interaction. As a contribution to sociological aspects of our knowledge of others, Simmel outlines important social features of our three senses. Seeing is a unique sociological phenomenon in the interaction between individuals, so much so that Simmel declares that two people looking at one another 'is perhaps . . . the most immediate and purest reciprocal relationship that exists'. The exchange of eye contact 'crystallises in no objective structure' since interaction can cease the moment the sensory function ceases. More poetically, the look, the glance can, as it were, unveil the soul of the other person. The object of the eye usually rests, of course, upon the expressive significance of the face (the subject of an essay by Simmel). The face is, as it were, 'the geometric location of knowledge of the other, the symbol of what the other is'. However, the reciprocity that is always present in eye contact is sometimes absent in the case of hearing. Conversely, although eye contact can be exchanged privately within a room, sound is available to all those who hear. Finally, unlike seeing and hearing which themselves form or seek out an object, the sense of smell, as a lower sense, 'remains trapped as it were in the human subject'. Nonetheless, Simmel highlights its significance for interaction and outlines the consequences of the development of artificial smells such as perfume for social relationships. And as he made clear in the original version of this note, these basic aspects of human interaction are every bit as significant for the development of sociation as are interactions within much larger social complexes such as social classes or the state.

The fifth and final dimension of spatial forms with whose structure communal life must reckon is the possibility of moving from one spatial location to another. This means that the spatial determinants of a group's or individual's existence is in flux. The classic form of sociation in which the group itself is on the move is provided by nomads. A second possibility is where part of a social group is on the move. Even in this instance the fact that only part of a group is on the move does not rule out the possibility that it will still have an effect upon the whole. Simmel gives the example of itinerant justices as contributing to the overall process of centralization or apprentice groups (journeymen's apprentices) on the move who took their means of production (hand tools) with them. In an appended note to this dimension of social space, Simmel examines briefly one of his most famous social types – the stranger – as instance of the individual on the move.

It is worth pointing out that this is the original context for Simmel's discussion of the stranger rather than it being an autonomous piece on 'the marginal person' as it is so often viewed. Yet this very brief note – perhaps because of its isolation from its original setting – 'as a stimulus both to studies on the role of the stranger and to work on the related concept of social distance, has probably been cited in more social science research than any other of Simmel's writings'. [91] Located within its original context we can see the significance of its opening statement that 'if wandering, considered as a state of detachment from every given point in space, is the conceptual opposite of attachment to any point, then the sociological form of "the stranger" presents the synthesis, as it were, of both of these properties . . . another indication that spatial relations not only are determining conditions of relationships among men, but are also symbolic of those relationships'. [92] And like the previous note on the senses, the brief discussion of the stranger is not merely an analysis of a social type but is also related to our sociological knowledge of others, insofar as Simmel indicates the relationship between detachment and objectivity.

Following on from his extensive treatment of the basic qualities of spatial forms with whose structure social groups must reckon, Simmel concludes with a briefer treatment of our spatial effects that arise out of the social group's own structures and energies. The first dimension is the division of a social group largely on a spatial principle which, Simmel argues, arises historically out of the transition from a class system to the organization of social life on a more mechanical, rational and political basis. The second dimension details the extent to which the exercise of power over human beings is documented in the spatial sphere. The third aspect deals with the extent to which social units come to be located in spatial forms – the family, the club, the regiment, the trade union all have their fixed localities, their 'house'. Ironically perhaps the most interesting and least obvious dimension of social space is the final one which Simmel considers: empty space. Empty space, for instance, as 'no-man's land' has a crucial importance for relations between antagonistic neighbours. It may be manifested in a neutral zone in which economic exchange takes place in primitive societies. And in the more general context of human interaction, empty spaces are those which no party has a particular interest in or around which there are no taboos. Indeed, Simmel concludes, 'empty space is itself revealed to be agent and expression of sociological interaction'. As a formal precondition for social interaction and as a neglected, rather blank space on the sociological atlas, its analysis has even today hardly been filled in.

In the same year in which Simmel first published two sections of his essay on the sociology of space, he also produced one of his most famous essays on 'The Metropolis and Mental Life' (1903) which belongs both to the same thematic area and to a synthesis of views already expressed in *The Philosophy of Money* on modes of experience in a metropolitan setting. In this respect it provides a fitting conclusion to some of the central themes raised in both domains. It also touches on many of the themes of his *Sociology*.

Within the context of a sociology of space, the city is 'not a spatial entity with sociological consequences, but a sociological entity that is formed spatially'. The metropolis is not merely the focal point of social differentiation and complex social networks, but also the location of indefinite collectivities such as crowds. The city's openness that brings together diverse social strata, contrasts sharply with the social distance signified by 'a concentrated minority' in the ghetto. In other words, it also provides the possibility for total indifference to one's fellow human beings. In a less extreme form, the social reserve prevalent in social interaction in the metropolis as a means of preserving social distance and the maintenance of the individual self faced with the threat of the tumult of continuously changing stimuli is related to a central theme of Simmel's work at the turn of the century.

In the opening passage of his essay on the metropolis, Simmel asserts that 'the deepest problems of modern life derive from the claim of the individual to preserve the autonomy and individuality of his existence in the face of overwhelming social forces' and are concentrated in the metropolis. The individual must 'resist being levelled down and worn out by a social-technological mechanism' such as the metropolis. Extreme subjectivism is the response to the extreme objectification of culture that is found there. Hence the individual's struggle for self-assertion, when confronted with the pervasive indifference of much metropolitan social interaction, may take the form of stimulating a sense of distinctiveness, even in an excessive form of adopting 'the most tendentious eccentricities, the specifically metropolitan excesses of aloofness, caprice and fastidiousness, whose significance no longer lies in the content of such behaviour, but rather in its form of being different, of making oneself stand out and thus attracting attention'. In part, this arises out of 'the brevity and infrequency of meetings' which necessitates coming to the point as quickly as possible and making a striking impression in the briefest possible time. The 'calculating exactness of practical life' – arising out of a money economy – also reinforces this tendency since

> The relationships and concerns of the typical metropolitan resident are so manifold and complex that . . . their relationships and activities intertwine with one another into a many-membered organism. In view of this fact, the lack of the most exact punctuality in promises and activities would cause the whole to break down into an inextricable chaos. If all the watches in Berlin suddenly went wrong in different ways even only as much as an hour, its entire economic and commercial life would be derailed for some time. [93]

In turn, this very diversity of interests that requires such exact co-ordination is itself the result of two further factors that Simmel had already dealt with – the division of labour and social and functional differentiation.

In this way, Simmel encompasses a whole range of themes that he had already dealt with. He also adds a theme of his work since the 1890s, namely 'the atrophy of individual culture through the hypertrophy of objective culture', a problematic which Simmel works through here in the context of the metropolitan psyche but which remains a permanent theme in his socio-cultural critique of modern society. In other words, the example of the themes clustered around the sociology of space – some of its basic formal features, social boundaries, sociology of the senses, the stranger as isolated individual, metropolitan life – indicates not merely a coherence of problem complexes in his *Sociology* but also a wider context for them that extends beyond their reduction to mere 'forms of sociation'.

What must remain an open question, however, with regard to the structure of Simmel's *Sociology* as a whole, is whether he intended to produce a coherent text and whether he was successful. At the start of the very last chapter of his *Sociology*, Simmel concedes that the themes around which the investigations of the individual chapters are assembled were 'individual concepts of the sociological domain as a whole' whose relevance and significance permeated a whole range of social spheres. In other words, the content of the individual chapters comprised merely 'a sum of propositions' to be found under the chapter's title. Only in the last chapter does Simmel start out with 'a proposition' rather than 'a concept'. The danger of this procedure was perceived by one of his students, Siegfried Kracauer, who suggested that Simmel's *Sociology* 'highlights an array of essential qualities of social life without, however, encompassing them in their totality, without subsequently asking whether they perhaps connect with one another and can be mastered according to some basic principle or other. Forms stand alongside forms, types against types in unending sequence and no law orders their diversity'. [94] In Simmel's defence it must be asserted that in his mature works he was always loth to seek out laws or a single basic principle. If his *Sociology* does cohere then it can only be either by means of a methodological tendency whose applicability is highlighted in a variety of social spheres or by means of a cluster or constellation of themes that are interrelated. Both possibilities suggest a view of the social world as a labyrinth through which the sociologist passes in tentative stages. A single key is not available.

NOTES and REFERENCES

[1]   See P. E. Schnabel, *Die soziologische Gesamtkonzeption Georg Simmels*, Stuttgart, Gustav Fischer (1974), pp. 40f.

[2]   Exceptions are P. Honigsheim, 'The Time and Thought of the Young Simmel' and 'A Note on Simmel's Anthropological Interests', and H. Maus, 'Simmel in German Sociology', all in K. H. Wolff (editor), *Essays on Sociology, Philosophy and Aesthetics by Georg Simmel et al.*, Columbia, Ohio State University Press (1959), New York, Harper Row (1965), pp. 167–200; H. J. Dahme, *Soziologie als exakte Wissenschaft*, Stuttgart, Enke (1981).

[3]   M. Lazarus and H. Steinthal, 'Einleitende Gedanken über Völkerpsychologie', *Zeitschrift für Völkerpsychologie und Sprachwissenschaft*, Vol. 1, 1860, pp. 1–73. On Lazarus and Steinthal see I. Belke (editor), *Moritz Lazarus und Heymann Steinthal: Die*

Begründer der Völkerpsychologie in ihren Briefen, Tübingen, Mohr (1971).

[4]   M. Lazarus, *Das Leben der Seele*, Berlin, Dümmler (1883), esp. pp. 323–411.

[5]   M. Lazarus and H. Steinthal, 'Einleitende Gedanken über Völkerpsychologie', p. 3.

[6]   *Ibid.*, p. 4.

[7]   *Ibid.*, p. 29.

[8]   K. Danziger, 'Origins and Basic Principles of Wundt's *Völkerpsychologie*', *British Journal of Social Psychology*, 1984 (forthcoming).

[9]   H. Böhringer, 'Spuren von spekulativem Atomismus in Simmels formaler Soziologie', in H. Böhringer and K. Gründer (editors), *Ästhetik und Soziologie um die Jahrhundertwende: Georg Simmel*, Frankfurt, Kolsterman, (1978), p. 112.

[10] H. J. Dahme, *Soziologie als exakte Wissenschaft*, p. 249.

[11] H. Spencer, *First Principles*, London, Williams and Norgate (1862), p. 228.

[12] *Ibid.*, p. 176.

[13] *Ibid.*, p. 495.

[14] H. J. Dahme, *Soziologie als exakte Wissenschaft*, p. 474.

[15] H. Böhringer, *op. sit.*, p. 110.

[16] G. Simmel, 'Steinthal, H., Allgemeine Ethik', *Vierteljahresschrift für Wissenschaftliche Philosophie*, Vol. 10, 1886, pp. 487–503.

[17] K. C. Köhnke, 'Von der Völkerpsychologie zur Soziologie',

[18] G. Simmel, 'Gerhardt Hauptmanns "Weber"', *Sozialpolitisches Zentralblatt*, Vol. 2, 1892–93, pp. 283–4.

[19] G. Simmel, 'Psychologische Glossen zur Strafgesetznovelle', *Sozialpolitische Zentralblatt*, Vol. 1, 1892, p. 174.

[20] G. Simmel, 'Jastrow, Dr J. Die Aufgaben des Liberalismus in Preussen', *Archiv für soziale Gesetzgebung und Statistik*, Vol. 6, 1893, pp. 622–7, esp. p. 725.

[21] *Ibid.*, p. 626.

[22] G. Simmel, 'Ein Wort über soziale Freiheit', *Sozialpolitisches Zentralblatt*, Vol. 2, 1892–93, pp. 283–4.

[23] G. Simmel, 'Soziale Medizin', *Die Zeit* (Vienna), Vol. 10, 13.10.1897. Translated by J. Casparis and A. C. Higgins, 'Georg Simmel on Social Medicine', *Social Forces*, Vol. 47, 1968, pp. 330–4.

[24] *Ibid.*, p. 334.

[25] G. Simmel, 'Der Frauenkongress und die Sozialdemokratie', *Die Zukunft* (Vienna), Vol. 17, 1896, pp. 80–4.

[26] G. Simmel, 'Sozialismus und Pessimismus', *Die Zeit* (Vienna), Vol. 22, 3.2.1900.

[27] G. Simmel, 'Sociological Aesthetics', in K. P. Etzkorn (editor and translator), Georg Simmel, *The Conflict of Modern Culture and other Essays*, New York, Teachers College Press (1968), p. 75. For a fuller discussion of Simmel's political position see my *Sociological Impressionism: A Reassessment of Georg Simmel's Social Theory*, London, Heinemann (1981), Chapter 5.

[28] See G. Schmoller, 'Die Thatsachen der Arbeitsteilung', *Jahrbuch für Gesetzgebung, Verwaltung und Volkswirtschaft*, Vol. 13, No. 3, 1889, pp. 57–128; G. Schmoller, 'Das Wesen der Arbeitsteilung und der socialen Klassenbildung', *Jahrbuch für Gesetzgebung, Verwaltung und Volkswirtschaft*, Vol. 14, No. 1, 1890, pp. 45–105; K. Bücher, 'Arbeitsgliederung und soziale Klassenbildung', in *Die Entstehung der Volkswirtschaft*, Tübingen, Laupp (1893). For a brief discussion in English see R. Dahrendorf, *Essays in the Theory of Society*, Stanford, University Press; London, Routledge (1968), pp. 160–3.

[29] E. Durkheim, *The Division of Labor in Society*, Glencoe, Free Press (1964), p. 46, note 11.

[30] G. Simmel, *Über soziale Differenzierung*, p. 19. My emphasis.

[31] *Ibid.*, p. 20.

[32] *Ibid.*, p. 44.

[33] *Ibid.*, p. 71.

[34] *Ibid.*, p. 85.

[35] Chapter Five on 'The Intersection of Social Spheres' and Chapter Six on 'Differentiation and the Principle of Energy Saving' are now translated in P. Lawrence, *Georg Simmel: Sociologist and European*, Sunbury, Nelson (1976), pp. 95–138. I have occasionally amended the translation but page references to these two chapters refer to the more accessible translation.

[36] *Ibid.*, pp. 100–1.

[37] *Ibid.*, p. 102.

[38] *Ibid.*, p. 108.

[39] *Ibid.*, p. 117.

[40] *Ibid.*, p. 130.

[41] *Ibid.*, p. 136.

[42] The comment is from a review of Simmel's book on the philosophy of history. See F. Meinecke, 'Die Probleme der Geschichtsphilosophie', *Historische Zeitschrift*, Vol. 72, p. 71.

[43] See O. Klose, *et al.* (editors), *Ferdinand Tönnies, Friedrich Paulsen, Briefwechsel, 1876–1908*, Kiel, Hirt (1961), p. 290.

[44]   F. Tönnies, 'Simmel, G., Uber soziale Differenzierung', *Jahrbücher für Nationalökonomie und Statistik*, Vol. 56, 1891, pp. 269–77, esp. p. 277.

[45]   B. Nedelmann, 'Strukturprinzipien der soziologischen Denkweise Georg Simmels', *Kölner Zeitschrift für Soziologie*, Vol. 32, 1980, pp. 559–573, esp. p. 563.

[46]   G. Schmoller, 'Simmels Philosophie des Geldes', *Jahrbuch für Gesetzgebung, Verwaltung und Volkswirtschaft*, Vol. 25, No. 3, 1901.

[47]   See the letters of 22.6.1895 and 13.12.1899 to Bouglé in W. Gephart, 'Verloren und gefundene Briefe Georg Simmels an Célestin Bouglé, Eugen Diederichs, Gabriel Tarde, in H. J. Dahme and O. Rammstedt (editors), *Die Aktualität Georg Simmels*, Frankfurt, Suhrkamp (1984).

[48]   See the following reviews: K. Joel, 'Eine Zeitphilosophie', *Neue deutsche Rundschau*, Vol. 12, 1901, pp. 812–26; G. H. Mead, 'Philosophie des Geldes', *Journal of Political Economy*, Vol. 9, 1901, pp. 616–19; S. P. Altmann, 'Simmel's Philosophy of Money', *American Journal of Sociology*, Vol. 9, 1904, pp. 46–68; F. Eulenburg, 'Georg Simmel. Philosophie des Geldes', *Deutsche Literaturzeitung*, 27.7.1901, columns 1904–8.

[49]   G. Schmoller, 'Simmels Philosophie des Geldes', *loc. cit.* p. 16.

[50]   E. Durkheim, 'Philosophie des Geldes', *L'Année Sociologique*, Vol. 5, 1900–1, pp. 140–5.

[51]   R. Goldscheid, 'Jahresbericht über Erscheinungen der Soziologie in den Jahren 1890–1904', *Archiv für systematische Philosophie*, Vol. 10, 1904, pp. 397–8.

[52]   *Ibid.*, p. 411.

[53]   B. H. Meyer, 'Philosophie des Geldes', *American Journal of Sociology*, Vol. 6, 1901, p. 852.

[54]   G. Simmel, 'Preface' to G. Simmel, *The Philosophy of Money* (Translated T. Bottomore and D. Frisby), London/Boston, Routledge (1978), pp. 53–6.

[55]   *Ibid.*, p. 56.

[56]   On Simmel's economic theory see my introduction to G. Simmel, *The Philosophy of Money*. Also A. Cavalli, 'Political Economy and Theory of Value in the *Philosophy of Money*', Paper presented at 10th World Congress of Sociology, Mexico City 1982; B. Accarino, *La Democrazia Insicura*, Naples, Guida Editori (1982), Ch. 3.

[57]   G. Simmel, *The Philosophy of Money*, p. 101.

[58]   *Ibid.*, p. 175.

[59]   *Ibid.*, pp. 178–9.

[60]   S. Kracauer, 'Georg Simmel', *Logos*, Vol. 9, 1920, p. 330.

[61]   G. Simmel, *The Philosophy of Money*, p. 377.

[62]   *Ibid.*, p. 385.

[63]   See my introduction to G. Simmel, *The Philosophy of Money*.

[64]   G. Simmel, *The Philosophy of Money*, p. 431.

[65]   *Ibid.*, p. 459.

[66]   G. Simmel, 'The Concept and Tragedy of Culture', in G. Simmel, *The Conflict in Modern Culture and Other Essays*, New York, Teachers College Press (1968), pp. 27–46.

[67]   M. Frischeisen-Köhler, 'Georg Simmel', *Kantstudien*, Vol. 24, 1920, p. 20.

[68]   Translated in K. H. Wolff (editor), *The Sociology of Georg Simmel*, New York, Free Press (1950), p. xxvi.

[69]   *Ibid.*, p. xxvi.

[70]   Letter to C. Bouglé 12.11.1896 in H. J. Dahme and O. Rammstedt (editors), *Die Aktualität Georg Simmels*.

[71]   G. Simmel, 'The Problem of Sociology', *Annals of the American Academy of Political and Social Science*, Vol. 6, 1895, pp. 61–2.

[72]   L. von Wiese, 'Neuere soziologische Literatur', Archiv für Sozialwissenschaft und Sozialpolitik, Vol. 31, 1910, esp. pp. 897ff. See also L. A. Coser (editor), *Georg Simmel*, Englewood Cliffs, N.J., Prentice-Hall (1965), pp. 53–7.

[73]   T. Masaryk, 'Simmels Soziologie', *Zeitschrift für Sozialwissenschaft*, Vol. 12, 1909, pp. 600–7, esp. p. 601.

[74]   D. Koigen, 'Soziologische Theorien', *Archiv für Sozialwissenschaft und Sozialpolitik*, Vol. 31, 1910, pp. 908–24, esp. p. 924.

[75]   A. Vierkandt, 'Literaturbericht zur Kultur-und Gesellschaftslehre für die Jahre 1907 und 1908', *Archiv für die gesamte Psychologie*, Vol. 17, 1910, pp. 57–138, esp. pp. 61f.

[76]   Quoted in K. H. Wolff, *The Sociology of Georg Simmel*, p. xxxiii.

[77]   D. Levine, 'Introduction' to Georg Simmel, *On Individuality and Social Forms*, Chicago, University of Chicago Press, pp. xxxif.

[78]   R. Mayntz, 'Simmel, Georg', *International Encyclopaedia of Social Science*, Vol. 14, New York, Macmillan & Free Press (1968), pp. 251–8, esp. p. 256f.

[79]   *Ibid.*, p. 256.

[80]   *Ibid.*, p. 257.

[81]   B. Nedelmann, 'Strukturprinzipien der soziologischen Denkweise Georg Simmels', *loc. cit.* pp. 559–73, esp. pp. 562f.

[82]   Translated in K. H. Wolff (editor), *Essays on Sociology, Philosophy and Aesthetics by Georg Simmel, et al.*, pp. 337–356.

[83]   G. Simmel, *Soziologie*, 5th edition, Berlin, Duncker und Humblot (1968), p. 570.

[84]   'How is Society Possible?', in K. H. Wolff (editor), *Essays on Sociology, Philosophy and Aesthetics by Georg Simmel, et al.*, p. 340.

[85]   U. Gerhardt, *Rollenanalyse als kritische Soziologie*, Neuwied and Berlin, Luchterhand (1971), pp. 27–40.

[86]   'How is Society Possible?', pp. 350–1.

[87]   *Ibid.*, pp. 352–3.

[88]   U. Gerhardt, *Rollenanalyse als kritische Soziologie*, p. 40.

[89]   J. O'Neill, 'How is Society Possible?', in his *Sociology as a Skin Trade*, London, Heinemann (1972), pp. 167–76.

[90]   'Sociability', trans. E. C. Hughes in Georg Simmel, *On Individuality and Social Forms*, pp. 127–40. The translation has been slightly amended here and below.

[91]   D. Levine, 'Simmel at a Distance', *Sociological Focus*, Vol. 10, 1, 1977, p. 16.

[92]   G. Simmel, 'The Stranger' in G. Simmel, *On Individuality and Social Forms*, p. 143.

[93]   G. Simmel, 'The Metropolis and Mental Life' in G. Simmel, *On Individuality and Social Forms*, p. 318.

[94]   Quoted in D. Frisby, *Sociological Impressionism*, p. 8.

5

A New Reception

Any attempt to suggest that a new look at Simmel's sociological work and its reception is called for must re-examine Simmel's social theory in relation to his contemporaries as well as in relation to more recent developments in sociology. A reassessment of Simmel's work in the light of that of his contemporaries and near-contemporaries might also have to challenge the Holy Trinity of Marx, Weber and Durkheim that dominates so many discussions of classical sociology. Though Simmel himself was also preoccupied with the figure three (and not merely in his discussion of triads), we need not remain captivated by only three giants and a whole range of pygmies. Is it not time that the balance between the two groups be questioned? In what follows, some brief indications of possible lines of reassessment are sketched out in the hope that this may take place in the future.

5.1 SIMMEL AND HIS CONTEMPORARIES

In his review of Simmel's *The Philosophy of Money* in 1901, Franz Eulenburg starts out by saying that 'if one is to speak of contemporary German social philosophy, then only two names come seriously into question – Tönnies and Simmel'. [1] And, of the two, Eulenburg is more impressed by Simmel who 'approaches problems with dialectical refinement, with infinite perspicacity and sagacity ... he is a much more conscious, superior artist that Tönnies', more in touch with and responsive to 'fashionable currents' than Tönnies. And with regard to Simmel's *The Philosophy of Money*, the reviewer finds that in this work the author cannot be criticized, as was the case for his earlier works, for their 'being too lacking in material content', with 'too few positive results'. Yet retrospectively we can see some connections between that work and Tönnies's earlier arguments in *Gemeinschaft und Gesellschaft* and, on rationality, Tönnies's earlier article on 'Historicism and Rationalism'. Tönnies himself had already reviewed critically two of Simmel's early works whilst, in turn, Simmel had criticised Tönnies's attack on Nietzsche in his *The Nietzsche Cult* (1897) – the only work by one of Simmel's German sociological contemporaries that he reviewed. For his part Tönnies modified his earlier more negative judgement of Simmel's social theory with the appearance of the latter's article 'The Self-Preservation of the Social Group' (1898) uopn which Tönnies declared that 'he has very much improved himself ... I should indeed be jealous. For much of that which he presents I myself have also outlined or similarly thought out'. [2]

Yet despite Simmel's own silence on his contemporary sociologists in Germany, some of his students were less inhibited in recognizing his significance for them. Again with reference to *The Philosophy of Money* and 'Simmel's importance for sociology', Georg Lukács declared that 'a sociology of culture, such as has been undertaken by Max Weber, Troeltsch, Sombart and others – however much they might all wish to distance themselves from him methodologically – has surely only been made possible on the foundation created by him'. [3] Earlier in 1915, Lukács had already singled out two works decisive for 'the clarification of the sociology of culture': Tönnies's *Gemeinschaft und Gesellschaft* and Simmel's *The Philosophy of Money*. [4]

Occasionally, Simmel's contemporaries compared his work with sociological developments beyond the German frontiers. As we have seen, Simmel's early mentor Gustav Schmoller compared his *The Philosophy of Money* with Durkheim's *Division of Labour in Society*, even though a more apposite comparison might be with Simmel's *On Social Differentiation*. And here, at first sight, the relationship seems to be very much a one-way one. Durkheim sometimes published Simmel's work in *L'Année Sociologique* and wrote several critiques of Simmel's sociological enterprise whereas Simmel never wrote on Durkheim. Further, Durkheim appears to have read Simmel's early writings at least and occasionally cited them in his own works. From the mid-1890s onwards this is possibly due to the mediating influence of one of his collaborators Celestin Bouglé who was in correspondence with Simmel and who even prefaced one of his own works by referring to his two sources of inspiration – Simmel and Durkheim. [5] Yet this did not lead, so far as is known, to any direct correspondence between Durkheim and Simmel. Indeed, in his correspondence with Bouglé, Simmel never once mentions Durkheim.

But as well as reviewing *The Philosophy of Money*, Durkheim, for his part, not only published Simmel's 'Self-Preservation of Social Groups' in his *L'Année Sociologique* but also sharply criticized Simmel's sociological project as a whole. This is outlined in his article 'Sociology and its Scientific Field' (1900). [6] There, Durkheim concedes that although Simmel had made 'a notable, almost violent, effort to trace the limits of the subject matter of sociology', his restriction of sociology to the study of forms of sociation 'serves merely to keep it tied to metaphysical ideology when it actually shows an irresistible need to emancipate itself from this sphere'. Durkheim is even more critical of Simmel's separation of form and content on the grounds that to assert that what is distinctly social lies merely in forms of sociation reduces the social group to

> a sort of empty trivial cast that can indifferently receive any kind of material whatever! The claim is that there are arrangements which are encountered everywhere, whatever the nature of the ends attained. But clearly, all these ends, despite their divergences, have characteristics in common. Why should only these common characteristics, and not the specific ones, have social value? [7]

In other words, Durkheim is saying that social forms cannot be separated out from the concrete specificity of their content (including the ends or goals of human sociation).

Indeed, Durkheim goes on to criticize the whole notion of form and content as crucial abstractions since 'the most general aspect of social life is not . . . either content or form . . . There are not two different kinds of reality which, though intimately connected, are distinct and separable; what we have instead are facts of the same nature, examined at different levels of generality'. To some extent, of course, Durkheim is here merely counterposing his own conception of sociology as the study of social facts. In this respect, Simmel's version of sociology omits any criteria for the degree of generality of analysis with the result that 'there is no rule for deciding in an impersonal manner where the circle of sociological facts begins and where it ends'. But Durkheim's most telling criticisms of Simmel's conception of sociology echo those that have often been made of his social theory. Durkheim concedes that though one may applaud Simmel's 'subtlety and ingenuity', it is

> impossible to trace the main divisions of our science as he understands it in an objective manner. No connection can be discovered among the questions to which he draws the attention of sociologists; they are topics of meditation that have no relation to an integral scientific system. In addition, Simmel's proofs generally consist only of explanations by example; some facts, borrowed from the most disparate fields, are cited but they are not preceded by critical analysis, and they offer us no idea of how to assess their value. [8]

If sociology is to go beyond 'philosophical variations on certain aspects of social life' – which is how Durkheim views Simmel's sociological work – then specific sociological problems must be formulated 'in a way that permits us to draw a logical solution'. This Durkheim finds wanting in Simmel's sociological reflections. In fairness to Simmel, however, the whole dimension of social interaction so crucial to his conception of sociology, is totally ignored by Durkheim.

With regard to Simmel's major sociological works, his *On Social Differentiation* receives merely a passing mention in Durkheim's *Division of Labour in Society*, whereas today their comparison might warrant further consideration. Durkheim does deal more fully with Simmel's next major sociological work *The Philosophy of Money*. Whilst one might imagine it to be 'of special interest to economic sociology', in fact it deals with issues which 'endlessly overflow this type of framework', so much so that 'there is scarcely a sociological problem that is not touched upon'. Durkheim not merely criticizes the first part of the book's economic presuppositions but also complains that its synthetic second part remains unclear since 'almost all these three hundred pages defy analysis; too many different issues are examined in turn, and it is not always easy to make out the thread that binds them into a unified whole'. Further,

> One will find in this work a number of ingenious ideas, pungent views, curious or even at times surprising comparisons, and a certain number of historical and ethno-

graphic facts, unfortunately imprecise and unwarranted as reported. The reading of the book, though laborious, is interesting and in places suggestive. But the objective value of the views that are proposed to us is not commensurate with their ingenuity. [9]

In short, the work is replete with 'illegitimate speculation' and is ultimately 'a treatise on social philosophy'.

This damning judgement of perhaps Simmel's most systematic work was not shared by Max Weber who not only studied *The Philosophy of Money* in detail prior to his first draft of the original articles that form the basis for his *Protestant Ethic and the Spirit of Capitalism*, but who praised Simmel's 'brilliant analysis' of the spirit of capitalism that it contained. Indeed, Weber argued that almost every one of Simmel's works 'abounds in important theoretical ideas and the most subtle observations'. It has in fact been suggested that 'in Simmel's *The Philosophy of Money* Weber found those methods outlined and in part carried out which he made use of in his later analysis of capitalism, *The Protestant Ethic and the Spirit of Capitalism*. He found a mode of procedure described there . . . which did not remain content with the derivation and application of mere ideal types but rather extended them into embodiments of whole complexes of meaning which grasped the distinctiveness of levels of historical development'. [10] Similarly, Levine suggests that in the same work Weber found 'a provocative interpretation of the all-pervasive effects of rationalisation in modern society and culture'. [11] Nonetheless, Weber himself argued that in Simmel's work 'the money economy and capitalism are too closely identified to the detriment of his concrete analysis', such that Simmel tends 'to move from a discussion of the money economy to the effects of capitalism without realising that there is a distinction between the two'. [12] This does not mean that Weber was not impressed by Simmel's analysis of the nature of economic rationality and in particular of means–ends rationality that found its way into Weber's own conception of purposive social action. The rationalization and functionalization of social relationships that Simmel portrays in the context of a money economy may also have influenced Weber's subsequent pessimistic philosophy of history.

But there are other dimensions of Simmel's writings that may have been important for the development of Weber's own sociological work. Though critical of Simmel's methodological and substantive works, Weber maintained that 'Simmel, even when he is on the wrong path, fully deserves his reputation as one of the foremost of thinkers, a first-rate stimulator of academic youth and academic colleagues'. [13] Weber intended to resolve his own 'contradictory judgements' of Simmel's work in 'a critique of Simmel's scientific style in his two major sociological writings': *The Philosophy of Money* and *Sociology*. Sadly, this critique was never completed but Weber did indicate some reasons why so many 'specialists' should find his work so irritating. Aside from Simmel's frequent use of diverse examples and dubious, 'playful' analogies to illustrate his sociological work, what is decisive is that 'where the specialist is dealing with questions of "facticity", empirical questions, Simmel has turned to look at the meaning which we can obtain from the phenomenon'. Indeed, even where Simmel is dealing with 'technical substantive questions' his 'ultimate *interests* are directed to metaphysical problems, to the "*meaning*" of life'. Further, it is likely that Weber would have reiterated the criticisms made earlier by Spann on the ultimately psychological grounding of society and sociology. And Weber was no less happy with Simmel's grounding of sociology in '"interactions" amongst individuals', largely because 'this concept of "interaction" extended so far that only with the greatest artificiality will one be able to conceptualise a pure "one-way" influence, i.e., an instance of one man being influenced by another where there is *not* some element of "interaction"'.

Yet despite these criticisms, it is true that Weber's own methodological standpoint, especially on *Verstehen*, owes something at least to Simmel's plea for the significance of interpretation in the second edition of his *Problems of the Philosophy of History* (1905). However, Weber notes somewhat cryptically in his *Economy and Society* that this work 'departs from Simmel's method . . . in drawing a sharp distinction between subjectively intended and objectively valid "meanings"; two different things which Simmel not only fails to distinguish but often deliberately treats as belonging together'. [14]

Nonetheless, the concept of the intentionality of social action as outlined by Simmel is not too far removed from Weber's notion of rational action. After discussing typification and idealization in Simmel's role theory – largely in the context of Simmel's essay 'How is Society Possible?' – Uta Gerhardt argues that 'it hardly requires additional evidence in order to make explicit the parallels between this determination of the *intentionality* of social action by Simmel and the conception of *rational* action by Weber', even though Weber 'sees in typification more a scientific method than a basic process of social interaction'. [15]

Such brief indications of possible parallels and divergences between the basic sociological concepts of Simmel and Weber should suggest the need for a new look at the relationship between the sociological projects of these two major social theorists.

5.2 SIMMEL AND MARXISM

At first glance, Simmel's relationship to Marxism appears a very tenuous one. Despite his early espousal of some aspects of a basically reformist socialism in the early 1890s, there is little evidence that this stimulated an interest in Marxism. And even when some dimensions of Marxism appear in his works, as in his early rejection of historical materialism or his critique of the labour theory of value in *The Philosophy of Money*, his response is largely critical. Even in the remarkable section of his study of money on the consequences of the division of labour, which some have seen as anticipating the discovery of Marx's *Paris Manuscripts*, the actual context is a theory of cultural alienation that is far removed from Marx's work. But if all this is true, how was it possible for writers like Goldscheid to suggest that *The Philosophy of Money* can be compared in some respects to parts of Marx's *Capital*? How was it possible for Georg Lukács to maintain that when his study of Marx commenced around 1908 'it was Marx the "socialist" that attracted me – and I saw him through spectacles tinged by Simmel and Max Weber' or that 'a properly scholarly use of my knowledge of Marx was greatly influenced by the philosophy and sociology of Simmel . . . not the least of reasons being that this approach brought me closer to Marx, though in a distorted way'? [16] Similarly, why did Walter Benjamin, the most original member of the Frankfurt School, say that after reading Simmel's *Philosophy of Money* he was 'struck by the critique of Marx's theory of value' and plead with Adorno that he 'recognise the cultural bolshevism in him'? [17]

This paradox cannot be resolved by recourse to Simmel's own intellectual development since we know so little of his early years. Even the extent to which Simmel studied some of Marx's works or gained a knowledge of them at second hand from his contemporaries has hardly been researched. The paradox in part hinges upon what we understand by Marxism and the reception of Marx's works within the Second International. Instructive is the statement made by Lukács – one of Simmel's favourite students and one clearly influenced by his work – who many years later confessed that he did not regret that 'I took my first lessons in social science from Simmel and Max Weber and not from Kautsky. I don't know whether one cannot even say today that this was a fortunate circumstance for my own development.' [18] Perhaps what attracted students such as Lukács to Simmel's work was not merely the subtlety and sensitivity of many of his writings on modern culture, and the dialectical turn in his mode of presentation, but also an apparently inspired attempt to relate culture to society in a manner that did not get locked into a restrictive base–superstructure dialectic so typical of the period.

Certainly the traces of Simmel's work in the writings of the young Lukács are only too apparent, especially in his work on the development of modern drama published in 1911. There, Lukács's emphasis upon the rationalization and objectification of modern culture draws heavily upon Simmel's analysis in *The Philosophy of Money*. Perhaps more surprising is the continuation of Simmel's influence after Lukács came to espouse Marxism in 1918. Even in his most important work of this period, *History and Class Consciousness* (1923), traces of Simmel's theory of alienation are still apparent. So too is the concept of reification – which we now associate most closely with Lukács – even though after Marx (who only used the concept itself once at the end of the third volume of *Capital*) its most explicit usage in a social context is to be found in Simmel's *Philosophy of Money*. Of course, Lukács's discussion of alienation (at least from around 1908 onwards) and reification is located in the context of a critique of bourgeois culture in a capitalist society and (after 1918) the renewal of a more dialectical Marxism – aims that are somewhat removed from those of Simmel's attempt to 'construct a new storey beneath historical materialism'. [19]

Nonetheless, Simmel facilitated Lukács's acquaintance with another of his favourite students, Ernst Bloch, who was also to become one of the central figures in western Marxism. His early major work *The Spirit of Utopia* (1918) contains a passage assessing Simmel's work and pointing to its ambiguity:

> Simmel has the finest mind among all his contemporaries. But beyond this, he is wholly empty and aimless, desiring everything except the truth. He is a collector of standpoints which he assembles all around truth without ever wanting or being able to possess it. [On the other hand,] Simmel has given to thought nuances and a heightened temperature which, if only taken out of the hands of a man born without a hard core, can indeed be of great service to philosophy. [20]

Many years later – and after Bloch had also sought to master the essay style of Simmel, amongst others – he reported with reference to Simmel's conception of society, that Simmel 'the impressionist philosopher . . . who must have known it to be true, once said that there are only fifteen people in the world but these fifteen move about so quickly that we believe there to be more'.

Even amongst those Marxists who were not Simmel's students it is possible to trace a positive response to his work. This is true, for instance, of the Austro-Marxist Max Adler. Aside from some favourable remarks on Simmel in his early contribution to the methodological dispute in the social sciences, Adler published a brief volume in praise of Simmel's work, *Simmel's Significance for Intellectual History* in 1919 which even today remains one of the better, brief assessments of Simmel's work as a whole. Later Adler came to criticize Simmel's foundation of sociology as being rooted in psychological presuppositions. In this respect he took up a criticism that had so often been voiced some decades earlier. [21]

Of greater contemporary significance is the relationship between Simmel's sociological and philosophical writings and the later work of Walter Benjamin. Benjamin said of Simmel's work that its

> typical dialectic stands in the service of a philosophy of life and is concerned with a psychological impressionism which, antithetical to systematisation, is orientated towards the essential knowledge of individual intellectual phenomena . . . Georg Simmel's philosophy already signifies a transition from strict academic philosophy towards a poetic or essayistic orientation. [22]

This somewhat negative judgement did not prevent Benjamin making considerable use of Simmel's work in his prehistory of modernity – the 'Arcades Project' – upon which he was engaged for over a decade. Indeed in the recently published notes to that project – of which only some sections on Charles Baudelaire have been published in English – Simmel's work is cited on many occasions. In fact, Simmel is the only sociologist whose writings are referenced. [23] What this suggests is that Benjamin found in Simmel's work the elements for a sociology of modernity that Simmel himself never systematically outlined. And on one occasion at least this interest in Simmel's work brought him into conflict with a younger member of the Frankfurt School – Theodor Adorno – who always maintained a highly ambiguous attitude towards Simmel's sociology and philosophy, quite possibly because its often essayistic form was rather too close to that of Adorno's.

This inadequate sketch of Simmel's connections with unorthodox strands of western Marxism suggests that the whole relationship with Marxism should be reopened. It is possible, for instance, that Simmel's analysis of money relations in *The Philosophy of Money*, if interpreted as an account of the world of commodities, might form a foundation for a Marxist phenomenology of experience in a capitalist money economy. And certainly Simmel's critical analysis of the apparent trivia of such a world – however much transposed into eternal forms – begins to fill a gap in more orthodox Marxist accounts of everyday life in a capitalist economy.

5.3 SIMMEL AND MODERN SOCIOLOGY

Insofar as much modern sociology has been dominated by sociological traditions in the United States, it is instructive to commence with Simmel's early reception there. Despite the fact that Albion Small – the key figure in the early Chicago School and founder of the *American Journal of Sociology* – translated many of Simmel's works for his journal around the turn of the century (which cannot be said of any other German sociologist of his time), Small probably became less impressed with Simmel's conception of sociology. In his review of Simmel's *Sociology*, Small lamented that 'Simmel restricts the content of the term "sociology" to a limit which no other first-rate sociologist in Europe, with the possible exception of Professor Tönnies, accepts . . . To Simmel sociology is merely the analysis of the forms of human groupings; it is a sort of social morphology, or crystallography. It is thus a mere fragment of the sociology which Americans have in mind when they use the term.' [24] Yet Small was not the only member of the early Chicago School to be interested in Simmel's work. Mead reviewed his *Philosophy of Money* favourably, whilst Robert Park had actually studied under Simmel in Berlin in 1899–1900 – in fact 'his only formal instruction in sociology'. As Levine has shown, Park stimulated work in the post-First World War period on themes drawn from Simmel's work such as social distance, the stranger and the metropolis. [25] Indeed, the early work of the Chicago School is perhaps the single concrete instance of the interaction between Simmel's sociology and empirical social research in the period prior to the Second World War.

Meanwhile, a potential aid to a broad reception of Simmel's

sociology in the United States was provided by Spykman's *The Social Theory of Georg Simmel* (1925) which at least offered some conception of his work as a whole. More influential, however, was Abel's largely negative treatment of Simmel as a formal sociologist in his *Systematic Sociology in Germany* (1926). Of even greater significance a decade later was the publication of Talcott Parsons's *The Structure of Social Action* (1937) which only in passing pointed to the untenability of Simmel's sociological programme – even though Parsons had prepared a chapter on Simmel's work which was not included in the published version. What is significant here is that Parsons's work influenced generations of American sociologists and gave them a cognitive map of the development of sociology (and especially a voluntaristic theory of social action) which excluded Simmel's contribution. [26] In contrast, another major figure in American sociology, Robert Merton, did utilize Simmel's work in relation to his own development, for instance, of role and reference-group theory.

But any conception of Simmel's work as a whole remained absent from American sociological discourse. Even the influence of the German emigration upon American sociology did not always lead to a renewal of interest in Simmel's sociology. The phenomenological tradition, especially that part of it centred around its institutional base the New School for Social Research and around Alfred Schutz, remained largely and remarkably silent on Simmel's sociology and either took up the work of Max Weber or that of less accessible figures such as Max Scheler. Indeed, it was Weber's work, as responded to by such figures as Honigsheim, Gerth or later Bendix (though Bendix did translate one of Simmel's important essays), that came to the fore rather than that of Simmel. The relatively brief emigration of members of the Frankfurt School, perhaps understandably given their hostile or, at most, ambiguous attitude, was also not conducive to the renewal of interest in Simmel's work. Only in the nineteen-fifties did Lewis Coser and, especially, Kurt Wolff make an impact upon the relative neglect of Simmel's work with significant translations of his work (Wolff's *The Sociology of Georg Simmel* (1950) and *Essays on Sociology, Philosophy and Aesthetics* (1959)) or monographs (Coser's *The Functions of Social Conflict* (1956)) that relied for their inspiration upon Simmel's sociology. Aside from the early work by Spykman, the collections assembled by these two writers represented the first attempt to take up Simmel's work as a whole.

Succeeding decades have seen the growth of empirical research that takes as its starting point themes from Simmel's sociology – on small group interaction, dyads and triads, the stranger, secret societies, conflict theory, exchange theory, interpersonal relations, and so on. [27] Valuable though much of this work may have been in the area of empirical sociology, it has perhaps had the effect of confirming a common response to major sociological traditions, namely, of conceiving them as quarries for fruitful testable hypotheses rather than as broader theories of society. Of course, it might be justifiably objected that Simmel's theory of society – and some conception of his sociological project as a coherent whole – has always been hard to extract from his works, even for those schooled in the traditions of German sociology from which he emerged. Further, Simmel himself was never too happy with his own identification merely as a sociologist. Hence, in this respect, Simmel's work perhaps deliberately provides few consolations for the specialist or the professional sociologist. The most striking sociological insights often come in those of his essays that are no longer classified as sociological at all.

Any renewal of interest in Simmel's social theory must break the bounds of professional sociology in order to grasp both the insights into social experience that cannot be easily compartmentalized and the theory of society that pervades Simmel's work. Only in this way can we see the continuity of themes such as social differentiation and the paradox and then tragedy of culture that span a lifetime's work. A social theorist who is fascinated by social processes sees them operating in the most unlikely places. As an intellectual wanderer he was at home everywhere, not merely in the study of the professional sociologist. His 'finely-spun net' could encompass almost any area of social life. But with his capacity for being everywhere, he was claimed by no one. With his unrivalled analysis and knowledge of the money economy, Simmel saw his future influence in this way:

> I know that I shall die without spiritual heirs (and that is good). The estate I leave is like cash distributed among many heirs, each of whom puts his share to use in some trade that is compatible with *his* nature but which can no longer be recognised as coming from that estate.

Is it not time to challenge Simmel's own judgement on the fate of his work?

NOTES AND REFERENCES

[1] F. Eulenburg, 'Georg Simmel, Philosophie des Geldes', *Deutsche Literaturzeitung*, 27.7.1901, no. 30, columns 1904–8.

[2] See letter of 25.10.1898 in O. Klose *et al.* (editors), *F. Tönnies – Friedrich Paulsen Briefwechsel 1876–1908*, Kiel, Hirt (1961), pp. 339–40.

[3] G. Lukács, 'Georg Simmel', *Pester Lloyd*, 2 October 1918, reprinted in K. Gassen and M. Landmann (editors), *Buch des Dankes an Georg Simmel*, Berlin, Duncker and Humblot (1958) p. 175.

[4] G. Lukács, 'Zum Wesen und zur Methode der Kultursoziologie', *Archiv für Sozialwissenschaft und Sozialpolitik*, Vol. 39, 1915, p. 216.

[5] C. Bouglé, *Les idées égalitaires. Etude sociologique*, Paris: Alcan (1899), esp. p. 20. On the relationship between Simmel and other key figures see also W. Gephart, 'Soziologie im Aufbruch. Zur Wechselwirkung von Durkheim, Schäffle, Tönnies und Simmel', *Kölner Zeitschrift für Soziologie*, Vol. 34, 1982, pp. 1–25.

[6] E. Durkheim, 'Sociology and its Scientific Field', in K. H. Wolff (editor), *Essays on Sociology and Philosophy by Emile Durkheim et al.*, New York: Harper & Row (1964), pp. 354–75.

[7] *Ibid.*, p. 357.

[8] *Ibid.*, p. 359.

[9] E. Durkheim, 'Georg Simmel. Philosophie des Geldes', in Y. Nandan (editor), *Emile Durkheim: Contributions to L'Année Sociologique*, New York/London: Free Press/Collier Macmillan (1980), p. 97.

[10] P Schnabel, 'Georg Simmel', in D. Käsler (editor), *Klassiker des soziologischen Denkens*, Vol. 1, Munich, 1976, pp. 288–9.

[11] D. Levine, 'Introduction', *Georg Simmel. On Individuality and Social Forms*, Chicago, University of Chicago Press, p. xlv.

[12] M. Weber, *The Protestant Ethic and the Spirit of Capitalism* (translator T. Parsons), London, Allen & Unwin (1930), pp. 185 and 193.

[13] M. Weber, 'Georg Simmel as Sociologist', *Social Research*, Vol. 39, 1972, p. 158f.

[14] M. Weber, *Economy and Society* (editors G. Roth and C. Wittich), Berkeley/Los Angeles/London, University of California Press (1978), p. 4.

[15]   U. Gerhardt, *Rollenanalyse als kritische Soziologie*, Neuwied and Berlin, Luchterhand (1971), p. 39, n. 30.

[16]   See G. Lukács, *History and Class Consciousness* (trans. R. Livingstone), London, Merlin 1971, p. ix, and F. Tökei, 'Lukács and Hungarian Culture', *New Hungarian Quarterly*, Vol. 13, no. 47, 1972, p. 110 respectively.

[17]   W. Benjamin, *Briefe* (editors G. Scholem and T. W. Adorno), Vol. 2, Frankfurt, Suhrkamp (1966), pp. 824f.

[18]   T. Pinkus (editor), *Conversations with Lukács*, London, Merlin, 1974, p. 100.

[19]   For a fuller discussion see my Introduction to G. Simmel, *The Philosophy of Money* (Translated T. Bottomore and D. Frisby), London/Boston, Routledge (1978), and my *The Alienated Mind*, London, Heinemann (1983), ch. 3.

[20]   E. Bloch, *Geist der Utopie*, Munich 1918, pp. 246–7.

[21]   See M. Adler, *Simmels Bedeutung für die Geistesgeschichte*, and M. Adler 'Soziologie und Erkenntniskritik', *Jahrbuch für Soziologie*, Vol. 1, 1925, esp. pp. 30f.

[22]   W. Benjamin, *Gesammelte Schriften: Werkausgabe*, Frankfurt, Suhrkamp 1980, Vol. 2.2, p. 810.

[23]   See W. Benjamin, *Gesammelte Schriften*, Vol. 5, Frankfurt, Suhrkamp (1980). For Simmel's influence on Benjamin see my *Fragments of Modernity: Georg Simmel, Siegfried Kracauer, Walter Benjamin*, London, Heinemann (1985) (forthcoming).

[24]   A. W. Small, 'Soziologie', *American Journal of Sociology*, Vol. 14, 1908–09, p. 544.

[25]   See D. Levine, 'Introduction' to *Georg Simmel on Individuality and Social Forms*, p. liv.

[26]   See D. Levine, *Simmel and Parsons*, New York, Arno Press (1980).

[27]   For a full discussion of Simmel in American sociology see D. N. Levine, *et al.*, 'Simmel's Influence on American Sociology', in H. Böhringer and K. Gründer (editors), *Ästhetik und Sociologie um die Jahrhundertwende: Georg Simmel*, Frankfurt, Kolosterman (1978), pp. 175–228.

Bibliography

SIMMEL'S MAJOR WORKS

The original works directly relevant to sociology are listed below. Since 1989 a twentyfour volume critical edition of Simmel's works has been in progress under the general editorship of Otthein Rammstedt and published by Suhrkamp Verlag, Frankfurt as the Georg Simmel *Gesamtausgabe*. Reference to this edition are given as GA with the volume number.

(Alongside literally hundreds of essays, there are other volumes on philosophy, aesthetics and metaphysics which are not cited below.)

1890   *Über sociale Differenzierung. Soziologische und psychologische Untersuchungen.* Leipzig: Duncker & Humblot. (GA2)

1892   *Die Probleme der Geschichtsphilosophie. Eine erkenntisffieoretische Studie.* Leipzig: Duncker & Humblot. (GA2)
        (Second fully revised edition 1905 and third revised edition 1907.) (GA9)

1892–93 *Einleitung in die Moralwissenschaft. Eine Kritik der ethischen Grundbegriffe.* Berlin: Hertz. 2 vols. (GA3, 4)

1900   *Philosophie des Geldes.* Leipzig: Duncker & Humblot, (Second enlarged edition 1907.) (GA6)

1908   *Soziologie: Untersuchungen über die Formen der Vergesellschaftung.* Leipzig: Duncker & Humblot. (GA11)

1911   *Philosophische Kultur. Gesammelte Essais.* Leipzig: Klinkhardt. (GA14)

1917   *Grundfragen der Soziolozie (Individuum und Gesellschaft).* Berlin/Leipzig: Goschen. (GA16)

(For the most comprehensive bibliography of Simmel's German works and translations [to 1958] see K. Gassen, 'Georg-Simmel-Bibliographie' in K. Gassen & M. Landmann (eds), *Buch des Dankes an Georg Simmel*. Berlin: Duncker & Humblot, 1958, pp. 309–65.)

ENGLISH TRANSLATIONS

1950   *The Sociology of Georg Simmel*. Translated with an introduction by Kurt H. Wolff, Glencoe, Ill.: Free Press.

1955   *Conflict and The Web of Group Affiliations*. Translated by Kurt H. Wolff and R. Bendix, with a foreword by Everett C. Hughes, Glencoe, Ill.: Free Press.

1958   *Essays on Sociology. Philosophy and Aesthetics by Georg Simmel et al.* Edited by K.H. Wolff, Columbus, Ohio: Ohio State University Press.

1959   *Sociology of Religion*. Translated by C. Rosenthal with an introduction by F. Gross, New York: Philosophical Library.

1968   *The Conflict in Modern Culture and Other Essays*. Translated with an introduction by K.P. Etzkorn, New York: Teachers College Press.

1971   *On Individuality and Social Forms*. Selected Writings, edited and with introduction by D.N. Levine, Chicago: University of Chicago Press.

1976   *Georg Simmel: Sociologist and European*. Translated by D.E. Jenkinson *et al.* with an introduction by P.A. Lawrence, Sunbury, Middx.: Nelson: New York, Barnes & Noble.

1977   *The Problems of the Philosophy of History*. Translated, edited and with an introduction by G. Oakes, New York: Free Press.

1978   *The Philosophy of Money*. Translated by T. Bottomore and D. Frisby with an introduction by D. Frisby, London/Boston: Routledge.

1980   *Essays on Interpretation in Social Science*. Translated and edited with an introduction by G. Oakes, Totowa, N.J.: Rowman & Littlefield; Manchester: Manchester University Press.

1984   *Georg Simmel: On Women, Sexuality and Love*. Translated and Introduced by G. Oakes, New Haven: Yale University Press.

1986   *Schopenhauer and Nietzsche*. Translated by H. Loiskandl, D. Weinstein and M. Weinstein, Amherst: University of Massachusetts Press.

1990   *The Philosophy of Money*. Second Enlarged Edition. Edited by D. Frisby, London: Routledge. New Enlarged Edition 2002.

1997   *Simmel on Culture. Selected Writings*. Translated by M. Ritter and others and edited by D. Frisby and M. Featherstone, with introduction by D. Frisby, London: Sage.

1997   *Essays on Religion*. Edited by H.J. Helle, New Haven: Yale University Press.

2002   *Georg Simmel on Rembrandt: A Philosophical Meditation on Art*. London: Routledge.

2003   *Englischsprachige Veröffentlichungen 1893–1910*. Frankfurt: Suhrkamp (GA18). (Collection of all Simmel's writings appearing during his lifetime in English).

Selected Bibliography of Secondary Sources

1 INTRODUCTIONS

Recent introductory sociological theory texts that cover Simmel include:

I. Craib, *Classical Sociological Theory*, Oxford: Oxford University Press (1997).
L. Ray, *Theorizing Classical Sociology*, Milton Keynes: Open University Press (1999).

2 ESSAY COLLECTIONS

American Journal of Sociology, 63, 6, 1958. Special Centenary issue on Durkheim and Simmel. Contains K.D. Naegle, 'Attachment and Alienation: Complementary Aspects of the Work of Durkheim and Simmel'; L.A. Coser, 'Georg Simmel's Style of Work'; T.M. Mills, 'Some Hypotheses on Small Groups from Simmel'.

Kurt H. Wolff (editor), *Essays on Sociology, Philosophy and Aesthetics by Georg Simmel, et al.*, Columbus, Ohio: Ohio State University Press (1958). As well as translations of some of Simmel's works, contains valuable essays on aspects of Simmel's sociology (e.g. by Levine, Tenbruck, Duncan, etc.).

Lewis A. Coser (editor), *Georg Simmel*, Englewood Cliffs, N.J.: Prentice-Hall (1965). Contains essays on aspects of Simmel's work as well as assessments by his contemporaries.

M. Kaern, B.S. Phillips and R.S. Cohen (eds.), *Georg Simmel and Contemporary Sociology*, Dordredit/Boston: Kluwer (1990).

M. Featherstone (editor), 'Georg Simmel', *Theory, Culture & Society*, volume 8, no. 3, (1991). Contains essays by M. Featherstone, K. Lichtblau, P. Watier, D. Frisby, D.N. Levine, D. Weinstein and M.A. Weinstein, G. Lukács, B. Nedelmann, F.J. Lechner, L.v. Vucht Tijssen, O. Rammstedt.

D. Frisby (editor), *Georg Simmel. Critical Assessments*, 3 volumes, London: Routledge (1994) (contains essays by Simmel, contemporary assessments, early reviews and reception, essays on Simmel and his contemporaries, essays on methodology, discussions of Simmel's major works, essays on substantive areas of his work, and Simmel in American sociology).

Simmel Studies. A journal devoted to Simmel research now in its twelfth year.

3 BOOKS

Y. Atoji, *George Simmel's Sociological Horizons*, Tokyo: Ochanomizu-shobo (1986).

M. Cacciari, *Architecture and Nihilism: On the Philosophy of Modern Architecture*, New Haven: Yale University Press (1993) Part 1 on Simmel.

D. Frisby, *Sociolozical Impressionism: A reassessment of Georg Simmel's Social Theory*, London: Heinemann (1981). Examines particularly the aesthetic dimension of Simmel's social theory. Second enlarged edition, London: Routledge (1991).

D. Frisby, *Fragments of Modernity*, Cambridge: Polity; Cambridge, Mass.: MIT Press (1985/1986).

D. Frisby, *Simmel and Since*, London: Routledge (1992).

B.S. Green, *Literary Methods and Sociological Theory. Case Studies of Simmel and Weber*, Chicago: Chicago University Press, (1988).

G.D. Jaworski, *Georg Simmel and the American Prospect*, Albany: State University of New York Press (1997).

W. Jung, *George Simmel zur Einführung*, Hamburg: Junius (1990).

K.C. Köhnke, *Der junge Simmel – in Theoriebeziehungen und sozialen Bewegungen*, Frankfurt: Suhrkamp (1996).

R.M. Leck, *Georg Simmel and Avant-Garde Sociology*, New York: Humanity Books (2000).

D.N. Levine, *Simmel and Parsons: Two Approaches to the Study of Society*, New York: Arno Press (1980). A valuable account of Simmel's sociology, usefully contrasted with the work of Parsons.

D.N. Levine, *The Flight from Ambiguity*, Chicago: Chicago University Press (1985), chs. 5, 6, 9.

K. Lichtblau, *Georg Simmel*, Frankfurt: Campus (1997).

G. Poggi, *Money and the Modern Mind*, Berkeley: University of California Press (1993). A detailed study of *The Philosophy of Money*.

N.J. Spykman, *The Social Theory of Georg Simmel*, New York: Atherton Press (1966) (reprint of 1925 edition). The first survey of Simmel's social theory as a whole.

F. Vandenberghe, *La Sociologie de Georg Simmel*, Paris: La Découverte (2001).

R.H. Weingartner, *Experience and Culture: The Philosophy of Georg Simmel*, Middletown, Conn.: Wesleyan University Press (1962). Looks especially at Simmel's later philosophy and philosophy of history. Should be supplemented by the two introductions by Oakes to his translations.

D. Weinstein and M.A. Weinstein, *Postmodern(ized) Simmel*, London: Routledge (1993). Makes the case for Simmel as postmodern theorist.

4 SELECTED ARTICLES AND ESSAYS

T. Abel, *Systematic Sociolgy in Germany*, New York: Columbia University Press (1926).

T. Abel, 'The Contribution of Simmel', in his *The Foundation of Sociological Theory*, New York: Random House (1970), ch. 4.

T. Abel, 'The Contribution of Georg Simmel: A Reappraisal', *American Sociological Review*, **24**, pp. 473–9. Modifies his earlier view of Simmel as a formal sociologist.

C.D. Axelrod, *Studies in Intellectual Breakthrough: Freud, Simmel, Buber*, Amherst: University of Mass. Press (1979). Deals with the fragmentary nature of Simmel's work.

I. Borden, 'Space Beyond', *Journal of Architecture*, 2, 1997, pp. 313–35.

T. Caplow, 'In Praise of Georg Simmel' in his *Two Against One*, Englewood Cliffs, N.J.: Prentice-Hall (1968), ch.2.

L.A. Coser, *Theories of Social Conflict*, London: Routledge (1956). A functionalist theory of conflict that relies heavily on Simmel's work.

L.A. Coser, 'The Sociology of Poverty', *Social Problems*, **13**, pp. 140–8. (The same issue also contains a translation of Simmel's work.

L.A. Coser, 'Georg Simmel's Neglected Contributions to the Sociology of Women', *Signs*, **2**, (1977) pp. 869–76. Points to some of the many essays on women by Simmel.

M.S. Davis, 'Georg Simmel and the Aesthetics of Social Reality', *Social Forces*, **51**, 1972/73, pp. 320–7.

N. Dodd, *The Sociology of Money*, Cambridge: Polity (1994) ch. 3.

R. Felski, *The Gender of Modernity*, Cambridge: Harvard University Press (1995), ch. 2. Critique of Simmel on women.

S.H. Frankel, *Money: Two Philosophies*, Oxford: Blackwell (1977) (on Simmel and Keynes).

J. Habermas, 'Georg Simmel on Philosophy and Culture', *Critical Inquiry*, **22**, 3, (1996), pp. 403–414.

H.B. Hawthorn, 'A Test of Simmel on the Secret Society', *American Journal of Sociology*, **62**, (1956), pp. 1–7.

L.E. Hazelrigg, 'A Re-examination of Simmel's "The Secret and the Secret Society"', *Social Forces*, **47**, (1969), pp. 323–30.

F. Jameson, 'The Theoretical Hesitation: Benjamin's Sociological Predecessor', *Critical Inquiry*, 25, 2 (1999), pp. 267–88.

S. Kracauer, 'Georg Simmel', *The Mass Ornament*, Cambridge: Harvard University Press (1995), pp. 225–58.

D.N. Levine, 'Simmel at a Distance', *Sociological Focus*, **10**, (1977), pp. 15–29. On Simmel's sociology of the stranger.

D.N. Levine, 'Sociology's Quest for the Classics. The Case of Simmel', in B. Rhea (editor), *The Future of the Sociological Classics*, London: Allen & Unwin (1981).

D.N. Levine et al., 'Simmel's Influence on American Sociology', *American Journal of Sociology*, **81**, (1976), pp. 813–45, 1112–32.

R. Lindner, *The Reportage of Urban Culture*, Cambridge: Cambridge University Press (1996). Sections on Park and Simmel.

S.D. McLemore, 'Simmel's "Stranger": A Critique of the Concept', *Pacific Sociological Review*, 13, (1970), pp. 86–94.

D. Miller, *Material Culture and Mass Consumption*, Oxford: Blackwell (1987), ch.5.

S. Moscovici, *The Invention of Society*, Cambridge: Polity (1993), ch. 7.

J. O'Neill, 'On Simmel's "Sociological Apriorities"', in his *Sociology as a Skin Trade*, London: Heinemann (1976).

L.A. Scaff, *Fleeing the Iron Cage*, Berkeley: California University Press (1989), ch. 4.

B.S. Turner, 'Simmel, rationalisation and the sociology of money', *Max Weber*, London: Routledge (1992), ch. 9.

J.H. Turner, 'Marx and Simmel Revisited. Reassessing the Foundations of Conflict Theory', *Social Forces*, **53**, (1975), pp. 618–27.

M. Weber, 'Georg Simmel as Sociologist', *Social Research*, **39**, (1972), pp. 155–63. Unfinished assessment of Simmel (around 1908/09) by Max Weber.

A. Witz, 'Georg Simmel and the Masculinity of Modernity', Journal of Classical Sociology, 1, 3 (2001), pp. 353–70.

Index